# REVISE BUSINESS STUDIES

## A COMPLETE REVISION COURSE FOR
# GCSE

EDUCATIONAL

David Floyd BA ACIS Adv DipEd Cert Ed
Senior Lecturer,
Wolverhampton Polytechnic

BPP Letts Educational Ltd

First published 1989
Reprinted 1991, 1992

Illustrations: Tek-Art

Text: © David Floyd 1989

© BPP (Letts Educational) Ltd
Aldine House, 7 Aldine Place
142–144 Uxbridge Road
London
W12 8AW

Printed and bound in Great Britain by
BPCC Wheatons Ltd, Exeter

**British Library Cataloguing in Publication Data**
Floyd, David C (David Charles)
    Business studies
    1. England. Secondary schools. Curriculum
    subjects: Business studies GCSE
    examinations. Techniques
    I. Title
    658'.0076

ISBN 1-85758-001-X

## Acknowledgements

The author and publishers are grateful to the following
organizations for permission to reprint material to which
they hold copyright:

Beecham Group plc
BICC plc
British Shoe Corporation Ltd
Cadbury Ltd
Controller of HMSO
Central Statistical Office
Courtaulds plc
Department of Employment
Department of Trade and Industry
GEC Turbine Generators Ltd
Guardian Newspapers Ltd
London East Anglian Group
Midland Examining Group
Northern Examining Association: ALSEB
    JMB, NREB, NWREB, YHREB
Northern Ireland Schools Examinations Council
RTZ Ltd
Shell UK Ltd
Shropshire Star
Southern Examining Group
STC plc
Texaco Ltd
THORN EMI plc
Welsh Joint Education Committee

# CONTENTS

# PREFACE

This book is designed to prepare candidates for the range of examinations and coursework found in GCSE Business Studies. It can also help students who are taking other business education courses: those studying for BTEC and similar qualifications should find that the book's content, examination questions and coursework material helps them in their studies.

*Revise Business Studies* has been written following a thorough analysis of the current GCSE Business Studies syllabuses (a table of analysis appears on page viii). The book contains detailed units on those syllabus areas and topics which are likely to be examined. It should therefore be used as the basis of an organized course of study, and not merely as a revision guide in the last few weeks of a course.

To help candidates in preparing for their GCSE Business Studies examinations, the book gives advice on how to prepare and revise for an examination. Each unit has a series of self-test questions which can be used by readers to check their progress. Details about the various examinations and types of exam question in the GCSE are also included: actual GCSE questions are provided, together with suggested answers.

A significant development of the GCSE – and an increasingly important element in all major Business Studies courses – is the inclusion of coursework. *Revise Business Studies* therefore includes actual GCSE coursework material and a range of possible coursework topics, together with guidance on how to approach this area of work.

I am grateful for the advice and assistance given by various colleagues at work and at Letts Educational. I would also like to record my thanks to the examination groups and other organizations for their help and permission to reproduce various materials.

Most of all, I am once again indebted to my wife, Val. Without her continual support and encouragement, the difficult task of writing this book would have been impossible.

**D.C.F.**

The author is Chief Examiner in Business Studies for one of the GCSE Examining Groups. He has also acted as Moderator for the Associated Examining Board's GCE Ordinary (Alternative) Level Business Studies examination, and as a Chief Examiner in three subjects for the Royal Society of Arts.

# INTRODUCTION

## Organization of the Book

*Revise Business Studies* has been designed for GCSE level candidates. It may also prove a valuable revision and study guide for other syllabuses. You must use the book properly to get the most out of it and this introduction explains how you can benefit from studying with *Revise Business Studies*.

Your first task is to check the name of the examination group which has published the syllabus you are studying. The syllabus coverage guide on page viii will tell you which topics could be included in your examination, but remember that this is only a general guide and that the examining groups are constantly updating and changing their business studies syllabuses.

The key content of the various syllabus topics is covered in Units 1 to 20 of the book. These are its **core units**. Each unit is divided into a number of different sections, to show you how the content develops logically and to help you to organize your study programme. The introductions to these units give an overview of the content and the summaries at the end include the main points that have been covered. Important words and phrases in each section have been printed in **heavy** type to give them a clear emphasis.

The core units have been organized in such a way that they follow logically on from one another. Although teachers organize their schemes of work in different ways, it is likely that many of them will teach this subject in the same order as the core units. Notes taken from the book can be slotted into your course notes, or kept as separate, 'backup', notes if required.

Once you have studied a core unit, you can refer to the Self-test Unit 21 (page 133) and answer questions on the unit studied. A summarized answer is given to each question asked in the Self-test Unit. If you have experienced any difficulty in answering these questions, then refer back to the relevant core unit and re-study the content areas that you have not fully understood. Try reading the content aloud, since we remember more if we see and hear something, than if we only read it. Also try to summarize the content, using your own words for the summary. You can then re-test yourself with the self-test questions, and study the answers provided.

Success in the GCSE examination and coursework assessment does not depend on your ability simply to remember the syllabus content. To achieve a high grade, you have to show that you fully understand business studies content and ideas by **applying** this knowledge. You must demonstrate what you know, understand and can do by answering examination questions which expect you to do a lot more than merely recall information. Both this unit and Unit 22 contain information about your examining group and your examination, which you will need to study carefully. In Unit 23, actual GCSE questions are provided for you to answer, and are then followed by suggested answers. To get the best out of this unit, you need to **attempt these questions before** you read the suggested answers. This gives you the opportunity to compare your answer with the one provided in the unit. You may well find that your answer contains detail not included in the 'model' answer, but check the answer supplied carefully to see if there are any areas that you may have missed out of your own answer.

The other area of work that tests what you know, understand and can do, is **coursework**. The coursework requirements of the different examining groups vary, this information being given in the 'Assessment patterns and weightings' section of this Introduction. Advice on how to meet the demands made by coursework is provided in Unit 24. This unit also contains actual GCSE coursework material and comments on the material, plus information on how your coursework may be assessed.

## Revision

Revision forms an important part of an overall plan of study. GCSE syllabuses are studied for at least one year, and usually two: you will study a great deal of information, and therefore need to plan and organize your study and revision time. Last-minute revision can help you, but it is of extremely limited value in GCSE Business Studies because the examinations do not test your ability to memorize chunks of information for a short time.

You will need to draw up a revision **programme**. If you are taking more than one examination, this programme will have to take into account the different dates of the various examinations, and your revision will have to be spread over quite a long period of time. The length of this programme will depend on several factors: the number of exams you are taking, the nature of the subject-matter you are studying (e.g. whether or not it is very descriptive) and how much study you have undertaken during the course. Doing coursework will probably help you learn effectively some of the business studies subject-matter during the course. Any further studying you can do before the last few months will be extremely valuable to you and will make your final revision period much easier. You cannot expect, in the GCSE, to leave most of your studying and revision until the end of the course: this is the recipe for a poor final grade.

Try to study and revise the business studies subject-matter in some logical **order**. The book's core units are organized into sections which follow on from one another, and the units themselves are in an order which many teachers may follow.

**Plan your study** and final revision sessions to ensure that you do more than read the book and your notes. Some points that might help you in studying and revising now follow.

1 Try to study in a **quiet place**, such as a library. This should help you to concentrate on the subject-matter without too many distractions.

2 Break up an overall study period into **shorter time periods**. You can only concentrate effectively for, typically, 20 to 30 minutes at a time: so build 5-minute or 10-minute breaks into your study sessions.

3 Remember to **allow for time lost** to breaks when you calculate how much study and revision you think you can do.

4 Plan to **avoid boredom**. Even the keenest students will become bored with studying and revising unless they vary the times they study, the topics they study and the ways they study (e.g. take notes, then read aloud, then answer a question, etc).

5 **Don't over-study.** All people at work need to take a break here and there: by not leaving everything until the last minute and then suddenly changing your lifestyle, the breaks that you do take from study will help to relieve tension and stress and will refresh you for further work.

6 Be prepared to use **your own words**: you will have to do this in your coursework and in the examination. To develop this skill, take notes from the book and summarize these notes without referring to the book. For example, the sections in Unit 6 dealing with economies of scale could be summarized as follows:

**Economies of scale:** unit costs fall as output increases,– i.e. it becomes cheaper to make the goods. Why?

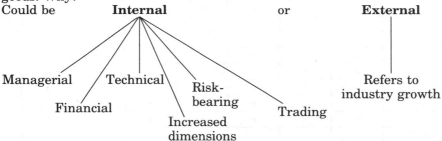

Could be **Internal** or **External**

Managerial / Technical / Risk-bearing / Trading

Financial

Increased dimensions

Refers to industry growth

Examples of internal:
Examples of external:
Problems?
**Diseconomies:** red tape, sheer size causing a problem.
Also some firms can't grow too large (e.g. localized demand for product/service).

## Syllabus Analysis

The GCSE National Criteria for Business Studies provides five essential areas for study:

1 External environment of the business
2 Business structure and organization
3 Business behaviour
4 People in business
5 Aiding and controlling business activity

The Examining Groups' syllabuses are based on these headings, although the amount and type of information included under the headings varies from Group to Group. The precise organization of the syllabus content also differs from syllabus to syllabus, which makes it difficult to analyse the exact content included under each heading. Although specimen and actual examination papers have been analysed to obtain further information, the GCSE is relatively new in education and full guidance is not always available. The syllabus analysis does follow a standardized classification but it is hampered by the lack of detail in some syllabus areas.

## Table of analysis of examination syllabus

| | London East Anglian (LEAG) | Midland (MEG) | Northern (NEA) Syllabus A | Northern (NEA) Syllabus B | Southern (SEG) | Northern Ireland (NISEC) | Wales (WJEC) | NBIS Project Business Studies | NBIS Project Business & Information Studies |
|---|---|---|---|---|---|---|---|---|---|
| **1 Economic framework** | | | | | | | | | |
| Concepts | • | • | • | | • | • | • | • | • |
| Specialization | • | • | • | • | | • | • | | |
| Systems | • | • | • | | • | • | • | • | • |
| Production | • | • | • | | • | • | • | • | |
| Markets | • | • | • | | • | • | • | • | |
| **2 Regional & national factors** | | | | | | | | | |
| Location of production | • | • | • | • | • | • | • | • | • |
| Population | • | • | • | | • | • | • | • | |
| Unemployment | • | • | • | | • | • | • | • | • |
| Regional policies | • | • | • | • | • | • | • | • | • |
| **3 International factors** | | | | | | | | | |
| Foreign trade | • | • | | • | | • | • | | |
| Balance of payments | | | | • | | • | • | | |
| Institutions | | | • | • | | • | • | | |
| Multinationals | • | • | • | • | • | • | • | • | • |
| **4 Business organizations** | | | | | | | | | |
| Private sector | • | • | • | • | • | • | • | • | • |
| Public sector | • | • | • | • | • | • | • | • | • |
| Other forms | • | • | • | • | • | • | • | • | • |
| **5 Business finance** | | | | | | | | | |
| Public sector sources | • | • | • | • | • | • | • | • | • |
| Private sector sources | • | • | • | • | • | • | • | • | • |
| Institutions | • | • | • | • | • | • | • | • | • |
| Stock Exchange | • | • | • | • | • | • | • | • | • |
| Banking services | • | • | • | | • | • | • | • | • |
| **6 Business risk & growth** | | | | | | | | | |
| Risks and insurance | • | • | • | • | • | • | • | | |
| Methods of growth | • | • | • | • | • | • | • | • | • |
| Economies of scale | • | • | • | • | • | • | • | • | • |
| **7 Structure of organizations** | | | | | | | | | |
| Charts | • | • | | | • | • | • | • | • |
| Functional organization | • | • | • | • | • | • | • | • | • |
| Terms | • | • | • | • | • | • | • | • | • |
| **8 Production** | | | | | | | | | |
| Costs | • | • | • | • | • | • | • | • | • |
| Breakeven analysis | • | • | • | | • | • | • | • | • |
| Production methods | • | | | • | | | • | | |
| Production department | • | • | • | • | | | • | | |
| **9 Purchasing** | | | | | | | | | |
| Purchasing department | | | • | • | • | | | | |
| Stock control | | | | • | | | | | |
| **10 The accounting function** | | | | | | | | | |
| Purposes | • | • | • | | • | • | • | • | |

| | London East Anglian (LEAG) | Midland (MEG) | Northern (NEA) Syllabus A | Northern (NEA) Syllabus B | Southern (SEG) | Northern Ireland (NISEC) | Wales (WJEC) | NBIS Project Business Studies | NBIS Project Business & Information Studies |
|---|---|---|---|---|---|---|---|---|---|
| **10 Accounting** continued | | | | | | | | | |
| Profitability & liquidity | • | • | • | • | • | • | • | • | • |
| Auditors | • | | | | • | | | | |
| Budgeting | • | • | • | • | • | • | • | • | • |
| Final accounts | • | • | • | • | • | • | • | • | |
| Interpretation | • | • | • | • | • | • | • | | |
| | | | | | | | | | |
| **11 Marketing** | | | | | | | | | |
| Marketing mix | • | • | • | • | • | • | • | • | • |
| Market research | • | • | • | • | • | • | • | • | • |
| Product lifecycle | • | | • | | | • | | | • |
| Pricing | • | • | • | • | • | • | • | • | • |
| Promotion | • | • | • | • | • | • | • | • | • |
| | | | | | | | | | |
| **12 Transport & distribution** | | | | | | | | | |
| Channels | • | • | • | • | • | • | • | | |
| Wholesalers | • | • | • | | • | • | • | | |
| Retailers | • | • | • | | • | • | • | | |
| Transport | • | | • | • | • | • | • | | |
| | | | | | | | | | |
| **13 The personnel function** | | | | | | | | | |
| Personnel department | • | • | • | • | • | • | • | | |
| Recruitment & selection | • | • | • | • | • | • | • | • | • |
| Training | • | • | • | • | • | • | • | • | • |
| | | | | | | | | | |
| **14 Work & its rewards** | | | | | | | | | |
| Human needs | • | • | • | • | • | • | • | | • |
| Wages & salaries | • | • | • | • | • | • | • | | • |
| Fringe benefits | • | • | • | • | • | • | • | | • |
| Gross & net pay | • | • | • | | • | • | • | | • |
| | | | | | | | | | |
| **15 Industrial relations** | | | | | | | | | |
| Trade unions | • | • | • | • | • | • | • | • | • |
| Employers organizations | • | • | • | • | • | • | • | | • |
| Bargaining and disputes | • | • | • | • | • | • | • | • | • |
| | | | | | | | | | |
| **16 Business documents** | | | | | | | | | |
| Trading documents | • | • | • | • | • | • | • | | |
| Documents in foreign trade | | | | • | | | • | | |
| | | | | | | | | | |
| **17 Business communication** | | | | | | | | | |
| Internal | • | • | • | • | • | • | • | • | • |
| External | • | • | | • | • | • | • | • | • |
| | | | | | | | | | |
| **18 Controlling business activity** | | | | | | | | | |
| Government | • | • | • | • | • | • | • | • | • |
| Pressure groups | • | • | • | • | • | • | • | • | • |
| | | | | | | | | | |
| **19 Aiding business activity** | | | | | | | | | |
| Government | • | • | • | • | • | • | • | | |
| Other sources | • | • | • | • | • | • | • | | • |
| | | | | | | | | | |
| **20 The impact of change** | | | | | | | | | |
| Changes affecting business | • | • | • | • | • | • | • | • | • |

## Assessment Patterns and Weightings

The Examining Groups differ in their approaches to GCSE assessment. The table on the next two pages summarizes assessment patterns for the 1990 Summer examinations.

Even though the GCSE is a relatively new examination, there have already been changes made to these patterns. More changes are likely in the near future. It is important, therefore, to check the exact position by asking your teacher, by reading the relevant syllabus details, or by contacting the appropriate Examining Group (the addresses of these Groups appear on page xiii).

A number of these syllabuses have provisions for **External Candidates**. Typically, external candidates do not have to submit the coursework assignments: instead, they undertake alternative work.

LEAG and SEG are examples of Examining Groups which allow external candidates to sit their GCSE Business Studies syllabuses. **LEAG** replaces coursework with a seen case study, sent to external candidates three to four weeks before the examination. **SEG** gives external candidates a case study (in place of coursework), which is based on a specified topic and completed during the course. Again, you will have to check the exact position with your teacher or with the relevant Group.

| London<br>East Anglian | Paper 1 | Papers 2A or 2B | Coursework |
|---|---|---|---|
| Weighting<br>Time<br>Features | 40%<br>1½ hours<br>Written paper:<br>Compulsory questions | 40%<br>1½ hours<br>Written paper:<br>10% compulsory<br>short-answer questions<br>30% choice of structured<br>questions | 20%<br><br>Six assignments set by LEAG<br>Candidates select and complete<br>two, each worth 10%, during the<br>Autumn and Spring terms of<br>year 2 |

*Scheme A candidates* take Papers 1 and 2A, and
Coursework. Grades E, F and G are not available
*Scheme B candidates* take Papers 1 and 2B, and
Coursework. Grades A and B are not available

*Skills*

Recall of knowledge

Application of knowledge ⎫  No specific syllabus guidance  40% maximum

Analysis ⎬

Judgment ⎭  No specific syllabus guidance  60% minimum

| LEAG and<br>the National Business<br>and Information Studies Project | Business Studies<br>(Single Option) | Business and Information Studies<br>(Double Option) |
|---|---|---|
| | Assessment is based completely on internally assessed coursework, 60% of which is controlled in classroom conditions<br>*Element A:* Portfolio Assessment<br>  90% of total marks: the Portfolio contains a selection of the candidate's learning assignments<br>*Element B:* Groupwork Assessment<br>  10% of total marks: the candidate's ability to be an effective member of a group is assessed | *Assessed Coursework*<br>40% of total, which is comprised of the following:<br>Portfolio of 4 of the learning assignments completed (8%)<br>Three mini-case studies (desk-based assignments), each worth 8%<br>Groupwork: assessment of candidate's ability to work as group member (8%)<br>*Final Case Study*<br>60% of total. Composed of three papers:<br>Paper 1 (Common Paper), attempted by all candidates<br>Paper 2 (General Paper), assesses performance over the grade range C-G<br>Paper 3 (Extended Paper), assesses performance over the grade range A-D |

| Midland | Paper 1 | Paper 2 | Coursework |
|---|---|---|---|
| Weighting<br>Time<br>Features | 70%<br>2 hours<br>Compulsory structured/<br>data response questions<br>and tasks | 70%<br>1¼ hours<br>Written paper based on<br>unseen case study | 30%<br>about 10 hours per assignment<br>Three assignments related to business<br>decisions or situations: maximum<br>1500 words each |

*Basic Scheme* candidates take Paper 1 and Coursework: grades A and B are not available
*Extended Scheme* candidates also take Paper 1 and Coursework, and in addition take Paper 2. Grades A and B
      are available, but candidates must have achieved grade C on the Basic Scheme. If a
      candidate obtains a lower grade on the Extended Scheme than on the Basic Scheme, he or
      she will be awarded the Basic Scheme grade

| Northern Syllabus A | Paper 1 | Paper 2 | Coursework |
|---|---|---|---|
| Weighting<br>Time<br>Features | 35%<br>1½ hours<br>3 compulsory structured<br>questions based on<br>stimulus material | 35%<br>1½ hours<br>Extended case study<br>with compulsory questions | 30%<br><br>Either:<br>1 assignment, up to 3000 words; or<br>2 assignments, up to 1500 words each; or<br>3 assignments, up to 1000 words each |

*Skills*

Knowledge  No specific syllabus guidance  40% maximum

Application ⎫

Analysis ⎬  No specific syllabus guidance  60% minimum

Judgment ⎭

(cont'd)

(cont'd)

## Northern Syllabus B

Candidates are assessed on coursework based on seven modules (no examination set by the Group)

| Module Title | Weighting | Assessment |
|---|---|---|
| Business foundation | 10% | Assessed on practical activity |
| Business communication | 10% | One problem-solving exercise assignment |
| Business organization and structure | 10% | Assignment on local business; unseen case study |
| People at work | 10% | Assignment on business decisions |
| Government and trade | 10% | Assignment on local, national or international business |
| Specialist study | 20% | In-depth study of one aspect of business activity |
| Coursework | 30% | Extensive study of business activity |

*Skills*

Recall and use of knowledge      40% maximum

Application, analysis, judgment 60% minimum

| Southern | Paper 1 | Paper 2A | or Paper 2B | Coursework |
|---|---|---|---|---|
| Weighting | 40% | 30% | 30% | 30% |
| Time | 2 hours | 1½ hours | 1½ hours | |
| Features | Five compulsory questions | Seen case study (common to both papers) is given to candidates 3-4 weeks before the examination | | Three assignments: more than three can be completed, and the best three submitted |

*Totals*

| Skills | Paper 1 | Paper 2A | Paper 2B | Coursework | General level | Extended level |
|---|---|---|---|---|---|---|
| Knowledge | 16 | 11 | 2 | 8 | 35 | 26 |
| Comprehension | 13 | 10 | 8 | 7 | 30 | 28 |
| Application | 9 | 6 | 11 | 10 | 25 | 30 |
| Evaluation | 2 | 3 | 9 | 5 | 10 | 16 |
| | 40 | 30 | 30 | 30 | 100 | 100 |

*General level candidates* take Papers 1 and 2A, and Coursework: grades A and B are not available

*Extended level candidates* take Papers 1 and 2B, and Coursework: grades E, F and G are not available

| Northern Ireland | Paper II | Paper I | or Paper III | Coursework |
|---|---|---|---|---|
| Weighting | 40% | 40% | 40% | 20% |
| Time | 1½ hours | 1½ hours | 1½ hours | |
| Features | Written paper: compulsory questions Taken by all candidates | Section A: ten compulsory short-answer questions (½ hour) Section B: three compulsory structured questions (1 hour) | Three compulsory structured questions | Two assignments |

Candidates entered for Papers II and III are eligible for grades A-D only

Candidates entered for Papers II and I are eligible for grades C-G only

| Skills | Papers II and I, Coursework | Papers II and III, Coursework | |
|---|---|---|---|
| Recall of knowledge | 40% maximum | 30% maximum | |
| High skills | 60% minimum | 70% minimum | |

| Wales | Paper 1 | Paper 2 | or Paper 3 | Coursework |
|---|---|---|---|---|
| Weighting | 30% | 40% | 40% | 30% |
| Time | 1¼ hours | 1½ hours | 1½ hours | Approximately 30 hours |
| Features | Written paper: Compulsory structured questions | Written paper: Compulsory structured questions | Written paper: Compulsory structured questions | Two, three or four assignments |

The highest grade a candidate taking Papers 1 and 2 can achieve is grade C

The highest grade a candidate taking Papers 1 and 3 can achieve is grade A

*Skills*

| Recall and understanding of knowledge | No specific syllabus guidance | 40% maximum |
|---|---|---|
| Application of knowledge } Analysis } Judgment } | No specific syllabus guidance | 60% maximum |

# Examination Boards: Addresses

## Northern Examining Association

*JMB*  Joint Matriculation Board
Devas Street, Manchester M15 6EU

*ALSEB*  Associated Lancashire Schools Examining Board
12 Harter Street, Manchester M1 6HL

*NREB*  Northern Regional Examinations Board
Wheatfield Road, Westerhope, Newcastle upon Tyne NE5 5JZ

*NWREB*  North-West Regional Examinations Board
Orbit House, Albert Street, Eccles, Manchester M30 0WL

*YHREB*  Yorkshire and Humberside Regional Examinations Board
Harrogate Office – 31-33 Springfield Avenue, Harrogate HG1 2HW
Sheffield Office – Scarsdale House, 136 Derbyshire Lane, Sheffield S8 8SE

## Midland Examining Group

*Cambridge*  University of Cambridge Local Examinations Syndicate
Syndicate Buildings, 1 Hills Road, Cambridge CB1 2EU

*O & C*  Oxford and Cambridge School Examinations Board
10 Trumpington Street, Cambridge CB2 1QB, and Elsfield Way, Oxford OX2 8EP

*SUJB*  Southern Universities' Joint Board for School Examinations
Cotham Road, Bristol BS6 6DD

*WMEB*  West Midlands Examinations Board
Norfolk House, Smallbrook Queensway, Birmingham B5 4NJ

*EMREB*  East Midlands Regional Examinations Board
Robins Wood House, Robins Wood Road, Aspley, Nottingham NG8 3NH

## London East Anglian Group

*London*  University of London School Examinations Board
Stewart House, 32 Russell Square, London WC1B 5DN

*LREB*  London Regional Examining Board
Lyon House, 104 Wandsworth High Street, London SW18 4LF

*EAEB*  East Anglian Examinations Board
The Lindens, Lexden Road, Colchester CO3 3RL

## Southern Examining Group

*AEB*  The Associated Examining Board
Stag Hill House, Guildford GU2 5XJ

*Oxford*  Oxford Delegacy of Local Examinations
Ewert Place, Summertown, Oxford OX2 7BZ

*SREB*  Southern Regional Examinations Board
Eastleigh House, Market Street, Eastleigh, Southampton SO5 4SW

*SEREB*  South-East Regional Examinations Board
Beloe House, 2-10 Mount Ephraim Road, Tunbridge Wells TN1 1EU

*SWEB*  South-Western Examinations Board
23-29 Marsh Street, Bristol BS1 4BP

## Wales

*WJEC*  Welsh Joint Education Committee
245 Western Avenue, Cardiff CF5 2YX

## Northern Ireland

*NISEC*  Northern Ireland Schools Examinations Council
Beechill House, 42 Beechill Road, Belfast BT8 4RS

# THE GCSE

The first series of GCSE exams, replacing the former GCE and CSE systems, took place in 1988. National Criteria have been published and all syllabuses called 'Business Studies' must conform to the National Criteria for Business Studies.

## Aims

The National Criteria list educational aims for all Business Studies GCSE courses. Key aims are summarized below.

Students should be able to:

1 develop knowledge and understanding of the business environment and its influence on businesses;
2 develop knowledge and understanding of various business-related groups and organizations;
3 develop understanding of the role of the economy's public and private sectors;
4 develop knowledge of how business organizations are financed, operated, organized and controlled;
5 appreciate the world of work and gain confidence in their dealings with it;
6 develop understanding of business language and decision-making techniques;
7 develop relevant skills such as numeracy, literacy and how to use information sources and select relevant information;
8 appreciate the importance of innovation and change to the business world.

## Core Content

The National Criteria state five content headings. These headings are:

1 External environment of the business
2 Business structure and organization
3 Business behaviour
4 People in business
5 Aiding and controlling business activity.

Although some descriptions and examples are provided in the National Criteria, the examining groups' syllabuses vary slightly in their interpretation of this detail. A syllabus analysis guide is provided on page viii.

## Assessment

### ASSESSMENT OBJECTIVES

The National Criteria establish six general assessment objectives.

Candidates will be expected to:

1 demonstrate a recall of knowledge in relation to specified syllabus content;
2 demonstrate an ability to use this knowledge in verbal, numerical and graphical form;
3 demonstrate an ability to explain and use, within the context of business, appropriate terminology, concepts, numerical calculations and elementary theories;
4 recognize, select, interpret and apply data;
5 organize information and apply it in an appropriate way to the solution of business problems;
6 distinguish between evidence and opinion, make reasoned judgments and communicate them in an accurate and logical manner.

The assessment objectives are weighted differently in the various Business Studies syllabuses, as shown in the section on assessment patterns and weightings (page x). The maximum weighting that can be given by any syllabus to the recall of knowledge is 40 per cent.

## ASSESSMENT TECHNIQUES

The National Criteria specify that all GCSE Business Studies courses should contain a compulsory coursework element, which accounts for between 20 and 40 per cent of the total marks available: the exact weighting again varies between the examining groups (see page x).

Other assessment techniques are not specified in the National Criteria, which point out that a range of different techniques – which must be appropriate to the objectives being assessed – can be used.

## GRADE CRITERIA

The National Criteria provide grade descriptions to give a general indication of the standards of achievement likely to have been shown by candidates who have received particular grades.

### Grade C

Candidates will normally have demonstrated:

1 ability to recall and use knowledge from the whole range of the syllabus;
2 ability to select and apply appropriate methods, techniques and procedures;
3 familiarity with the vocabulary and theory appropriate to the syllabus and ability to use numerical methods;
4 ability to organize and apply data to a variety of problems;
5 some ability to analyse and discuss;
6 ability to communicate effectively in writing.

### Grade F

Candidates will normally have demonstrated:

1 some ability to recall knowledge from some areas of the syllabus;
2 some ability to select and apply commonly used methods, techniques and procedures;
3 familiarity with vocabulary central to the course and ability to make simple calculations;
4 some ability to apply data to the solution of simple problems;
5 some ability to communicate effectively.

# 1 THE ECONOMIC FRAMEWORK OF BUSINESS

## 1.1 Introduction

The Business Studies syllabuses require you to be familiar with the purpose of economic activity, some key economic problems such as those of scarcity and choice, and the main types of production systems and markets that exist.

**Economics** tries to explain how we can best use the various resources which are at our disposal. Many decisions have to be made about business resources: managers must decide, for example, whether to employ more or fewer people, or whether to invest in a new machine. Decisions are usually made on the basis of some information about the business, such as that gathered by an accountant (Unit 10).

There are many influences on business. Some of these may be **local** or **national** (Unit 2), whereas others may come from **international** dealings (Unit 3). Business organizations cannot afford to isolate themselves from the rest of the business world: they will need to **communicate** with other organizations (Unit 17), as well as needing their own efficient communication systems.

Businesses vary in many ways:

1 In their **organization**.
2 In the **goods or services** they produce.
3 In their **size and complexity**.
4 In the nature of their **markets**, which could be local (such as that for a hairdresser), national (e.g. BBC television) or international (for example, Fiat cars).

The economies in which these various firms operate will also vary, from the **planned economies** of the Eastern Bloc countries to the **market-oriented economies** of the West.

## 1.2 The Purpose of Economic Activity

Economic activity takes place within a society such as the United Kingdom. It sets out to **satisfy the needs of the society**. Through economic activity taking place, wealth is created and distributed, so the members of the society can share in this wealth.

### Factors of production

A society needs to produce the goods and services demanded by its consumers: it will use resources to do this. These resources are known as 'factors of production.'

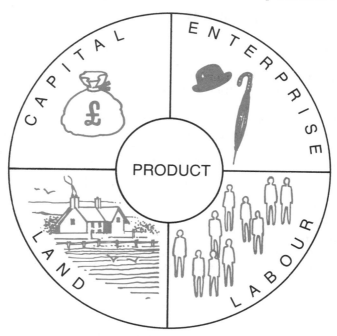

**Fig. 1.1** The four factors of production

1

1 **Capital**, available for investment in new machines, new companies, etc.
2 **Enterprise**, referring to the people who are willing to take the risk of setting up in business and making business decisions.
3 **Land**, which is used for agriculture, housing development, leisure and for providing natural resources such as minerals.
4 **Labour**, the number of men and women available and willing to work.

### Scarcity and choice

One of the main problems that any society faces is that it cannot satisfy all the wants of its members. These **wants are unlimited**, and yet there are **limited resources** available to the society to provide the various goods and services. There is not an endless supply of the factors of production: capital, enterprise, land and labour are all scarce resources, which means that society has to make a series of **choices**.

There are a number of key questions that the society must ask itself:

#### What to produce

In many cases, the **price mechanism** will help to decide what is produced and what is not produced; or the **government** might take a more important role in saying what is or what is not provided. This is covered in detail later in the unit.

#### How to produce

To produce goods and services, the four factors of production should be combined in the most efficient way possible. To lower the costs of production, for example, a firm may decide to substitute new capital equipment in place of a number of employees (i.e. automation). Decisions such as these, which may increase the firm's efficiency, can lead to inefficient use of the factors of production in the economy generally, e.g. through the creation of a large pool of unemployed labour.

#### Where to produce

The availability and situation of the factors of production – such as the availability of inexpensive building land and of a suitably skilled workforce – will be a major influence in deciding where firms produce their goods and services. Governments often use **regional policy** to influence where new firms are established, for example by awarding grants to encourage firms to set up production in certain regions of the country (Unit 2).

### Opportunity cost

The problem of having limited resources and unlimited wants is that **some wants are unsatisfied**. Consumers have to choose how they spend their money or their time.

If you have a choice of, say, going to the cinema or going to a football match, by choosing to go to the cinema you are giving up the alternative of the football match. The opportunity cost of the cinema is the football match: watching the film has cost you the opportunity of seeing the football. 'Opportunity cost' therefore results from having to go without one thing to obtain another. It is a lost opportunity.

## 1.3 Specialization

In advanced economies, such as that of the United Kingdom, production tends to be **indirect** rather than direct. This means that people do not produce only for themselves but instead work with others in order to produce goods and services which are then sold to all. They **specialize** in what they do best, which leads to greater efficiency and higher economic output.

Firms take advantage of this specialization. A **division of labour** takes place: employees gain management or clerical skills, they learn and become efficient at welding, driving, assembling, operating machinery and so on. This allows the firm to use complicated production processes, and its work can be divided into different functions such as personnel, purchasing and sales, which can then be staffed by specialists.

### Advantages and disadvantages of specialization

#### Advantages

1 There are **reduced unit costs**, since manufacturing processes can take place more easily and quickly.
2 **Specialist equipment** can be used, leading to quicker and more efficient production.
3 **Employees become specialized** and therefore more efficient.

#### Disadvantages

1 The risk of **boredom** for employees, leading to **lower job satisfaction** and greater chance of labour disputes. The quality of the finished product may suffer.
2 A single group of workers taking industrial action can **halt the whole production line**.
3 Problems of unemployed workers, who possess specialist, narrow and **out-of-date skills**.

**Fig. 1.2** Specialized Production: Steam Turbines  Courtesy: *GEC Turbine Generators Ltd*

# INTERDEPENDENCE THROUGH SPECIALIZATION

The various 'parts' that make up the economy, such as firms and workers, start to depend on each other as a result of specialization.

## Specialization of firms and countries

### Firms

By specializing, **firms become dependent on other firms.**

A farmer, specializing in growing vegetables, relies on others to distribute, pack and sell his vegetables to the public. A car manufacturer relies on the expertise of an advertising agency to promote the cars and on a chain of garages to sell them.

Firms specializing in various products will **compete** with one another in the same market: they may also **cooperate** with each other. Unit 15 explains the role of trade associations and similar bodies which exist to help individual businesses.

*Countries*

Countries will also specialize in a limited range of products or services. In many cases, this specialization is based on the country's **climate and natural resources**: for example, Bolivia and tin production, some Mediterranean countries and tourism, South Africa and gold mining. There may be **historical influences**, such as the development of banking and financial services in Great Britain helping to establish a strong service sector in our economy.

A country is therefore not self-sufficient and has to depend on other countries to supply those goods and services it cannot provide itself. **International trade** (Unit 3) takes place, which increases the interdependence that exists between countries.

### Specialization of people

People are trained for particular occupations, such as teachers, nurses, welders, and insurance clerks. Regardless of the type of job they do, these people will have broadly similar demands: for televisions, cars, washing machines and other 'consumer durables', as well as for various specialist services such as TV repair, car servicing, and plumbing services for installing a washing machine.

This leads to people becoming **dependent on others** to provide them with these goods and services. A teacher may use the specialist skills of the garage mechanic and the plumber: at the same time, this teacher may be contributing to the education of their children. This interdependence relies on the use of money to purchase the various goods and services, rather than the use of the old, inefficient barter system.

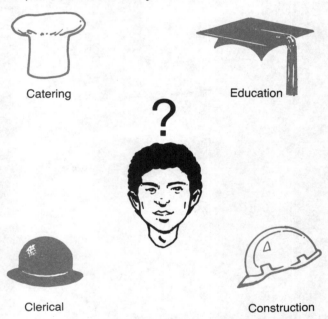

Catering

Education

Clerical

Construction

**Fig. 1.3** Specialization of people

## 1.4 Economic Systems

There are three main types of economic system: **free market** (capitalist), **planned** (command) and **mixed**. The difference between the three systems stems from the amount of government interference which takes place in the production and distribution of the goods and services.

### THE FREE MARKET SYSTEM

This is also known as the **capitalist** system, or the **laissez-faire** system.

#### Features of this system

In the free market system, there is no government interference in the workings of the economy. The **price mechanism** is its main feature, prices of goods and services being determined by the demands made by the consumers and by the willingness of producers to supply these goods and services. As shown by fig 1.4 opposite, different levels of demand and supply will exist at different price levels.

As the curves show, a price of £5 would lead to 30 000 being supplied but only 5000 demanded. If the price of the item was only £1, the demand level would be 30 000 but only 5000 would be supplied.

Demand, supply and price tend to interact. If demand exceeds supply (e.g. in fig 1.4, when the price is £1), the price will tend to rise. Higher prices reduce overall demand because some people cannot afford the higher prices. They also encourage greater supply to take place:

higher prices may mean higher profit margins and encourage new firms to enter the market. This should therefore lead to supply meeting demand.

If the supply level of a product is greater than the demand for that product, its price will fall: more people can now afford it, thus increasing demand. Fewer products are likely to be made because of the lower price and so the supply level will fall to meet the new level of demand.

In the free market economy, **resources are owned by individuals**, not by the State. The various factors of production are again dependent on the workings of the price mechanism. If the price of labour is too high, it may not be employed (demanded) by firms. If the rate of interest for bank loans – a form of capital – falls, more loans will probably be taken out by firms.

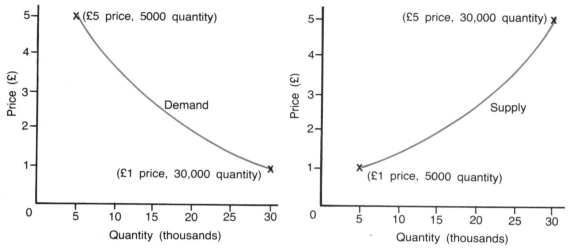

Fig. 1.4 Demand and supply curves

**Advantages of the free market system**

1 **Incentive.** People are encouraged to work hard, because opportunities exist for individuals to accumulate high levels of wealth.
2 **Choice.** People can spend their money how they want; they can choose to set up their own firm, or they can choose for whom they want to work.
3 **Competition.** Through competition, less efficient producers are priced out of the market: more efficient producers supply their own products at lower prices for the consumers, and use factors of production more efficiently. The factors of production which are no longer needed can be used in production elsewhere. Competition also stimulates new ideas and processes, which again leads to efficient use of resources.

**Disadvantages of the free market system**

1 **Unequal distribution of wealth.** The wealthier members of the society tend to hold most of the economic and political power, while the poorer members have much less influence. There is an unequal distribution of resources and sometimes production concentrates on luxuries, i.e. the wants of the rich. This can lead to excessive numbers of luxury goods being produced in the economy.
2 **Public services.** The price mechanism may not work efficiently where services need to be provided for the benefit of society as a whole (such as defence, education, and health services).
3 **Profit motive.** Since the profit motive is all-important to producers, they may ignore social costs of production, such as pollution. Short-term profit performance may be considered more important than long-term growth (a criticism often levelled at speculation which takes place on the Stock Market).
4 **Hardship.** Although in theory factors of production such as labour are 'mobile' and can be switched from one market to another, in practice this is a major problem and can lead to hardship through unemployment. It also leads to these scarce factors of production being wasted, by not using them to fullest advantage.
5 **Wasted or reduced competition.** Some firms may use expensive advertising campaigns to sell 'new' products which are basically the same as many other products currently on sale. Other firms, who control most of the supply of some goods, may choose to restrict supply and therefore keep prices artificially high: or, with other suppliers, they may agree the prices to charge and so price will not be determined by the interaction of supply and demand.

## THE PLANNED SYSTEM

This is also known as the **command** system or the **collectivist** system.

### Features of this system

Unlike the market economy, where the government plays no direct role in deciding what is produced, **the planned system relies exclusively on the State**. The government will decide what is made, how it is made, where it is made, how much is made and how distribution takes place.

The resources – the factors of production – are controlled by the government on behalf of producers and consumers. Price levels are not determined directly by the forces of supply and demand but are fixed by the government.

Although division of labour and specialization are still found, the planned economies tend to be **more self-sufficient** and to **take part in less international trade** than market economies.

### Advantages of the planned system

1  **Use of resources.** Central planning can lead to the full use of all the factors of production, so reducing or ending unemployment.
2  **Large-scale production.** Economies of scale become possible due to mass production taking place.
3  **Public services.** 'Natural monopolies' such as the supply of domestic power, or defence, can be provided efficiently through central planning.
4  **Basic services.** There is less concentration on making luxuries for those who can afford them and greater emphasis on providing a range of goods and services for all the population. There are less dramatic differences in wealth and income than in a market economy.

### Disadvantages of the planned system

1  **Lack of choice.** Consumers have little influence over what is produced and people may have little say in what they do as a career.
2  **Little incentive.** Since competition between different producers is not as important as in the market economy, there is no great incentive to improve existing systems of production or work. Workers are given no real incentive to work harder and so production levels are not as high as they could be.
3  **Centralized control.** Because the state makes all the decisions, there must be large influential government departments. The existence of such a powerful and large **bureaucracy** can lead to inefficient planning and to problems of communication. Furthermore, government officials can become overprivileged and use their position for personal gain, rather than for the good of the rest of society.

## THE MIXED ECONOMY

There are no economies in the world which are entirely 'market' or 'planned': all will contain elements of both systems.

Most modern western countries have mainly market economies. The USA is a typical example of a largely market-based society but its government still plans certain areas of the economy such as defence and provides very basic medical care for those who cannot afford medical insurance. In the 1980s, the United Kingdom has become increasingly market-based, for example through the Government's policies of **privatizing** former state monopolies such as British Gas.

Some western countries such as Sweden run their economies with a great deal of state planning: better-known examples include the Soviet Union and China, although even here these economies are not totally planned.

### Features of this system

The mixed economy includes elements of both market and planned economies. The government operates and controls the **public sector**, which typically consists of a range of public services such as health and education, as well as some local government services. The **private sector** is largely governed by the price mechanism and 'market forces', although in practice it is also controlled by various regulations and laws (Unit 18). The relative strength of these two sectors will depend on political factors: in the UK, for instance, the Labour party often puts greater emphasis on the public sector than does the Conservative party.

Some services may be subsidized: provided at a loss but kept for the benefit of society in general (many national railways, for example, are loss-making). Other services, such as education or the police, may be provided free of charge (though they are really paid for through the taxation system).

The private sector is **regulated**, i.e. influenced by the price mechanism but also subject to some further government control, such as through pollution, safety and employment regulations.

### Advantages of the mixed economy

1  **Necessary services are provided.** In a true market economy, services which were not able to make a profit would not be provided.

2 **Incentive.** Since there is a private sector where individuals can make a lot of money, incentives still exist in the mixed economy.

3 **Competition.** Prices of goods and services in the private sector are kept down through competition taking place.

### Disadvantages of the mixed economy

Just as the 'best of both worlds' argument applies to the mixed system, it can also suffer from the disadvantages of both planned and market systems. For example, **large monopolies** can still exist in the private sector, and so competition does not really take place. Since a public sector exists in a mixed economy, there is likely to be a lot of **bureaucracy** and 'red tape' found.

## 1.5 Types of Production

Workers in less developed countries often satisfy their wants **directly**, by providing the goods or services they require themselves. As countries develop economically, increased specialization and the division of labour lead to **indirect** production taking place, where workers are paid for their part in the production process. The money that they earn is used to buy the finished goods and services.

The firms that exist in these various economic systems will be involved in **production** which is classified under the three headings in fig. 1.5

### PRIMARY, SECONDARY AND TERTIARY PRODUCTION

All **primary production** involves some form of **extraction**.
Areas of work in the primary sector are:

1 Mining and quarrying
2 Fishing
3 Farming
4 Forestry

Firms taking part in **secondary production** are either involved in manufacturing or construction:

**manufacturing** either the finished article, such as a car, or parts for further assembly and manufacture (e.g. making spark plugs or seat upholstery to go into the car);

or

**construction** of houses and other buildings, roads, etc.

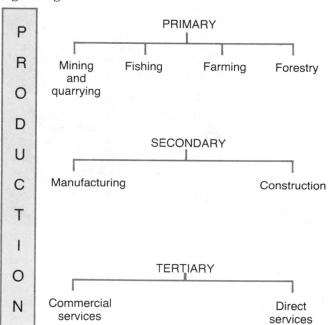

**Fig. 1.5** Types of Production

**Fig. 1.6** Agriculture: primary production

**Fig. 1.7** Processing the produce: chocolate manufacture (secondary production) Courtesy: *Cadbury Ltd*

Items that have been grown, extracted, made or constructed have to be passed from producer to consumer. Although the producer may sell the goods directly to the consumer – for instance, a farmer selling farm-produced foodstuffs to callers – it is more likely that the goods will need to be transported, stored, advertised, financed in some way and insured.

There are a range of commercial services and activities which make up **tertiary production**. These are shown in fig. 1.8.

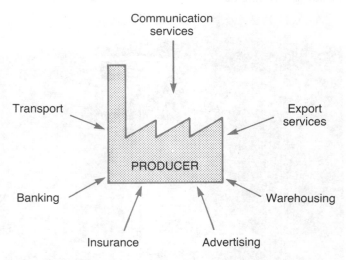

**Fig. 1.8.** Commercial services which assist producers

There are also **direct services** provided for the benefit of the community. These include occupations such as teachers, the police, health workers and firemen.

## 1.6 Markets

A market is a **place where buyers and sellers are in contact with one another**; it is where goods and services are bought and sold.

### Types of market

Many different types of market exist. They can be grouped under two headings.

*Consumer Markets*

For consumer goods and services, which consist of:

1 **Single-use** consumer goods, such as foodstuffs and domestic power.
2 **Consumer durables**, e.g. videos, TVs, freezers.
3 Consumer **services**, such as dentists and hairdressers.

*Industrial markets*

These markets supply the goods and services required by firms, such as:

1 **Capital goods** like new office or factory machinery.
2 **Industrial services**, e.g. cleaning services, printing company logos, or transporting business products and mail.

### Market price

The market system relies on the working of the price mechanism, market price being determined by the forces of supply and demand (see page 4).

## 1.7 Summary

Business Studies takes some of its subject-matter from other subjects. The main concepts of Economics – scarcity, opportunity cost and specialization – form the background to the study of the business world. Terms such as 'market', which have a special meaning in economics, are also important in Business Studies.

Although the theoretical extremes of the market and planned economies are not found in the real world, all mixed economies include their elements to a greater or lesser extent. The price mechanism, influenced by supply and demand, itself influences all business activity. The actions of a government can also be a major influence on the world of business.

# 2 REGIONAL AND NATIONAL FACTORS

## 2.1 Introduction

Countries are made up of different regions and these regions will have their own individual characteristics. In the UK, for example, there are major differences between the south-west and north-east of England; different dialects and differences in climate are obvious examples.

The **economies** of regions and localities will also vary. Historically, both the north-east and south-west of England were important centres of mining: coal in the former area, tin and clay in the latter. Nowadays, the South-West is noted more for its tourist industry, while centres of population in the North-East try to attract new work to replace their declining traditional industries of mining and shipbuilding.

Many changes have taken place in the various regions of the country in the last decade or so. Some of these changes are due to **local or regional influences**. For example, the discovery of North Sea oil, as well as being of benefit to the UK economy in general, started a boom in the economy of Aberdeen and its surrounding area.

**Fig. 2.1** North East Shipbuilders, Wearside: one of the firms and areas affected by deindustrialization
Courtesy: *The Guardian*

Other changes have been on a **national** scale. Two notable national trends in the 1980s have been:

1  **Privatization**. The government has followed a policy of denationalizing various industries: important examples include British Telecom and British Gas.
2  **Deindustrialization**. The 1980s have seen a reduction in the importance and influence of the traditional heavy engineering and manufacturing industries, with the tertiary sector of the economy becoming far more important than before.

New industries have been established, or have grown substantially in recent years: the information technology and telecommunications industries are two examples. These require workers with new skills, and the owners of these new businesses must decide where they are to be based.

## 2.2  The Location of Production

Many factors will have influenced where a firm is located. These factors have changed in relative importance in recent years: for example, the quality of modern-day transport and

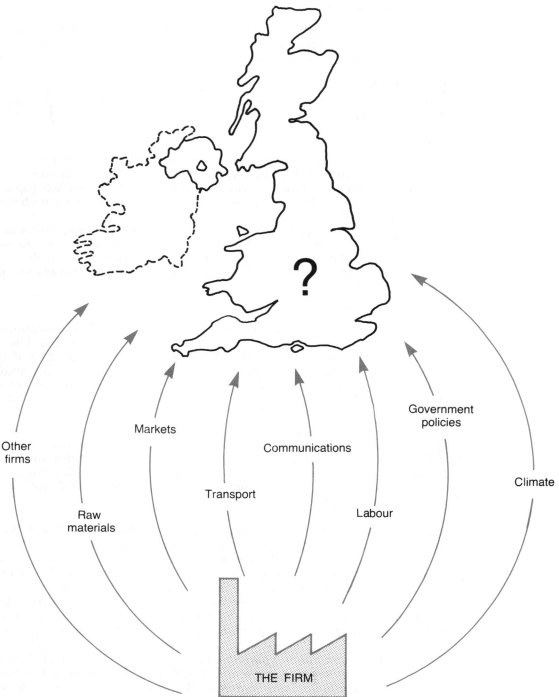

**Fig. 2.2** Influences on the location of a firm

communications means that it is less important nowadays for a firm to be based either near the source of its raw materials, or very close to the market for its finished products.

The various 'pulls' on a firm are shown in fig. 2.2 on page 11.

### Historical factors

The availability of power used to be a significant factor in the location of a firm: nowadays this is a far less important influence, with electricity and gas supplies available nationally.

Many industries originally grew up near to the **supply of their raw materials**, such as the china industry in the Potteries. Other firms were based by **fuel supplies** such as a coal mining area, because of the high cost of transporting this fuel. Again, location by a firm's raw material supply is less important nowadays due to improved, efficient methods of transport.

### Natural advantages

These can influence where industries or firms are located. The availability of water and an appropriate **climate** were important factors in establishing the cotton and woollen industries in the north of England and the brewing industry in the north Midlands; and good climate, drainage and soil will always help in deciding whether an area will be used for agriculture.

### Transport and communications

Location near to an effective **transport network** has always been a major influence: **canals** and **railways** were influential forms of transport, and today being close to **motorway** networks, **airports** and **seaports** is important in deciding a firm's geographical location.

### Labour supply

Owners of a firm will be encouraged to locate it where there is an **available, adequately skilled workforce**.

### Markets

As a general rule, if a firm's raw materials were bulky and costly to transport, it would be located near the source of these materials. If, however, it was in a 'weight-gaining' industry – that is, the final product gained weight or bulk during production (e.g. the brewing industry) – it would be located near the market for its product. This would save high costs of transporting the finished products.

The distribution of **population** is a second market influence. Firms providing consumer goods would be tempted to locate near areas of high population, such as south-east England (although other factors, such as the high cost of land, may of course discourage this).

Finally, certain firms, mainly in the service sector (e.g. hairdressers and plumbers), need to be located near their customers.

### External economies

Also known as **economies of concentration**, these external economies arise where one industry is concentrated in a particular area. For example, the UK car industry has traditionally been concentrated in the Midlands. This means that there exists a ready supply of labour having relevant skills; there are local colleges experienced in running courses which are designed to train car workers; and so on. New car firms may therefore be encouraged to set up in the same area.

### Personal choice

When it comes to locating a business the owners of the business will be influenced by their own likes and dislikes. Some may have many personal 'ties' in one area of the country and therefore will not be prepared to set up in business elsewhere. Others may be attracted by areas they see as clean or attractive to live and work in (e.g. because of the surrounding countryside).

### Government influences

Central government, particularly since the end of the Second World War, has become an increasingly important influence in helping to decide where firms are to be located. New towns such as Telford and Milton Keynes have been built and central government has offered **financial incentives** to business people to move to these areas. The Government has also offered these incentives to encourage firms to be set up in particular regions of the country: typically, those regions which have suffered high levels of unemployment due to the run-down of their traditional industries (e.g. the North-East and shipbuilding). These incentives will vary from government to government, but usually consist of benefits such as rent-free factories and tax incentives.

Central government has also played a more direct part in locating industry, by setting up its own departments in areas facing economic difficulty. Examples of this policy include basing the DVLC (the vehicle licensing centre) at Swansea and the National Girobank plc at Bootle, Merseyside.

## 2.3 Population

A country's population is one of its most important natural assets. The population provides the economy with the **supply of labour**, to produce goods and services. The **demand** for these items also comes from the population. Any change, therefore, in the **structure** or **size** of the population can have a major effect on the country's economy.

### World population

Total world population in 1988 was approaching five billion (five thousand million). It is expected to increase to over six billion by the year 2000, and to eight billion by 2025. The overall rate of increase is expected to decline from the present rate of one and two thirds per cent each year, to about one per cent per annum. This will vary from country to country: the developing countries—many African countries, for example—typically have population growths of between two and three per cent each year, while the industrialized countries, such as the UK, usually have a yearly population growth rate of about one per cent.

World population growth is influenced by a number of factors:

1 **Medical epidemics**, for example the Bubonic Plague in Europe in the Middle Ages, recent diseases such as smallpox and the current AIDS problem.
2 **Natural disasters**; floods and famine are obvious examples.
3 **Wealth and levels of education**; richer countries tend to have lower birth rates, but also lower infant death rates and a population with a greater life expectation.

Population growth in other countries can influence the performance of the United Kingdom's economy. For example, the successful economic growth of much of the Far East has led to the UK importing many of its electronic and electrical products from this area and has affected the UK's own manufacturing performance. This is partly due to the existence of large numbers of low-paid workers in many of these countries.

### UK population

The population of the United Kingdom was 56.7 million in 1986 and it is expected to rise to about 58 million by the end of the century. The fastest rate of growth was during the 19th century: there had always been a high birth rate but during the last century the death rate fell dramatically due to improved hygiene, sanitation and medical knowledge.

### Influences on population size

The overall size of a country's population is influenced by several factors.

*Birth rate*

The rate at which children are born—the **fertility rate**—is a major influence on population size. This rate is expressed as the number of births per thousand of the total population per year. The UK birth rate in 1986 was 13.2 children per thousand population.

This figure is influenced by:

1 The number of women capable of having children;
2 the number who are willing to bear children;
3 the average number of children born per woman.

Further influences here are:

4 Education about parenthood.
5 Attitudes to family size.
6 Knowledge and availability of birth control.
7 Legal factors (e.g. relating to the minimum age for marriage).

The UK has recently faced a **declining birth rate**. In 1900 it was 28.6 children per thousand, but has remained at around 13 per thousand since 1974. There are a number of likely reasons for this, including the desire by many couples to delay having children, improved knowledge of birth control methods and the availability of cheap and effective methods of birth control.

*Death rate*

The death, or mortality, rate of the UK is currently below 12 people per thousand each year. This rate has shown a steady decline in this country. It is influenced by the following:

1 Living standards, i.e. the quality of food, clothing and housing (shelter and warmth).
2 Medical advances, e.g. discovery of new drugs and improvements in transplant and other surgical techniques.
3 Environmental standards; mainly the clean and safe disposal of all waste products, as well as the provision of safe drinking water.

### Migration

'Migration' is the difference between the total of people entering a country (**immigration**) and the total of those leaving it (**emigration**).

The United Kingdom has a history of both net emigration and net immigration. In recent years, more people have tended to emigrate from this country than to enter it as immigrants, as shown below.

| Year | Inflow to the UK (thousands) | Outflow from the UK (thousands) | Balance (thousands) |
|------|------|------|------|
| 1976 | 191 | 210 | −19 |
| 1981 | 153 | 233 | −80 |
| 1986 | 250 | 213 | +37 |

**Fig. 2.3** Migration into and out of the UK  Source: *Office of Population Censuses and Surveys, CSO 'Blue Book' 1988 edition*

It is not only the number who enter or leave the country that is important: we must also consider the **skills** that they bring with them or take from the country. In the last 20 or 30 years, the UK has been said to have suffered a 'brain drain', with the loss of many highly skilled and educated people. One reason for the Government policy in the 1980s of having low direct taxes (notably income tax) for the high wage earners is an attempt to halt this trend, but there seems no evidence that it is having any major success.

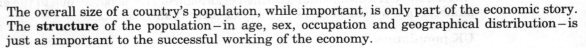

## 2.4  Population Structure and Employment

The overall size of a country's population, while important, is only part of the economic story. The **structure** of the population – in age, sex, occupation and geographical distribution – is just as important to the successful working of the economy.

### Age structure

While the United Kingdom has a reasonably fixed total population, the age structure within this total is changing quite noticeably. Both government and business can use this information to **predict changes in the total demand for their products and services**. For example, there is a predicted increase in the number of over 65s and under 5s by the year 1995. This will lead to an increased demand for health and related services for the elderly and an increased demand for baby and toddler products.

It is also likely that the number of 15 to 19 year olds will fall by about a million by 1995. This will affect the number entering the labour market and therefore firms' recruitment policies.

### Problems of an aging population

The average age of the UK's population is increasing: by the year 2045, the Government Actuary's Department estimates that the number of over 75s will increase from the present 3.7 million to about 6.2 million. The major economic effects of an aging population are as follows:

1 There are **increased demands for social services**, such as health services.
2 There is **increased dependence** on those in work, to provide the tax and other contributions to pay for these various social services.
3 There will be **changes in demand**: for example, there will be an increased demand for warmer clothing, smaller houses and flats, and public transport.

### Sex structure

There are approximately one million more women than men living in the UK at present: although the number of male births exceeds female births, women live for longer on average.

### Geographical distribution

The population has tended to be concentrated in our major towns and cities, following the Industrial Revolution of the last century. In recent years, there has been some movement out of inner-city areas into either the suburbs or rural areas.

On a national basis, there is a continual **drift of labour to the South-East**, encouraged by the opportunity of work but facing the problem of housing shortages and costs and a generally higher cost of living.

### Employment

In June 1987 there were an estimated 21.3 million employees in Great Britain, of whom 11.9 million were men and 9.4 million were women. There were also 2.8 million self-employed, of whom over a quarter were women. The present characteristics of employment are:

1 The continuing growth in the numbers of women workers.
2 The continuing growth in part-time and temporary jobs.
3 The continuing growth in the numbers of self-employed workers.
4 A slight fall in the numbers of men in full-time jobs.

Fig 2.4 illustrates the key trends.

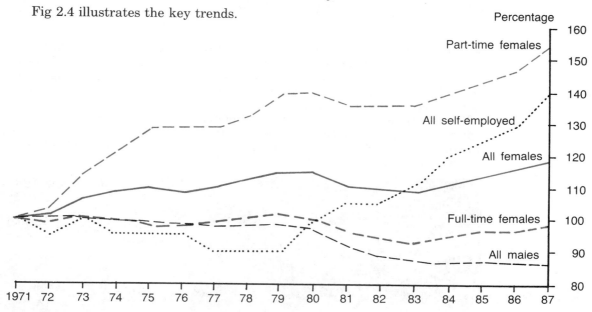

**Fig. 2.4** Employment trends, 1971 to 1987 (1971=100)
Source: *Department of Employment, 1987*

In the United Kingdom today there are fewer people employed in the primary and secondary sectors of the economy and more employed in the tertiary sector. The **status** of those working has also changed in recent years, with more people setting up in business for themselves. In 1987, approximately 15 per cent of men and 7 per cent of women in employment were self-employed.

*Occupation by sector*

| Sector | 1976 *(thousands)* | 1986 *(thousands)* |
|---|---|---|
| Central government | 2 364 | 2 337 |
| Local authorities | 2 956 | 3 010 |
| Public corporations | 1 980 | 1 199 |
| Private sector | 17 544 | 17 996 |

**Fig. 2.5** Employed labour force by sector
Source: *CSO 'Blue Book' 1988 Edition*

Fig. 2.5 shows the occupational distribution found in the United Kingdom. Another way of classifying by sector is shown in fig. 2.6, which shows the changes in employment totals in some of the main industries and occupations.

| | *June 1981* *(thousands)* | *June 1987* *(thousands)* |
|---|---|---|
| Agriculture, forestry, fishing | 343 | 302 |
| Coal, oil and gas extraction and processing | 344 | 196 |
| Mechanical engineering | 901 | 705 |
| Motor vehicle manufacture | 361 | 238 |
| Textiles, leather, footwear, clothing | 614 | 543 |
| Construction | 1 102 | 984 |
| Hotels and catering | 930 | 1 095 |
| Banking, finance, insurance | 1 712 | 2 299 |
| Other services | 1 282 | 1 609 |

**Fig. 2.6** Employees in employment: industry Source: *Department of Employment,
'Employment Gazette', July 1988*

The primary – extractive – sector of the economy employs some 3 per cent of the working population of the UK. Improved mechanization and other developments, such as greater farming yields through better fertilizers, has led to a continual reduction in the numbers employed in this sector.

Certain areas of manufacturing and construction have declined greatly in the last decade: the textile and heavy engineering industries are examples of where fewer people are employed than formerly.

The tertiary sector shows the most marked increase: banking and insurance are examples of where more people are now being employed.

### Women in employment

One recent trend which is related to the sex structure has been the **increase in the number of women working**, especially those employed in part-time jobs. This is especially noticeable in the electronics field, where women possess the advantage of having greater manipulative skill – their typically smaller and more nimble hands and fingers are often more efficient at assembling small components.

The service sector has, for many years, employed a large number of women workers, often on a part-time basis, e.g. in shops, offices and banks. The part-time nature of the work suits many women with young children at school; and the clerical and secretarial skills which they often possess are relevant to this sector of the economy.

**Fig. 2.7**  Women employed in a 'high-tech' industry

## 2.5 Unemployment

Unemployment has been a major economic problem in the United Kingdom during the 1980s. There are different types of unemployment which affect the different groups found in the population, the various industries which make up the economy, and the various regions of the country.

### Frictional unemployment

This form of unemployment is temporary and voluntary, occuring when **people change jobs**. It represents the time spent looking for the new job.

### Structural unemployment

This form happens when there is a **long-term change in demand or supply**: for example, when a product or a skill becomes out-of-date or unfashionable.

Structural unemployment has affected whole industries in the UK, such as iron and steel, textiles and cars. Overseas competition has often led to UK companies becoming uncompetitive, with a resulting fall-off in jobs in these industries.

### Cyclical unemployment

Now often referred to as 'Demand deficient' unemployment, it arises from a general **lack of demand** for goods and services in the economy.

*Seasonal unemployment*

This occurs in industries such as tourism and agriculture, where the **seasonal nature of the work** leads to people being made unemployed at certain points during the year.

*Technological unemployment*

This type of unemployment arises from the fact that, in more and more areas of work, it is becoming possible to substitute **machines for people**: for example, the use of robots on production lines to replace welders, assembly workers, etc.

## Groups unemployed

Although no one is immune from the risk of being unemployed, certain groups and individuals stand a higher chance of becoming unemployed.

*Younger and older workers*

Those coming onto the labour market face problems in both getting jobs and keeping them (younger workers are less expensive to be made redundant). Older workers, those aged 50 or over for example, also find it relatively difficult to get other jobs and are less likely to want to retrain for other work. People with **temporary jobs** also tend to be either at the beginning or the end of their working lives: about 15 per cent of 16 to 19 year olds in work in 1986 were in jobs classed as temporary.

*Unskilled workers, and workers having out-of-date skills*

Most jobs in the newer industries are for skilled or semi-skilled workers: many of the people made redundant from the older industries have been doing unskilled work, or they may possess skills that are no longer required by these newer industries.

*Ethnic minorities and women*

In 1986, The Department of Employment calculated that 10.3 per cent of white workers were unemployed, compared with 19.8 per cent of ethnic minority workers. Where white and non-white applicants for jobs have similar qualifications, evidence suggests that the white applicant stands a greater chance of being employed due to the existence of racial prejudice against non-whites. Various Acts have been passed (Unit 18) in an attempt to stop discrimination taking place.

Although there has been a growth in part-time work and the employment of women workers in some areas of the economy, sexual discrimination against women in other areas appears to exist. Governments have also passed Acts to prevent sexual discrimination (Unit 18).

## Industries and regions

Fig 2.6 shows that jobs have been lost in the primary and secondary sectors. **Deindustrialization** has taken place: factories have closed down and manufacturing industry nowadays makes a lower contribution to the output of the UK's economy than formerly. The service sector of the economy has grown and increased in overall importance as a provider of work.

Unemployment varies from region to region. Even in the less-affected regions such as south-east England, there will be pockets of relatively high unemployment. In the UK, areas such as Northern Ireland and the north-east of England have been hit badly by structural unemployment. The next sections explain further the regional problems faced by the Government and the country.

## 2.6 The Mobility of Labour

In trying to solve the problem of unemployment, one alternative is to **move work to the workers**, for example by the Government using policies to help regions facing special difficulties. The other alternative is to **encourage the workers to move to the work**, either by moving **area** or by changing **occupation**.

### Geographical mobility of labour

Workers can move from area to area to get work but there are a number of factors which discourage people from moving.

1 **Family ties,** such as problems of children at school, or relatives in the area where the worker is currently living.
2 **Costs.** The high costs of housing in London, the South-East and East Anglia mean that many workers cannot move to those areas. Rented accommodation may not be available, or council house waiting lists may be too long. This brings difficulties to companies which need to recruit skilled labour and sometimes leads to firms offering house purchase schemes.
3 **Prejudice.** Workers may not be prepared to live in certain areas of the country.

### Occupational mobility of labour

If a worker cannot or will not move areas to find work, it may be possible to change occupations. This can again prove difficult, for the following reasons:

1  **Ability.** An individual may not have the inborn ability or skill to do certain work.
2  **Training and retraining.** People may regard themselves as too old to be retrained; facilities for training or retraining may not be available and retraining may be regarded as too long or too expensive.
3  **Pay levels.** Training or starting pay may be too low to attract potential workers.

## 2.7  Regional Problems and Policies

Those regions which have relied on traditional manufacturing industries to provide work for the population have faced the worst problems of unemployment. In the West Midlands, for example, difficulties faced by the car and other engineering industries led to a decline in this once prosperous area in the early 1980s. Unemployment climbed from 120 000 in 1976 to 343 000 by 1983.

Regions may also face other problems. Most will have cities which are suffering from 'inner-city decay'; those who can afford to, have tended to move out of the inner-city areas, leaving a population which often lacks money and amenities, and many social problems can then arise.

Even the most prosperous area of the country, the south-east of England, has its own problems. The **high cost of living** discourages workers in low-pay jobs from living or moving there and this may lead to understaffing in service industries such as nursing and public transport. **Congestion** of traffic and of living space is another problem that London and parts of the South-East in particular have to face. For example, the cost of congestion on the M25 – London's orbital motorway – has been estimated at £1 billion per year through time wasted in

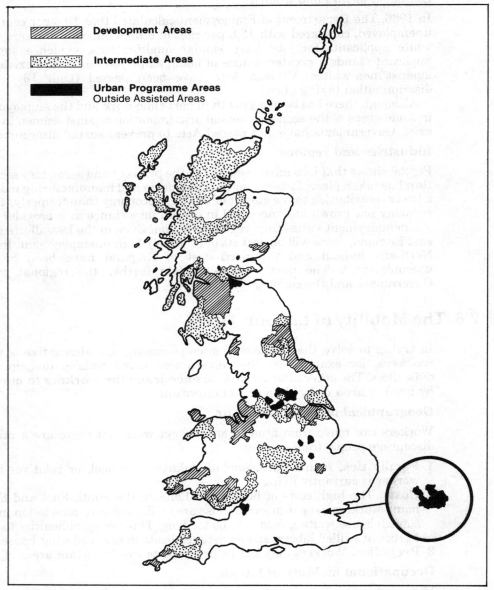

**Fig. 2.8** Assisted areas, as defined in 1984  Source: *DTI, 1988*

traffic hold-ups. The Confederation of British Industry (Unit 15) has also estimated that congestion in 1988 could have cost up to £300 for an average family.

**Policies to solve the problems**

To try and solve the various problems that exist in our regions, central and local government, together with other organizations, can adopt a range of policies.

*Training schemes*

To help those who have limited or outdated skills, various Government schemes have been set up, such as the Youth Training Scheme and the Employment Training Scheme (Units 13 and 19).

*Government regional policies*

If workers cannot, or will not, go to areas where there is work, then governments can adopt policies which encourage work to go to the workers. Firms have been encouraged to move to areas such as Northern Ireland and Scotland by being offered various incentives. Specific examples are given in Unit 19, and fig. 2.8 illustrates the country's Development Areas, Intermediate Areas and other Urban Programme Areas.

*Other policies*

These include:

1 Initiatives taken by non-government organizations, such as the Confederation of British Industry Task Force, set up to help halt the decline of inner-city areas in cities such as Newcastle.
2 Initiatives by central and local government to halt inner-city decay, e.g. by setting up Enterprise Zones to encourage firms to move back into inner-city areas.
3 Finance from the European Community through its Social Fund to help improve road systems, to counter the problems of congestion.

## 2.8 Summary

During the 1980s, the Government's stated priority was to control the rate of inflation. Unemployment has grown substantially, for a variety of reasons. All regions face the problem of unemployment: some are more bady affected, because the industries which originally based themselves there suffered a great decline in competitiveness or in the demand for their products.

Although jobs are available, many of the unemployed workers do not have the relevant skills, or cannot afford to move to the areas where the jobs are presently available. Action is taken by central government and other bodies to encourage business to locate in certain areas and to persuade people to train for, and move to, the work that is available.

# 3 INTERNATIONAL FACTORS

## 3.1 Introduction

Although some countries may be capable of producing all the food, manufactured products or services needed by their population, they will normally **specialize** in the production of only some of these goods or services. By specializing, **surpluses** are created which can be **traded** with other countries.

A country may lack natural resources: although the UK has discovered and used North Sea oil, it lacks reserves of many minerals such as iron ore. The country will therefore have to obtain what it lacks naturally from other countries, again by trading its own surplus products.

The United Kingdom depends on foreign trade. **Imports** are received from other countries and paid for by the UK. **Exports** are sent overseas, for which the country receives payment. Our trade consists of both 'visibles' and 'invisibles'. Visible trade consists of **goods** which are imported or exported. Invisible trade is made up of **services** such as banking, insurance and tourism, which are also imported and exported.

**Fig. 3.1** North Sea oil: an important UK export  Courtesy: *Shell UK Ltd*

## 3.2 International Trade

A country benefits from trading with other countries. These benefits come from greater competition, greater specialization and greater choice.

### Greater competition

Importing goods and services from abroad provides home-based producers with competition they would not otherwise have to face. This competition should lead to **lower prices** for consumers and help to guard against monopolies being created in the home country.

Firms will have **larger markets** available through exporting their goods or services to other countries. This can result in higher production levels: through being able to bulk-buy raw materials and make other savings, lower unit costs (i.e. although total costs increase, each batch of products made are now cheaper to make than the previous batches) can be passed onto the consumer.

### Greater specialization

Just as individuals build up expertise by specializing in careers, so countries can also develop specialist expertise in providing particular goods or services. The United Kingdom has a high reputation for its financial services; Japan produces quality electrical and electronic goods; Denmark is noted for its foodstuffs. Specialization should lead to **higher output** (and therefore surpluses, which will be traded) and greater efficiency.

### Greater choice

Differences in **climate and natural resources** mean that, if international trade did not take place, some goods would never be available in certain countries: e.g. tropical fruit in northern Europe, oil in Japan.

Consumers benefit from greater choice when international trade takes place. Goods are available that would otherwise not be and there is often a wider choice of the same type of product: for example Japanese, Swedish, French, Italian and other overseas manufacturers provide UK consumers with alternatives to cars made by British companies.

## 3.3 The UK and Foreign Trade

The United Kingdom needs to trade with other countries for many reasons:

1 It **lacks natural resources and raw materials**. The type of climate means that certain foodstuffs cannot be grown naturally and minerals not found here will have to be imported.
2 It needs **foreign currency** to buy what it cannot produce, and this foreign currency is gained by selling exports.
3 Its manufacturers gain from **wider markets**, allowing greater production and economies of scale.
4 As trade increases, **unemployment may fall**, which benefits the country as a whole, as well as individual workers.
5 Its population gains from the **wider choice** of goods and services now available.

### Changes in UK trade

Until recently, the United Kingdom was regarded by other countries as essentially a producer of manufactured goods for export, with raw materials and foodstuffs being imported in return. Exports of manufactured goods and 'semi-manufactures' are still very important, as the statistics in fig. 3.2 below show, and are boosted nowadays by the export of North Sea oil.

The largest imports to the UK are now also finished manufactured goods, with foodstuff imports taking a smaller proportion of the total than previously.

The major goods trade of the UK is shown in fig. 3.2.

| TYPE OF GOODS | EXPORTS (£ million) | (£ million) | IMPORTS (£ million) | (£ million) |
|---|---|---|---|---|
| Foodstuffs: e.g. cereals, meat, beverages, sugar | | 4 506.1 | | 8 950.1 |
| Fuels and lubricants: petroleum and related products | | 16 795.5 | | 10 663.6 |
| Manufactured goods (total): | | 52 506.1 | | 58 312.2 |
| chemicals and related products | 9 411.7 | | 6 900.8 | |
| leather, paper, textiles, other materials | 10 430.2 | | 14 342.3 | |
| industrial, office and other machinery, vehicles | 24 667.5 | | 26 937.5 | |
| other manufactured items | 7 996.7 | | 10 131.6 | |

**Fig. 3.2** Major UK trade in goods, 1985
Source: *Department of Trade and Industry, CSO 'Blue Book' 1988 edition*

*Reasons for change*

These are the main reasons which have led to the decline in importance of the UK as a manufacturing nation:

1  The growth in importance of the manufacturing sector in other countries. This has led to **increased competition** from areas such as the Far East.
2  **Lower costs** in competing countries. Lower wage costs may exist in the overseas country, which will probably lead to cheaper total costs of making the item and therefore a more competitive price may be charged.
3  **Less competitive and efficient UK management and workforce.** For example, there may be an unwillingness to learn foreign languages or a lack of investment in new machinery and processes.
4  **Poor quality, design and marketing** of UK-manufactured products.

## 3.4  The Balance of Payments

The 'Balance of Payments' records the inflow and outflow of a country's foreign currency. Inflows of foreign currency come from the export of goods and services: outflows of foreign currency occur when imports of goods and services are paid for.

The Balance of Payments is made up of the import and export of 'visibles' and 'invisibles'.

### The Balance of Trade

The Balance of Trade, or 'visible balance', is calculated by:

**visible exports less visible imports**

Visible exports and imports are of **goods only** and do not include services: engineering products, textiles, foodstuffs and chemicals are examples of visible trade.

If visible exports are greater than visible imports, there is a **surplus** on the country's balance of trade: if visible imports are larger than visible exports, there is a **deficit** on the balance of trade. Fig. 3.3 illustrates the United Kingdom's recent position with its balance of trade.

| VALUE (£ million) | 1977 | 1981 | 1985 |
|---|---|---|---|
| Exports | 31 728 | 50 977 | 78 111 |
| Imports | 34 012 | 47 617 | 80 289 |
| Visible balance | −2 284 | +3 360 | −2 178 |

**Fig. 3.3** UK visible trade  Source: *Department of Trade and Industry, CSO 'Blue Book' 1988 edition*

### The Balance of Payments on current account

The Balance of Payments 'on current account' includes the information contained in the Balance of Trade and also takes into account all **invisible** exports and imports. These 'invisibles' are **services**, such as the banking, insurance and other financial services which are provided by British companies to overseas clients.

The Balance of Payments is calculated by:

Visible exports − Visible imports
(= Balance of trade)
+
Invisible exports − Invisible imports
=
Balance of payments

| | 1985 (£ million) | | 1986 (£ million) | |
|---|---|---|---|---|
| **VISIBLE TRADE** | | | | |
| Exports | | 78 111 | | 72 843 |
| Imports | | 80 289 | | 81 306 |
| Visible balance | | −2 178 | | −8 463 |
| **INVISIBLES** | | | | |
| Credits ('Exports') | 79 784 | | 76 188 | |
| Debits ('Imports') | 74 687 | | 68 581 | |
| Invisible balance | | 5 097 | | 7 607 |
| *CURRENT BALANCE* | | 2 919 | | −856 |

**Fig. 3.4** UK Balance of Payments on current account, 1985 and 1986
Source: *Department of Trade and Industry, CSO 'Blue Book' 1988 edition*

A country's Balance of Payments may be **favourable** or **adverse** (unfavourable). If a country has a favourable balance of payments, the total value of its visible and invisible exports is greater than the total value of its imports. An adverse balance of payments exists when a country's total value of imports (visible and invisible) is greater than the total value of exports. The UK's performance on balance of payments is shown in fig. 3.4.

## 3.5 Exporting

Both countries and individual firms benefit from exporting. An exporting firm gains from the wider markets and therefore stands a better chance of surviving in the competitive world of business as well as receiving larger profits. Firms that do export, however, face many difficulties.

### Problems of exporting

1 Differences in **measurements**, such as different weights, sizes and electrical voltages.
2 **Language** difficulties: there will be problems of communicating over the telephone, by letter, designing sales brochures and product labels, etc.
3 **Trading risks:** there is, for example, the risk of granting credit to new overseas clients.
4 **Payment:** the overseas clients will pay their debts using foreign currency, which needs converting to sterling.
5 **Costs:** as well as typically higher delivery and insurance costs compared to selling on the home market, there may be a fluctuation in value of the overseas currency against the UK pound during the time it takes to sell the goods abroad (this can be very costly for exporters).
6 **Import restrictions:** a country may set up limits on the numbers or the value of certain goods that can be imported into that country.
7 **Documentation:** there are many complicated procedures that the exporting firm must comply with.

### Assistance to exporters

Governments, because they realize the advantages gained from international trade, will encourage and support their exporters (Unit 19). Other assistance will be provided by trade associations and local Chambers of Commerce (Unit 15) and by commercial banks (Unit 5).

## 3.6 Restrictions on International Trade

Governments in all countries tend to take action to restrict international trade. The following are the main types of action normally taken.

### Tariffs

Tariffs are import duties, such as the customs and excise duties of the United Kingdom. These have the effect of **raising the price of the imported goods** and therefore making them less competitive when compared to home-produced goods. Import duties can be an important source of government income.

### Quotas

Quotas are physical **restrictions on the amount of goods** that can be imported into a country over a period of time. For example, the UK Government has set a limit on the number of Japanese cars that can be imported into the United Kingdom.

### Subsidies

These are **given to home producers**, which makes their goods cheaper and therefore more competitive when compared with the prices of imported goods from overseas competitors.

### Embargoes

Embargoes are **bans on importing** certain items from overseas.

### Reasons for restricting trade

A government may decide to restrict imports into a country for a number of good reasons:

1 To **raise revenue** (from tariffs).
2 To **protect existing industries** from overseas competition.
3 To **protect newer, 'infant' industries** which are not yet strong enough to compete with established overseas firms.
4 To **restrict 'dumping'** of foreign goods (goods which are exported at very low prices by countries wishing to establish a market in another country).

There are disadvantages that arise when a government carries out measures to restrict free trade with other countries. The main one is that when one country introduces some form of restriction on trade, other countries could then follow this example: this can lead to a fall-off in total trade, and world economic recession.

## 3.7 Institutions Found in International Trade

### THE EUROPEAN COMMUNITY (EC)

#### Its influence on trade

The EC was established in 1957 by the Treaty of Rome, and now consists of 12 member nations, including the United Kingdom. One of the reasons for its formation was to promote trade between its members; Unit 18 explains one of its other roles, that of regulating and controlling business activity.

Its main effects on trade are given below.

#### Subsidies

These are provided, e.g. to those in agriculture through the 'Common Agricultural Policy' (CAP). This should result in EC farmers becoming more competitive with the rest of the world. The CAP, however, is often criticized for creating 'butter mountains', 'wine lakes' and other surpluses; and the high CAP budget means that less money is available for other EC projects and policies.

#### The free movement of labour and investment

This takes place between the Member States and helps lead to increased efficiency and trade.

#### Other Community policies

These provide further money and resources, e.g. for training, which helps in making EC firms more competitive in world markets.

#### The Common External Tariff

For the purposes of trading with other countries, the Community has established the Common External Tariff (CET). There are no internal tariff barriers between member states, and the use of a common external tariff means that goods coming into the Community – wherever they enter – are subject to the same tariff.

#### Membership of the EC

The 'Common Market' is presently the largest single market in the western world, with a population of over 320 million consumers. This 'single market' aspect will be further strengthened in 1992.

| Original members, 1957 | 1972 | 1980 |
|---|---|---|
| Belgium | UK | Greece |
| France | Denmark | |
| Italy | Eire | |
| Luxemburg | | **1986** |
| Netherlands | | Portugal |
| West Germany | | Spain |

**Fig. 3.5** EC membership 1988

#### Trade with the EC

Fig. 3.6 is a summary of the United Kingdom's trade with both the Community and the rest of the world. The importance of trading with EC countries is clearly seen from these figures. Since the UK's entry into the Common Market, trade with it has continually grown. In 1972 the 11 other countries now in the EC took **one third** of UK exports: currently, **half** the exports and imports from the United Kingdom take place with EC countries.

#### The 'Single Market' in 1992

The UK is increasing its trade with the Community countries: by 1993 it will be linked physically to the rest of Europe by the Channel Tunnel. The 'single market' proposals for 1992 come from the Single European Act (SEA) which came into operation in 1987: they are wide-ranging and will influence all UK exporters and importers in a number of ways:

1 **Common EC standards** of quality and safety for many goods will be established. The various national standards and rules for these products will be abolished, and UK industry must ensure that its products meet these new requirements.
2 There will be **open markets** in information technology and telecommunications. Common standards are planned and equipment made by UK companies will again have to meet these new standards.

| IMPORTS TO AND EXPORTS FROM | IMPORTS (£ million) 1985 | EXPORTS (£ million) 1985 |
|---|---|---|
| 1 The European Community | 39 004.8 | 36 233.8 |
| 2 The rest of Western Europe (e.g. Norway, Sweden, Austria) | 14 571.5 | 9 430.6 |
| 3 North America (USA and Canada) | 11 709.1 | 13 331.5 |
| 4 Other developed countries (e.g. Japan, Australia, New Zealand) | 6 379.3 | 3 791.1 |
| 5 Oil exporting countries (e.g. Nigeria, Kuwait, Iraq, Venezuela) | 1 876.5 | 5 952.1 |
| 6 Other developing countries (e.g. Ghana, Egypt, India, Jamaica) | 8 512.0 | 7 923.5 |
| 7 Centrally planned economies (e.g. USSR, East Germany) | 1 893.2 | 1 587.2 |

**Fig. 3.6** Value of UK imports from and exports to the European Community and other areas
Source: *Department of Trade and Industry, CSO 'Blue Book' 1988 edition*

3 Restrictions on **financial services** will be removed. British companies, such as banks and investment houses, will compete more openly with other EC firms.

4 Changes in **transport** services are planned. Increased freedom for shipping services, road haulage and civil aviation should allow UK transport firms greater opportunities to compete in other countries.

5 The **Single Administrative Document** was introduced in 1988. It has replaced about 100 trade forms and is leading to all Member States using the same documentation.

## THE INTERNATIONAL MONETARY FUND (IMF)

The IMF was established in 1947. Its aims include:

1 Keeping the exchange rates of the world's different currencies stable (see below).
2 Helping nations which are experiencing balance of payments problems.
3 Promoting world trade in general.

Most countries outside the Communist Bloc are members of the IMF: they contribute to its fund and can receive financial assistance if they are experiencing temporary balance of payments problems.

*Exchange rates*

The advantage of stable exchange rates for firms involved in foreign trade is that they can **calculate exactly how much they will earn** from exporting to another country.

For example, under a stable, or **'fixed' exchange rate** system, a UK manufacturer exporting to the USA knows that if the current exchange rate is two dollars to the pound, this will still be the rate at which he converts the US dollars he earns to UK pounds when payment is made for his goods. This fixed rate also helps him price his goods in the overseas market. Under a system of **'floating' exchange rates**, there is more of a gamble: by the time payment is made, the exchange rate between dollars and pounds may have altered, costing the exporter money.

The **European Monetary System** attempts to stabilize the values of most of the EC member countries' currencies: as yet, the UK has not joined the European Monetary System.

## THE GENERAL AGREEMENT ON TARIFFS AND TRADE (GATT)

Like the IMF, GATT was also set up in 1947, following World War II. It attempts to reduce trade barriers and to promote free trade. There are some 80 member countries, including the UK, which meet in Geneva to try to achieve the specific aims of:

1 **Reducing tariffs,** by cutting them in 'tariff rounds'.
2 **Reducing quotas.**

GATT's importance has declined as a result of the growth of the EC and other trade groupings. These will have their own rules on free trade, such as the European Community's CET (see page 24).

## UNCTAD

The **United Nations Conference on Trade and Development** (UNCTAD) was first held in 1964 and now takes place every four years. Its aim is to encourage the wealthy, developed

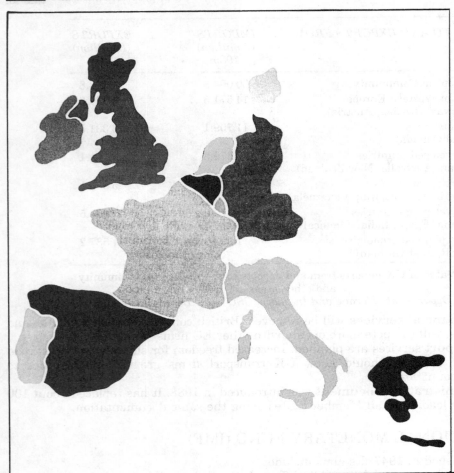

**Fig. 3.7** The Single Market
Courtesy: *DTI 1988*

countries to assist the economically poorer countries. It sets out to achieve this aim by a number of measures:

1 Trying to **stabilize the prices of certain commodities**, so that countries which depend on the export of these commodities (e.g. Zambia and copper, Bolivia and tin) are not so badly hit should the price of the commodity fall drastically.
2 Encouraging the better-off, developed countries to give a set percentage of their earnings as **aid to underdeveloped countries**.
3 **Reducing or eliminating export restrictions** (tariffs and quotas) which are placed on exports from developing countries.

# 3.8 Multinationals

A multinational company is one which **produces in more than one country**.

The ownership of a multinational is based in only one country: for example, it may operate as a holding company (a company set up to **hold** overall control over other countries, which then do business under their own name) which has subsidiaries in other countries. In some cases, the multinational will be organized so that the various stages of production take place in different countries.

Multinationals are responsible for approximately one third of total world production. In the UK, especially since joining the European Community in 1970, multinational companies have gained an increasing share of total production.

Fig. 3.8 illustrates the structure of BICC plc, an example of a multinational company.

## Effects on the UK economy

There are many benefits to an economy such as the United Kingdom through allowing overseas multinationals to set up in business. These are now listed.

1 **Reduced unemployment:** e.g. Nissan starting car production in the North-East, Epson producing printers in the West Midlands, both regions having been badly affected by high unemployment levels.

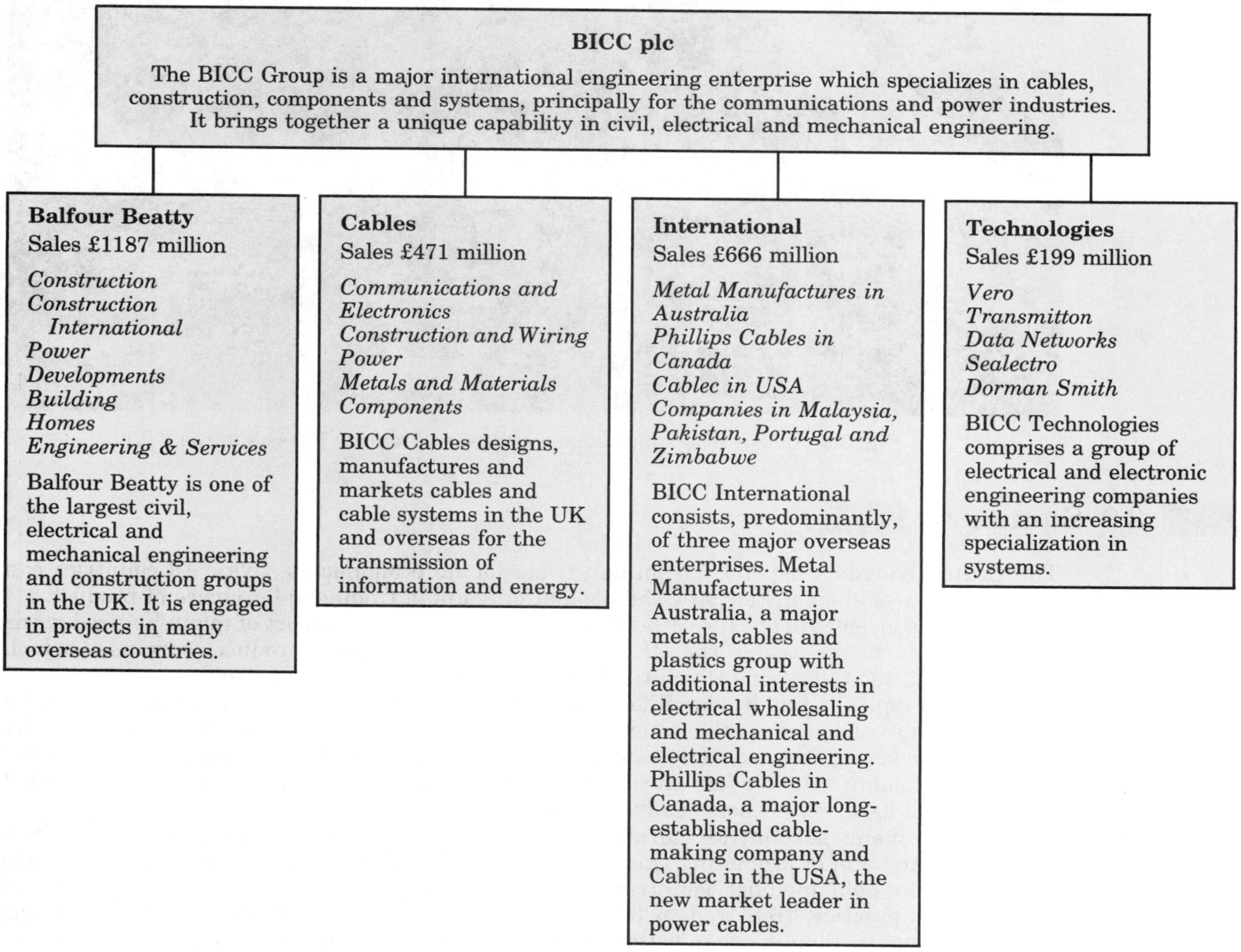

---

**BICC plc**

The BICC Group is a major international engineering enterprise which specializes in cables, construction, components and systems, principally for the communications and power industries. It brings together a unique capability in civil, electrical and mechanical engineering.

---

**Balfour Beatty**
Sales £1187 million

*Construction*
*Construction*
*    International*
*Power*
*Developments*
*Building*
*Homes*
*Engineering & Services*

Balfour Beatty is one of the largest civil, electrical and mechanical engineering and construction groups in the UK. It is engaged in projects in many overseas countries.

---

**Cables**
Sales £471 million

*Communications and*
*Electronics*
*Construction and Wiring*
*Power*
*Metals and Materials*
*Components*

BICC Cables designs, manufactures and markets cables and cable systems in the UK and overseas for the transmission of information and energy.

---

**International**
Sales £666 million

*Metal Manufactures in*
*Australia*
*Phillips Cables in*
*Canada*
*Cablec in USA*
*Companies in Malaysia,*
*Pakistan, Portugal and*
*Zimbabwe*

BICC International consists, predominantly, of three major overseas enterprises. Metal Manufactures in Australia, a major metals, cables and plastics group with additional interests in electrical wholesaling and mechanical and electrical engineering. Phillips Cables in Canada, a major long-established cable-making company and Cablec in the USA, the new market leader in power cables.

---

**Technologies**
Sales £199 million

*Vero*
*Transmitton*
*Data Networks*
*Sealectro*
*Dorman Smith*

BICC Technologies comprises a group of electrical and electronic engineering companies with an increasing specialization in systems.

---

**Fig. 3.8** The BICC Group structure (1987) Courtesy: *BICC plc*

2 The **introduction of new technology**: Honda's presence in the UK, for example, helping Rover to design and produce cars.
3 **Training in up-to-date skills:** multinationals often provide efficient training schemes, or link up with other providers, such as local colleges, to improve the skills of the local workforce.
4 **Other benefits,** such as providing other work for the local economy: e.g. work for local catering firms supplying meals to the company or for local suppliers of components which are required by the multinational.

There are disadvantages to the UK and other countries through these multinationals being allowed to operate. The following are typical problems that can arise.

1 The multinational may **import expertise** of its own managers and trained workers, rather than recruit locally.
2 The multinational may introduce different countries' working practices, which may lead to **industrial relations problems**: 'single-union' and 'no-strike' agreements have not always been introduced easily or successfully.
3 It can **send the profits out of the country**, to its 'home' country.
4 There may be **difficulties of control**: because of their size, multinational companies can exert great influence over a government's economic policies, the government finding it difficult to control the operations of the company.

**Fig. 3.9** An overseas multinational company producing TV sets in the UK

## 3.9 Summary

The United Kingdom depends on foreign trade for its economic survival. All countries can benefit from trade, for instance by the population gaining from a wider choice of product.

Countries concentrate on their relative strengths, such as the export of manufactured goods and 'invisibles' in the case of the UK. Specialization by countries produces surpluses, which can then be traded for goods which the home country cannot produce itself.

Firms will typically find it more difficult to export their goods than to sell them on the home market because of specific problems such as exchanging currency, or transport difficulties. By exporting, however, they not only contribute to their own profitability; they also help their country by earning valuable foreign currency. The country's balance of payments is a record of the success of its firms in their dealings with the rest of the world.

The governments of countries can choose to join a number of organizations, such as the EC, which have the aim of promoting trade between nations. Other bodies, such as the IMF, are established to help member countries facing temporary problems with their balance of payments. In practice, 'free' trade is limited by governments using restraints to trade such as tariffs and quotas, though organizations like the EC devote their energies to removing these barriers to free trade.

# 4 BUSINESS ORGANIZATIONS

## 4.1 Introduction

The UK's economy is mixed: the 'mix' is made up of private sector and public sector organizations. The main organizations are shown in fig. 4.1.

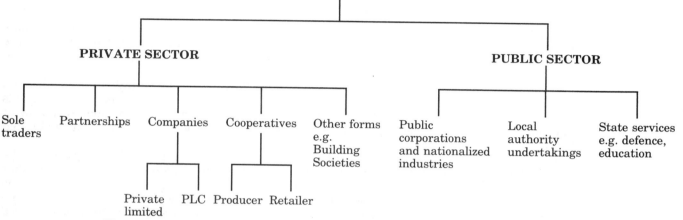

**Fig. 4.1** Business organizations in the UK economy

**Private sector** firms are owned by individuals, not by the State. These firms can be large or small, owned by one person or by thousands. By producing and selling their goods or services, they attempt to make profits for their owners.

As fig. 4.1 shows, the four main types of firm in the private sector are sole traders, partnerships, private limited companies and public limited companies. These are not the only types of private enterprise: other forms of ownership, such as cooperatives, are also found in this sector of the economy.

The **public sector** forms the second important part of the economy. It consists of both central government and local government organizations. The firms and industries which make up this 'public enterprise' are operated under state control. Ownership is therefore not in the hands of private individuals, although public sector organizations are run for the benefit of the general public.

## 4.2 The Private Sector

Businesses which operate in the private sector have a series of objectives. Their owners will want them to **survive** in the very competitive world in which they operate. If losses are made in the short-term, these may be put up with in the hope that business will improve in the future. The businessman or woman may also set out to gain a larger share of their local, regional or national market. They may therefore cut their prices to achieve this **larger market share** and so be willing, again for a short time, to accept lower profits.

Firms in the private sector are set up to make a profit. This **profit motive** encourages people either to invest in existing businesses—by buying their shares on the Stock Market, for example—or to establish themselves in business, perhaps on their own or in partnership with a friend. Most firms in the private sector are either sole traders (one person owning the firm), partnerships or limited companies.

A typical example of a **sole trader** is the traditional corner shop selling groceries, newspapers, sweets and tobacco, which may be open for long periods and which is likely to be owned by the person serving in the shop. **Partnerships** are often found in the main streets of towns and villages; the 'professions', such as dentists and accountants, often operate as partnerships. **Limited companies** are also widely found; the larger public limited companies, such as Marks and Spencer, Boots and Sainsburys, are household names, but there are many more (typically smaller) private companies.

### Unincorporated and incorporated businesses

Sole traders and partnerships are **unincorporated businesses**. The effects of a business being unincorporated are:

1 There is **no separate legal existence** from its owner or owners. This means that these firms cannot enter contracts in their own names and so the owners will be fully responsible for the business debts.
2 Sole traders and partners have **unlimited liability** for these business debts.
3 **Few formalities** are necessary to set up in business, compared to those involved in setting up a limited company.

Limited companies are examples of **incorporated businesses**. Unlike sole traders and partnership firms, limited companies have **many formalities** to go through before being established. Another important difference is that limited companies have a **separate legal existence** from their owners (their shareholders). This means that a limited company can **sue and be sued in its own name**, and that the owners are not personally responsible for the business debts: they gain from the principle of **limited liability**.

*The advantages of limited liability*

Two people who both have £5000 to invest will have many options to choose from. One may decide to set up in business as a sole proprietor in the hope of making profits from the firm; the other could buy £5000 worth of shares in a limited company and expect to receive a return on this investment through the company paying out dividends on the shares.

If the sole trader's business fails, he or she is liable to pay, from **personal savings**, all those **business debts** that the firm cannot meet out of its own resources. If the limited company fails and is 'wound up', the shareholder who has invested the £5000 may lose this money, but he or she will not have to use personal assets or savings to pay for any further debts that the limited company cannot meet from its own money.

The liability of the sole trader – like the partner – is unlimited. The liability of the shareholder is limited, to the value of the investment in the limited company. The fact that limited companies are forced by law to use the terms 'ltd' (for 'limited') or 'plc' (the abbreviation for 'public limited company') acts as a **warning** to those who trade with the company that its liability is limited, and so they will not be able to recover their amounts owed if the company cannot itself meet these debts.

Limited liability has a great advantage to those who want to invest money in companies. Potential investors realize that they can only lose so much money and no more. This should encourage people to invest money in companies, which gives those companies the chance of raising more capital than would otherwise be the case.

## 4.3  The Sole Trader

These are the most commonly found type of business in the UK. They are owned and controlled by one person, who provides all the capital required by the business. Formation is relatively simple, and the organization of the business is usually quite straightforward.

Many sole traders provide **specialist services**, such as plumbers, carpenters and hairdressers. Although many sole traders will employ a few workers, the ownership remains in the hands of the sole trader.

**The advantages and disadvantages of being a sole trader**

The following are the main advantages gained by sole traders:

1 The business is usually small-scale and so **small amounts of capital** are required to set it up. It is easy for the owner to **keep overall control**, because of the small-scale nature of the firm.
2 It is **easy to set up** in business, requiring few formalities.
3 The owner is his own boss: **quick decisions** can therefore be made.
4 **Profits do not have to be shared** with others.

Sole traders also face a number of problems that they have to cope with:

1 **Unlimited liability:** the risk of the sole trader having to sell personal assets to pay for business debts.
2 It may be **difficult for the business to continue** if the owner dies, is ill, or takes time off.
3 **Long hours and few holidays** are typical for sole traders.
4 The limited amount of capital can lead to **difficulties in expanding** the business and sole traders usually find it more difficult than large-scale organizations to borrow more money.
5 **Responsibility cannot be shared** and the absence of a partner may mean that there is a **lack of new ideas**.

## 4.4  Partnerships

Partnerships can also be formed easily. The partners normally draw up a **deed of partnership** which sets out the essential details. It will contain details of the **number** of partners, the **type** of partnership, the amount of **capital** contributed by each partner, how profits **and losses** are to be shared, and whether one or more of the partners is to receive a **salary** for working in the partnership.

If the partners have not drawn up a deed of partnership, the **1890 Partnership Act** lays down a series of rules:

1 Profits and losses are shared equally.
2 Partners are not entitled to salaries.
3 Loans made to the partnership by partners receive 5 per cent interest.
4 There is no interest awarded on the capital invested by the partners.

Partners, like sole traders, contribute all the capital: some partners, known as **sleeping partners**, only invest money in the business, and do not take part in its running.

### The advantages and disadvantages of partnerships

Partnerships can be formed almost as easily as sole trader businesses. They have a number of advantages when compared to sole traders, as shown below.

1 Since there must be at least two partners, they can **divide control** of the business between them. Division of labour becomes possible, with partners specializing in certain aspects of the business.
2 Management and responsibility can be **shared** by the partners, allowing greater time off and more holidays than are possible for sole traders.
3 Partnerships typically have **more capital** than sole trader businesses (there are more owners to contribute). Expansion is therefore easier for a partnership than for a sole trader.
4 There is **greater continuity** than a sole trader (although the death of a partner will end the partnership).

The disadvantages of operating as a partnership include the following points:

1 There is **unlimited liability**, like sole traders.
2 **Disputes** can take place between the partners.
3 Partnerships also tend to be small-scale, and so **expansion is still difficult**.

## 4.5 Limited Companies

The 1980 Companies Act identified and distinguished two types of limited company: **public limited companies** (PLC) and **limited companies** (ltd co), often called private limited companies. The most important differences between these two forms is that shares of the PLC

**Fig. 4.2** A well-known 'high street' company

are 'quoted', i.e. sold, on the Stock Exchange. These shares can therefore be sold to members of the public (which explains the word 'public' in the name), unlike the ordinary limited companies.

Both forms of company must indicate their status in their names: this is usually done by the abbreviations 'PLC' or 'ltd'. It warns traders with them that their liability is limited, and therefore the traders cannot recover trading debts from the personal funds of the company shareholders.

### Features of limited companies

Both types of limited company can be formed by a minimum of two shareholders (there is no maximum). The key features are as follows:

1 There is **limited liability**: the liability of shareholders is limited to the amount of their investment in the company.
2 There is a **separate legal existence**. A limited company is a 'separate legal entity' in the eyes of the law: this means that it can sue and take legal action in its own name, own property and other assets, and enter legal contracts in its own name.
3 The company gains from greater **continuity**: its separate legal existence is not affected by events such as the death of one of its shareholders.
4 There is a **separation of ownership and control**. Unlike partnerships and sole traders, where the owners usually run the business themselves, the owners – the **shareholders** – of limited companies have little say in the running of these companies. It is the **directors**, elected by the shareholders at the AGM (Annual General Meeting) of the company who will control the company, even though they may not hold any shares. Directors will also appoint managers and other staff to assist them. Policies are decided by the Board of Directors and are carried out – with some delegation – by the Managing Director.

### Private and public limited companies

Compared to the sole trader and partnership, the private limited company has the advantages of limited liability, greater continuity and a separate legal existence. Its business affairs, however, are not as private as its name might suggest: unlike the unincorporated businesses, the private company must have its accounts audited and available for inspection.

Compared with a PLC, however, the ordinary limited company does not have the same opportunity to raise extremely large amounts of capital by offering its shares to the public.

**Multinational companies** (Unit 3) usually operate as PLCs in the United Kingdom.

### The advantages and disadvantages of PLCs

This form of business ownership also has the same advantages of limited liability, greater continuity and a separate legal existence as the private limited company. Its main advantage over the private limited company is in its ability to raise **capital from the public**: this is done by advertising its shares for sale. The other advantages it has as a form of business ownership come from its **size**, as follows:

1 It benefits from economies of scale such as bulk buying.
2 A PLC finds it is easier to borrow money because of its size and the security it can offer.
3 Through its size, a PLC can easily specialize, e.g. by establishing specialist departments and through using specialist equipment.

There are certain disadvantages associated with PLCs:

1 They may be **too large** and so suffer from 'red tape' and inefficiency.
2 Ownership can change overnight – **takeover bids** can be launched by rivals buying the PLCs shares on the Stock Exchange.
3 Their annual accounts are open to **public inspection** – the public company is not as private as the private company.
4 Because ownership and control have become separate, the **directors' interests may differ from those of the shareholders**. For example, the directors may have long-term plans to obtain a larger market share but the shareholders of the PLC may be expecting immediate, large returns on their investment in the company.
5 The PLC may be dominated by only a few shareholders, for example by **institutional investors** such as pension funds and insurance companies, which own large proportions of the shares.
6 Formation of the company is **complicated and expensive**.

## SETTING UP A LIMITED COMPANY

There are a number of steps to take in setting up a limited company. Fig. 4.3 shows the main steps.

If a business wishes to become a limited company, it must become **registered** with the Registrar of Companies. There are a number of documents that must be delivered to the Registrar, including the Memorandum of Association and the Articles of Association.

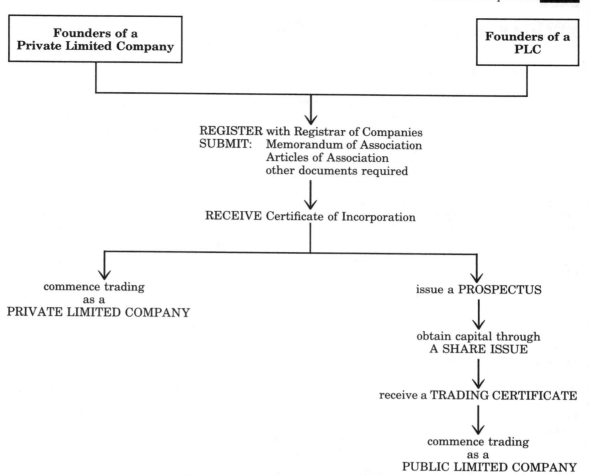

**Fig. 4.3** Setting up a limited company

*The Memorandum of Association*

This document contains details of the **external relationship** of the limited company with the world at large. There will be a number of clauses:

1 The **Name** clause, which is to ensure that it will have a different name from other limited companies.
2 The **Objects** clause, giving the purpose for which the company was formed (e.g. to make tyres, or to construct buildings).
3 A **Situation** clause, which states where the company has its registered office.
4 A **Liability** clause, to state that liability of its members is limited.
5 The **Capital** clause, which gives the amount of capital the company is registered with and the types of its shares (Unit 5).
6 The **Association** clause, which is signed by at least two of those forming the company to declare that they are taking up their shares in the company.

*The Articles of Association*

This document governs the **internal workings** of the limited company. It is signed by those who have signed the Memorandum of Association and it must not conflict with the Memorandum. The articles include:

1 How **directors** are elected.
2 Their **number, rights and duties**.
3 How **meetings** are called and conducted.
4 How **profits** are divided.

*Registration of the company*

Other documents must also be submitted. These include the **Statutory Declaration**, which is a declaration that the requirements of the Companies Acts have been followed. If the Registrar is happy that the correct formalities have been met, he will issue a **certificate of incorporation**. The company now has a separate legal entity.

At this point, the private company can start trading but the PLC must set about raising its capital from the public. It will issue a **prospectus** – which gives details about the plans of the PLC – to invite the public to subscribe capital. Once sufficient capital has been raised, the Registrar issues a **trading certificate** and the PLC can now start trading.

## 4.6 The Public Sector

The public sector of the economy consists of those firms and industries for which **central or local government** are mainly responsible. This sector includes such activities as state education, the National Health Service and the armed forces. These are paid for through the taxation system, and their purpose is to provide services for the whole population.

Other public sector activity involves **public corporations** (including nationalized industries) and **local authority undertakings**. These also provide services to the public, often competing with firms in the private sector. The differences between the two sectors are summarized in fig. 4.4.

| SECTOR OF THE ECONOMY | OWNERSHIP | SOURCES OF FINANCE | REASON FOR EXISTENCE |
|---|---|---|---|
| PRIVATE SECTOR | PRIVATE INDIVIDUALS | INDIVIDUALS AND FIRMS | PROFIT MOTIVE |
| Sole traders | One person | Sole trader | Profit for owner |
| Partnerships | Two or more individuals | Partners | Profit for partners |
| Limited companies | Two or more shareholders | Shareholders | Profit for shareholders |
| | | Other sources, e.g. commercial banks | |
| PUBLIC SECTOR | CENTRAL & LOCAL GOVERNMENT | PUBLIC FUNDS | SERVICE MOTIVE |
| Public corporations | Central government | Taxation and trading | To provide a service, and break even or make profit |
| Local authority undertakings | Local government | Local finance and trading | To provide a service, and break even or make profit |

**Fig. 4.4** Private and Public Sectors: the main differences

### Reasons for public ownership

The Government may decide to take a firm or industry into public ownership for a number of reasons:

1 To control a 'natural' monopoly, e.g. to ensure the safe processing and distribution of water.
2 To take over the control of a private sector monopoly, which would otherwise exploit the public.
3 To make sure that unprofitable but essential services, such as health services, are provided.
4 To protect an industry, and therefore to protect jobs.
5 To ensure national security and safety by controlling defence and, for example, atomic energy.
6 To avoid wasteful duplication, e.g. in allowing several different railway companies to operate between the same towns.
7 To provide capital for important large-scale developments.

### The advantages and disadvantages of public ownership

Public ownership brings a number of advantages. **Essential services** will be provided, even if they are unprofitable. Secondly, **everyone shares in the profits** from public ownership. **Wasteful duplication** of services can be avoided and planning can be coordinated through centralized control.

Public ownership, however, can lead to problems of **inefficiency**. Diseconomies of scale can arise due to the great size of the organizations involved, and the absence of a profit motive may give a lack of incentive to employees. Any losses must be met by the taxpayer and political interference can take place, affecting the ability of the organization or industry to work efficiently.

## 4.7 Public Corporations and Nationalized Industries

Care must be taken to distinguish between a **public limited company** and a **public corporation**. The PLC is an important type of business organization in the private sector, which has been formed to make profit for its shareholders. A public corporation, however, is quite different: it lies in the public sector, and has different objectives.

**Nationalized industries** are one form of public corporation: well-known examples include British Rail, British Coal and the Post Office. A nationalized industry – unlike other public corporations, such as the Bank of England – will **sell its goods or services directly** to the general public, therefore receiving its revenue directly from them as well.

### Features of a public corporation

A public corporation is formed by an **Act of Parliament**, which sets up its functions and organization. Its day-to-day policy is decided by its **Board**, appointed by the Minister responsible and which consults with the government. The public corporation has a legal identity which is separate from the government and it is set financial targets by the government, such as to break even or to make a profit.

A public corporation is **financed** through a number of sources (Unit 5). The Treasury provides it with funds through general taxation and may also make loans to the corporation. It may also receive income from its trading activities: any profits which are made can be used to pay interest on its loans or its capital, to repay part of its capital, or to expand.

A public corporation is **controlled** in the following ways:

1 **The Cabinet** will establish its overall policy, which the appropriate Minister must then follow.
2 **The Minister:** each corporation will have a government minister, who influences the appointment of the corporation's Chairman and Board members. The Minister will also negotiate with the Treasury to obtain funds for the corporation.
3 **Parliament:** MPs are free to question the Minister on the performance of nationalized industries, and parliamentary **Select Committees** will examine the workings of public sector corporations.
4 **Consultative Committees,** which are set up to listen to complaints from members of the public about public corporations.

### Privatization

During the 1980s, many nationalized industries have been privatized by the Government: this means that they have been **transferred from the public sector to the private sector**, losing their status as public corporations and becoming PLCs.

Other public corporations, which are still in the public sector, may be affected by privatization through **deregulation** (to allow greater competition to take place with the corporation), or by **using private sector services**—such as a private sector cleaning firm being used by a hospital—where these services are cheaper.

There are usually three arguments given for privatizing a public corporation:

1 Greater competition will take place, which can result in higher efficiency and lower prices for consumers.
2 A wider share ownership in the population will result from privatization.
3 Privatization leads to lower levels of government interference.

**Fig. 4.5** Privatization makes the news Courtesy: *The Guardian*

## 4.8 Local Authority Undertakings

Also known as 'municipal undertakings', these are businesses which the local authority operates on a commercial basis. The **finance** for their operation is raised locally, and they receive income from selling their services. Profits made can be 'ploughed back' to improve or expand the service. Day-to-day **control** of these services is provided by their managers, with overall policy being influenced by local councillors.

Some of these undertakings may compete with private sector firms, for example where local authority highways or buildings departments compete with other construction companies.

## 4.9 Other Forms of Business Organization

Many other forms of business organization are found. Some forms of business structure, such as the holding company, exist to control large organizations; other important forms which are widely found in the UK economy include cooperatives and franchising agreements.

## COOPERATIVES

There are two main types of cooperative: worker cooperatives and retail cooperatives.

### Worker cooperatives

Worker cooperatives are becoming increasingly popular forms of business ownership, with an estimated 1500 in the UK in 1988, and a growth in number of 250 per year. The federation of worker cooperatives – **ICOM** – was formed in 1971, and supports its member cooperatives through providing business information, training and other services.

Worker cooperatives vary both in size and in organization. In the United Kingdom, they have sometimes been formed by groups of workers 'buying out' their company, which may have been in severe financial or trading difficulties. By cooperating, the members can share experience, buy and share more expensive equipment and gain from economies of scale. In worker cooperatives, the members will contribute the capital and share the profits, and run the cooperative on democratic lines, with the managers often being elected from amongst the group of workers. Some specialists, such as an accountant, will be employed.

Areas of the economy where new workers cooperatives were established in 1987 included:

1 Printing, publishing and design (9 per cent of new cooperatives set up, 1987).
2 Foodstuffs (8 per cent).
3 Engineering and general manufacture (8 per cent).
4 Textiles and fashion (7 per cent).

### Retail cooperatives

Started by the 'Rochdale Pioneers' in 1844 because they were being exploited by local shops, the 'Coop' is a well-known retail outlet in most towns. These Cooperative Retail Societies (CRS) have the following features:

1 They have **wider aims** than most other business organizations. For example, the cooperative movement sponsors many Labour MPs, since it has political and social, as well as financial, objectives.
2 **Anyone can join** the Society, by buying shares (£1 each) from it: these shares cannot be bought and sold on the Stock Exchange.
3 There is **one vote per member** (shareholder), regardless of the number of shares held.
4 **Members share the profits** and also **elect the management committee**.

The retail cooperatives are supplied by the CWS – the Cooperative Wholesale Society – which allows them to take advantage of bulk-buying economies.

## FRANCHISING AGREEMENTS

In 1977 eight firms, including Wimpy, launched the British Franchise Association (BFA). The BFA currently has over 100 member companies, who operate over 80 000 outlets.

Franchising typically involves a company allowing someone to use its logo (its trade mark) and sell its products. In franchising, the **franchisees** are the people who pay for the use of the company's products: the **franchisor** (the company) will supply the products, fit out the shop in the accepted company style, and provide a wealth of marketing support, e.g. through national advertising.

It is probably best known in the 'fast food' industry, such as Wimpy and Kentucky Fried Chicken, but many variations are found, as shown below.

1 The manufacturer-retailer franchise: popular examples are petrol stations and car dealerships.
2 The wholesaler-retailer franchise: 'voluntary groups' (Unit 12) such as Spar are supplied by a group of wholesalers.
3 The trade mark-retailer franchise: the franchisor's product or service is marketed under a common trade name through standardized outlets, e.g. the 'fast food' business, and cleaning and copying services.

## 4.10 Summary

The United Kingdom's mixed economy contains many forms of business organization. There are a number of influences that will help to decide the type of organizations that exist or which are newly formed.

The **objectives** of the organization are a key factor. For example, if the profit motive is important, the business will be owned by private individuals and based in the private sector: organizations that provide services for the benefit of the local or national community are in the public sector.

In the private sector, sole traders, partnerships and limited companies are the main forms of business ownership. The limited company has the advantage of having a separate legal existence from its owners, whose liability is also limited to the extent of their investment in the shares of the company. Limited companies are, however, more complicated and expensive to form.

In the public sector, public corporations control a large share of the economy. Although recent government policies have led to the selling of certain public enterprises—e.g. British Gas, British Telecom and British Airways—this form of ownership still makes a significant overall contribution to the economy.

# 5 BUSINESS FINANCE

## 5.1 Introduction

All businesses need to obtain finance, to start and to grow. Firms will have to meet short-term debts, which come from trading activities such as buying goods on credit. This short-term finance is a firm's **working capital** (Unit 10). Any business which has a lack of working capital will face difficulties in surviving. It will not be able to take advantage of cost-saving discounts, since it does not have the cash available: and its creditors will be demanding payment of the money they are owed by the firm. In this last instance, they could take legal action to recover the amount owed by the firm, forcing it to close down and sell off its assets to get the required money.

Firms also need **long-term capital**, in order to expand. There are many sources of long-term capital: personal savings of sole traders and limited company shares are two well-known examples of such sources. Without sufficient capital, firms will find it impossible to grow.

## 5.2 Sources of Finance for the Public Sector

The two forms of business organization in the public sector outlined in Unit 4 were the public corporation and the local authority undertaking.

*Public corporations are financed by:*

1 General taxation, given in the form of Treasury grants.
2 Borrowing from the Treasury.
3 Retained profits which the corporations make from their trading activities.

*Local authority undertakings are financed by:*

1 Locally raised income by the authority, given to the undertakings in the form of a grant.
2 Borrowing from the local authority.
3 Retained profits from their trading activities.

Retained profits are an example of **internal sources** of funds, because the funds come from within the business itself. Both public corporations and municipal undertakings have other internal sources of funds (see below). Their grants and borrowing are illustrations of **external sources** of finance, because these funds come from sources outside the business.

## 5.3 Sources of Finance for the Private Sector

Private sector firms – principally sole traders, partnerships and limited companies – also have both internal and external sources of finance available to them.

### Internal sources of finance

Firms can raise funds internally, through these methods:

1 **Retained profits:** profits which are held back and not taken by the owners, i.e. they are not distributed as dividends to shareholders, but kept as **reserves**.
2 **Selling assets** which are no longer required.
3 **Trade credit:** firms may take greater advantage of credit offered by suppliers and reduce the credit periods offered to their customers.
4 **Investing surplus cash,** receiving interest on this investment.
5 **Reducing stocks,** to release the cash 'tied up' in this stock.

### External sources of finance

Sole traders, partnerships and limited companies can obtain funds from many outside sources. Items 1 to 3 below are sources of long-term, 'fixed' capital: items 4 and 5 are shorter-term sources which can be used to improve the firm's working capital position.

1 **Personal savings,** or loans from friends or relatives.
2 Bank and building society **loans or mortgages**: central and local government may also make loans or grants available.
3 Using **finance houses**, through:
   (a) leasing equipment such as photocopiers (the firm rents the piece of equipment and saves

the cost of buying it);

**(b)** hire purchase: the equipment is bought in instalments, and the firm gets the use of the equipment before having to pay for it in full.

**4 Overdrafts** from banks.

**5 Factoring.** Firms which have debts owed to them by their customers (their debtors) can sell these debts to a company, and receive most of the cash owed to them by the debtors. The factoring company then chases the debtors for payment.

## 5.4 Shares and Debentures

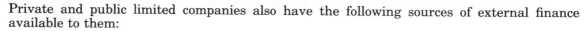

Private and public limited companies also have the following sources of external finance available to them:

**1 Share issues.** Shares indicate that their holders 'own a share' of the company. The public company (PLC) is allowed to sell its shares to the general public, through a prospectus: 'second-hand' shares are then sold on the Stock Exchange. The private limited company, however, must sell its shares privately: they cannot be exchanged on the Stock Exchange.

**2** Issuing **Debentures** (the name of the documents which are given to the lenders of long-term capital to a company). The lenders receive interest and will have this loan capital paid back at an agreed date.

### TYPES OF SHARES

There are two main types of share that can be issued by companies.

*Ordinary shares*

Ordinary shares, or 'equities', allow their holders to **vote** at company meetings. The rate of dividend – the reward for holding the shares – depends on the company profits: it is a **variable rate**. Ordinary shareholders will be the **last to be paid out of profits**, and so they risk not receiving any dividend when profits are poor. They are also the **last to have capital repaid** if the company is wound up. Ordinary shares, therefore, are regarded as rather risky investments, but which bring the chance of large returns (for example, when profits are high, large dividends can be declared).

*Preference shares*

Companies may also issue Preference shares. Unlike Ordinary shares, these do not normally give their holders a vote at meetings. The preference shareholders **receive priority** over ordinary shareholders in both payment of dividend and repayment of capital. The preference dividend, which is a **fixed dividend**, is therefore more likely to be paid. Preference shareholders also stand a greater chance of getting their investment repaid than do the ordinary shareholders (who are last in the queue for repayment). Preference shares are thus a safer investment than ordinary shares but they will not receive high returns when profits are high – their dividend is a fixed amount.

Some preference shares are **cumulative**. If profits in one year are not large enough to allow the preference shareholders their full dividend, the amount that they are owed is carried forward to the next year and will be paid when profits are large enough to allow this. Fig. 5.1 summarizes the differences between ordinary and preference shares.

| | ORDINARY | PREFERENCE |
|---|---|---|
| *VOTING RIGHTS* | Normally one vote per share | Usually non-voting |
| *PAYMENT OF DIVIDEND* | Variable: high or low depending on level of profits. | Fixed: often cumulative |
| | Paid after Preference | Paid before Ordinary |
| *REPAYMENT OF CAPITAL* | Repaid after Preference shareholders: a riskier investment | Repaid before Ordinary shareholders: a safer investment |

**Fig. 5.1** Ordinary and Preference shares

### DEBENTURES

Debentures, also called **loan stock**, are a long-term loan to a company. The debenture holders are therefore **creditors** of the company and not owners, unlike shareholders. The loan is normally **secured** against company assets: if the company cannot repay the loan, the debenture holder can then sell the asset to recover the value of the loan.

In return for making the loan, the debenture holder receives a **fixed rate of interest** on the loan: this payment must be made by the company, whether it is making profits or losses. This debenture interest is a normal business expense, and not paid out of the company's net profit.

Like other loans, debentures will normally be **repaid** at some future date (which is agreed in advance between the company and the debenture holder).

The key differences between shareholders and debenture holders are summarized in fig. 5.2.

|  | *SHAREHOLDERS* | *DEBENTURE HOLDERS* |
| --- | --- | --- |
| *STATUS* | Own a share of the company, often having a vote | Creditors: a loan is made to the company, with no say in its affairs |
| *REWARD* | Dividend (fixed or variable) is paid out of profits | Fixed rate of interest paid whether profits are made or not |
| *REPAYMENT* | Share capital not normally repaid: if company wound up, repaid after debenture holders | Debentures normally repayable at a future date: if company wound up, repaid before shareholders |

**Fig. 5.2** Shareholders and Debenture holders

## 5.5 Institutions through which Finance is Obtained

**Savings institutions** are key providers of long-term capital to business. The most important forms of savings institutions for business capital are described below.

### Pension funds

These are formed from the contributions made by groups of workers towards their private pensions (which are in addition to the State pension scheme). Trustees manage the funds and invest them to try to get the highest possible safe return on this investment for the benefit of those making the contributions.

### Insurance companies

Insurance premiums, paid by individuals and businesses, are invested by the companies to make a profit as well as to provide income to meet the insurance claims that they must pay.

### Unit trusts

These institutions tend to compete with building societies for the savings of the general public. The savings from a group of small savers are invested by professionals in a range of stocks and shares for safety; part of their ensuing profit is used to pay their investors.

### Investment trusts

These are companies which issue shares to the general public and use the income to invest elsewhere, for example in government securities or company shares.

### Other institutions

**Investors in Industry** is an organization, independent of the government, which provides long-term capital and a range of advisory services to all types and sizes of firms. It is funded by the Bank of England and the high street banks.

**Banks** (see p. 42) and **building societies** are also important providers of business finance.

## 5.6 The Stock Exchange

The Stock Exchange (based in London, with some regional exchanges) acts as the most important **market** for capital in the UK. Since it is a market, it brings together sellers and buyers – in this case, the institutions, such as insurance companies, which **supply funds** and the companies (together with central and local government) which want to **borrow funds**.

The Stock Exchange is the market for **second-hand securities**, i.e. the shares and debentures of PLCs, and government stock. Smaller companies can trade on the **Unlisted Securities Market** (USM), which is linked to the main Stock Exchange, but which has less demanding rules for admitting companies to it.

The existence of the Stock Exchange makes it easier for companies, and the government, to raise long-term finance. It also encourages investment in new share issues, because companies and investors realize that these shares can easily be traded on this second-hand share market. Finally, the Stock Exchange establishes share prices. Shares have a 'nominal' (face) value, but their price on the Market will vary, for example due to the profit performance of the company.

**Fig. 5.3** Activity on Wall Street, one of the world's most important financial markets
Courtesy: *The Guardian*

The company can then sell any new shares issued at the current market price.

A popular criticism of the Stock Exchange is that it over-emphasizes short-term gains. As share prices fluctuate and investors **speculate** (gamble) on these prices, they often buy shares on the basis of short-term profit records, rather than because of any long-term business plans of the company.

## 5.7 Factors Affecting the Method of Finance Chosen

Firms do not normally rely on one method of long-term finance. There are usually alternative sources of funds, and alternative methods of providing the funds, from which it can choose its finance. The main factors influencing the method and source of finance are shown in fig. 5.4.

The **nature of the project** may determine the source of finance. For example, long-term projects may need injections of finance at particular points in time (perhaps a series of share issues could be made), whereas a short-term project could be financed by a bank loan. Companies with projects involving a lot of highly technological equipment could lease, rather than buy, these items, to ensure they keep using the most up-to-date equipment.

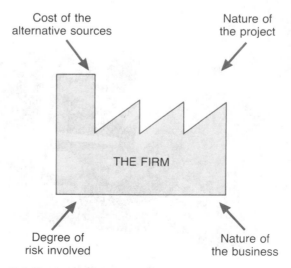

Cost of the
alternative sources

Nature of
the project

THE FIRM

Degree of
risk involved

Nature of
the business

**Fig. 5.4** Factors influencing the sources of finance chosen

The **nature of the business** can also determine the method of finance: some methods and sources are only available to certain forms of business (shares are an obvious example). Firms in **high-risk** areas, and smaller firms, may also find that their sources of finance are restricted and that the **cost of the finance** – the rate of interest charged – is higher than average.

## 5.8  Banking Services to Business

Commercial or 'high street' banks, such as Barclays, Lloyds or NatWest, are public limited companies, and are one of the institutions which provide business capital. They can offer both long-term capital, in the form of loans and mortgages, and short-term capital (bank overdrafts). The commercial banks also provide a wide range of other services to business.

### Business accounts

Banks will be used by firms to keep their money safely, to help them to obtain it and use it quickly, and to ensure they make the most effective use of their money. The most commonly used accounts by business are:

*Current accounts*

Firms will pay in cheques and cash received and use this account when they pay their bills by cheque. In addition to using cheques, firms may also use **direct debits** or **standing orders** for paying bills, or for receiving payments for customers. Direct debits are used when payments vary in amount and standing orders when these amounts are fixed.

Companies also use **credit transfers**, to pay into the current accounts of others and to receive credit transfer payments from customers. One very common use of this system is when a company pays its employees' salaries straight into their bank accounts.

*Deposit accounts*

These pay interest on the account balance, unlike most current accounts. Firms may use these accounts to keep **surplus cash** in for short periods.

*Other accounts*

Banks may provide a firm which trades overseas with a **foreign currency** account, into which the firm could pay the foreign currency that it has earned.

### Assistance on exporting

Banks will provide **advice** to companies engaged in exporting; they can also provide **foreign currency**, help to **finance exports**, and assist with **Bills of Exchange** (a method of payment widely used in international trade).

**Fig. 5.5** Some banking services for business

### Other services

Many other services may be offered. For example, **night safes** are provided by banks, in which firms can deposit money (usually their daily 'takings') when the bank is closed. If firms do not use the bank giro system for paying wages and salaries, banks can provide the **cash** required, analysed into its correct denominations. Finally, banks will provide a wealth of **advice** on all financial matters, on setting up in business and on taxation and legal matters.

## 5.9 Summary

Money has been called 'the lifeblood of any business'. All firms – whether they are based in the public sector or the private sector – require capital to commence business, and capital to expand.

There are many sources of capital: which one is used by a firm depends on a number of factors. Some business organizations are not allowed by law to use certain sources of finance: for example, the private limited company, unlike the PLC, cannot advertise its shares for sale to the public at large.

The major market for capital is the Stock Exchange: it brings together the sellers of capital such as insurance companies, and the buyers of that capital. It is a 'second-hand' market, because the shares that it deals with are being resold. These shares vary in type and are different from debentures, which can also be traded. Shareholders gain from limited liability, which encourages people to invest in companies and therefore bring extra capital into the business world.

# 6 BUSINESS RISK AND GROWTH

## 6.1 Introduction

The **profit motive** exists mainly in the private sector of the economy. People set up in business to make a profit, but risk making a loss and going out of business. They can protect themselves against some risks faced, in the same way that individuals can: through taking out **insurance**. There are, however, other risks which cannot be insured against by the business owner.

Successful firms will **grow** in size. There are many advantages that a large-scale business has: for example, it can buy in bulk more cheaply than a smaller firm, and it has other economies of scale. It will find, however, that there are limits to growth, such as the size of the market for the firm's products.

## 6.2 Insurance Services to Business

Of the four factors of production (Unit 1), it is 'Enterprise' which is most closely associated with the risks of business. The **Entrepreneur** – the businessman or businesswoman – is the person who decides to start a business and who takes the main risks of the business not succeeding.

The business may fail for various reasons. Its products may be badly designed, made or marketed; they may be too expensive, when compared with the competition; they may become quickly out-of-date or unfashionable; or a new law may make them illegal. These are **uninsurable risks**: the entrepreneur cannot take out an insurance policy against the business being unsuccessful. The reason for this is that the insurance companies cannot

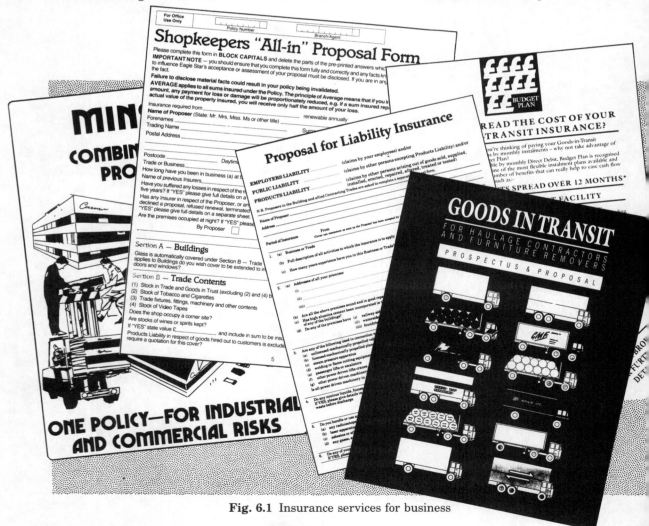

**Fig. 6.1** Insurance services for business

44

accurately calculate the **probability** – that is, the likelihood – of a firm being able to sell its products and be successful, and so cannot work out a suitable premium to charge.

There are other reasons why businesses fail. The buildings may burn down; its stock or takings may be stolen; it may be sued successfully by an employee who has been badly injured whilst at work. These are some examples of **insurable risks**: the probability of these events happening can be calculated and a premium can be set by the insurance company.

Insurance is therefore a valuable 'aid to trade': it allows firms to reduce some business risks and so stay in business. The main insurable business risks are described below.

### Fire damage

Firms can insure their **property** against fire damage. Buildings and their contents are insured against not only fire but also flooding and other natural disasters.

**Consequential loss** insurance is often taken out. When fire damages property or its contents, it is likely that the firm's trading – and therefore its profits – will be badly affected. This 'loss of profits' insurance will cover the firm for loss of earnings due to the fire and will pay its fixed costs (such as rent) which still have to be met.

### Theft insurance

Firms can insure against property being stolen from their premises.

**Fidelity guarantee** insurance can be taken out by firms to protect themselves against thefts of their property by an employee.

### Liability insurance

Should an employee suffer injury or illness at work due to the negligence of the employer, **Employers' Liability Insurance** – which must be taken out – provides compensation for the employee.

**Public Liability Insurance** is similar to employers' liability insurance: this insurance will cover the cost of damages (financial compensation) if a member of the public is injured, suffers illness or has property damaged as a result of the firm's negligence.

**Product Liability Insurance** can be taken out by a firm, to provide the cost of compensating a member of the public who has been injured by one of the firm's products.

### Motor vehicle insurance

Delivery vans, staff cars and other vehicles owned by a firm will be covered under a **fleet** policy.

### Bad debts insurance

A firm can protect itself by insuring against the risk of customers – debtors – failing to pay for the goods they have bought on credit from the firm.

### Other risks

Firms can also ensure their **goods in transit** against all risks, such as fire or theft.

Those firms with large plate glass windows, which are very expensive to replace, can take out **plate glass** insurance.

## 6.3 Size and Growth of Firms

A firm will seek to expand and grow in size for a number of reasons. Firstly, larger size leads to **economies of scale** which can make the firm more competitive. Secondly, a larger firm often has a **better chance of surviving** in the business world. It is likely to have a larger market share, it can borrow funds more easily and it will probably depend less on the profitability of a single product, having a wider range of products to sell than a smaller firm. Finally, the directors may seek the **power and status** that can come from being in charge of a larger firm, and so they will try to expand its operations.

A firm's **size** can be measured in different ways. Fig. 6.2 illustrates these.

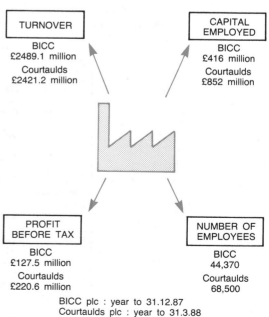

TURNOVER

BICC
£2489.1 million
Courtaulds
£2421.2 million

CAPITAL EMPLOYED

BICC
£416 million
Courtaulds
£852 million

PROFIT BEFORE TAX

BICC
£127.5 million
Courtaulds
£220.6 million

NUMBER OF EMPLOYEES

BICC
44,370
Courtaulds
68,500

BICC plc : year to 31.12.87
Courtaulds plc : year to 31.3.88

**Fig. 6.2** Measuring a company's size

The most popular criteria used are **turnover, net profit, capital employed** and the **number of employees**. As fig. 6.2 shows, Courtaulds had a slightly lower turnover than BICC and could therefore be thought of as 'smaller': but it has a larger net profit and capital employed figure, and Courtaulds also employed more workers than BICC.

## 6.4 Methods of Growth

Growth can take place slowly or quickly. Most firms will grow slowly through **internal expansion**. Many companies choose to expand more quickly, by deciding to take over, or merge with, other companies: mergers and takeovers are methods of **integration**.

**Fig. 6.3** Takeovers and mergers making the headlines  Courtesy: *The Guardian*

### INTERNAL EXPANSION

A firm can expand through:

1 Producing and selling more of its current products in its existing markets.
2 Selling these products in new (e.g. overseas) markets.
3 Making and selling new products.

### INTEGRATION

A **takeover** occurs when one company buys enough of another company's voting shares to allow it to take control. The directors of the company being taken over could try to oppose the takeover, but may be powerless to stop it. Fig. 6.4 illustrates the importance of takeovers as a means of expansion.

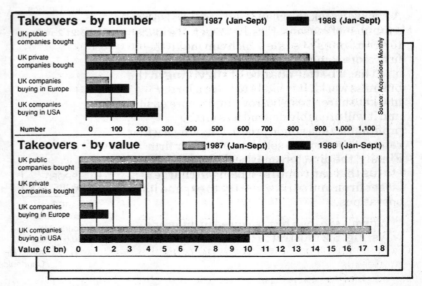

**Fig. 6.4** Takeovers by number and by value  Courtesy: *The Guardian*

A **merger** takes place between two companies through their agreement, unlike many takeovers. The two companies are completely reorganized following the merger.

Integration through either mergers or takeovers allows firms to expand quickly. There are three forms of integration:

1 Horizontal integration.
2 Vertical integration.
3 Lateral, or conglomerate, integration.

Fig. 6.5 summarizes these forms of integration.

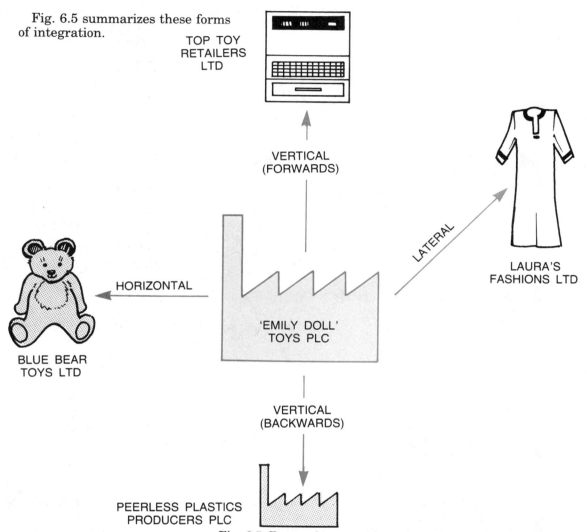

**Fig. 6.5** Forms of integration

### Horizontal integration

A horizontal merger or takeover occurs between firms **in the same industry** and **at the same stage of production**. For example, the mergers of the National Provincial and Westminster banks to form NatWest, the confectionery makers Rowntrees and Mackintosh, and the shoe chains Dolcis and Manfield.

Horizontal mergers lead to **larger-scale production** and therefore to economies of scale. Another advantage is that the new company has a larger market share, which gives it much **greater market power**.

### Vertical integration

Vertical integration also occurs between companies **in the same industry** but which are at **different stages of production**. Many breweries control their own public houses (retail outlets), tyre manufacturing companies such as Dunlop will own rubber plantations, and oil companies like Esso and Texaco have their own refineries and filling stations.

**Vertical backwards** integration occurs when a company starts to control firms supplying it with its raw materials: it is moving back down the chain of production. This form of integration has the following advantages:

1 The company is now directly in control of the **supply, quality and delivery** of its raw materials.
2 The **profits** of the firm under its control now belong to the company.
3 **Economies of scale** are possible.

- Exploration for oil in the North Sea
- Production of oil
- Refining at its refinery at Pembroke
- Distributing products throughout the country
- Selling products direct to commerce and industry, and through a modern chain of service stations.

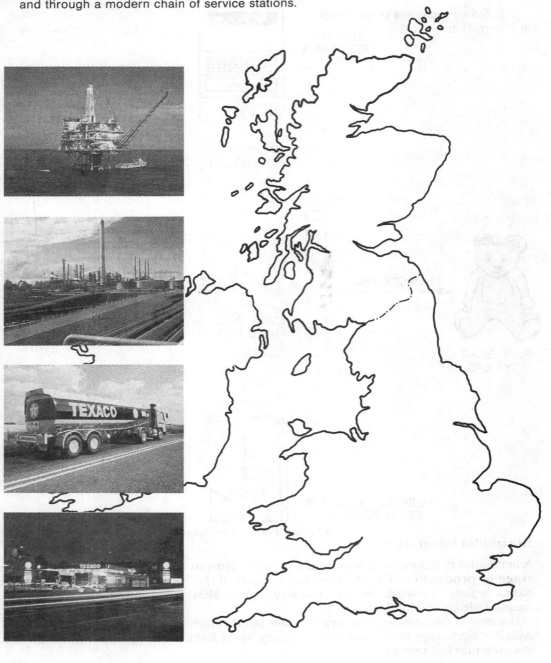

**Fig. 6.6** Texaco Ltd: vertical integration  Courtesy: *Texaco Ltd*

**Vertical forwards** integration is found where a company merges with, or takes over, firms further along the chain of production (e.g. a producer taking over retail outlets). The advantages from this type of integration are:

1 The company has a **better access** to its market, by being able to control **advertising and** promotion, the quality of the outlet, etc.
2 The **profits** of the retail outlet now belong to the company.
3 **Economies of scale** are again possible.

### Lateral integration

Lateral integration – also known as 'conglomerate', or 'diversified' integration – occurs when **firms in different industries** merge: the goods or services they produce are not related. One example is where the major tobacco companies, facing the reducing home demand for their tobacco products, take over other firms in expanding areas of the economy. British-American Tobacco plc has taken over companies such as Yardleys (cosmetics), Argos (retailing) and Eagle Star (insurance).

The advantages of lateral integration are as follows:

1 By diversifying into other areas, **risk is reduced**: the company no longer depends on a single type of product (such as tobacco).
2 A company's current products may dominate, or 'saturate', the market; it cannot expand in this market and so it needs **new markets for expansion**.

## 6.5 Economies of Scale

Producing on a large scale can bring many benefits to a firm. These 'economies of scale' result in the firm gaining from a **reduction in the average cost per unit** manufactured: total costs will increase as production increases but average costs of production can fall, leading to the firm becoming more competitive.

Firms can benefit from **internal economies**: these are specific to the firm itself. It can also gain from **external economies**, which are associated with the industry in which it operates.

**Fig. 6.7** Technical economies of scale  Courtesy: *The Guardian*

## INTERNAL ECONOMIES OF SCALE

There are a number of different internal economies of scale.

### Technical economies

Firms with large-scale production can use **more advanced machinery**, or use their existing machinery more efficiently. Mass production allows specialization and **division of labour**, which should increase efficiency and reduce costs.

### Managerial economies

The principle of the division of labour also applies here: highly qualified, **specialist and expert managers** can be employed by the larger-scale firms. In addition, the costs of management will probably not increase at the same rate as the growth of the firm: if the firm doubles in size, it still only has one managing director, one sales manager, etc, resulting in **falling management costs per unit** of output.

### Trading economies

Large-scale operations can take advantage of **bulk buying**, where suppliers offer the goods at lower unit prices because the firm is such an important, large customer. **Marketing** costs are spread over a large output: unit costs of advertising, packaging and delivery can therefore fall.

### Financial economies

**Costs of borrowing** are usually cheaper for the larger firms: banks may offer them loans at lower rates of interest, for example.

### Economies of increased dimensions

These economies are available to larger firms. For example, the use by oil companies of massive oil tankers which may have 20 times the capacity of smaller tankers, yet only cost 3 or 4 times as much to operate.

### Risk-bearing economies

Large conglomerates – created through lateral integration – are based on these economies: they spread their risks by producing a number of different products, using a wide range of suppliers and selling in many different markets. Smaller firms cannot spread their risks to the same extent.

## EXTERNAL ECONOMIES OF SCALE

When an industry grows in size, its firms can benefit from this growth in the following ways:

1 **Concentration.** Where the industry is mainly located in one part of the country, this encourages its suppliers to base themselves in the same region (e.g. many of the suppliers of components to the West Midland car industry are based in that region). These suppliers benefit from the growth of the industry: they can specialize and gain themselves from internal economies.
2 Through concentration, **skilled labour and management** are found in the area. **Specialist training schemes** are also encouraged.
3 The **reputation** of the area – for example, the reputation of the Potteries for producing quality china goods – can help the individual firms that are based there.
4 Firms in the area can link together to provide joint **information** and **research and development** schemes, from which all can gain.

##  6.6 The Limits to Growth

Although there are many benefits arising from increased size, firms do not simply grow larger and larger. There are limits to the amount of growth that can take place.

### Diseconomies of scale

Firms may simply grow **too large** and suffer from diseconomies of scale. The larger the firm, the greater the number of levels there are that decisions must go through. This **bureaucracy** can lead to a lack of personal contact between management and the workforce, which in turn can cause these problems:

1 Employees become apathetic, and do not feel part of the company, which affects the quality and quantity of their work.
2 Decisions take much longer to implement, because of all the channels that they must go through.
3 Labour relations are more difficult to manage, which can lead to a 'them and us' attitude by both sides and an increase in labour disputes.

**Survival of the small firm**

In 1987, the Business Statistics Office calculated that there were just over 150 000 manufacturing 'units' or firms in Great Britain. Of these, over 100 000 had fewer than 10 employees and there were under 500 firms employing 1000 people or more. Approximately 5 million people worked in manufacturing in 1987: half of them were employed by firms with a total workforce of under 200.

Small firms suffer from a number of important weaknesses. They cannot gain economies of scale and so face higher costs of borrowing and other higher unit costs, compared with larger companies; they often rely on a single product, which increases their level of risk; and they lack the expertise (especially in management skills) present in larger firms.

They also have a range of strengths, when compared to a typical larger company. Small firms tend to be **more adaptable and flexible** in meeting the needs of their market; they are **quicker to take decisions** (there is less 'red tape' to go through); and they usually have **better labour relations** than larger firms, because the owners tend to be in closer contact with the 'shop floor'.

Several factors lead to firms remaining small in size:

1 Their market is local; for example, hairdressers, dentists and plumbers.
2 They provide specialist or luxury items, for which there is a very limited total demand.
3 There is a lack of ambition on the part of the owners, who prefer to keep business small-scale and therefore relatively uncomplicated.

## 6.7 Summary

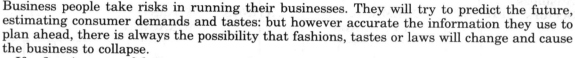

Business people take risks in running their businesses. They will try to predict the future, estimating consumer demands and tastes: but however accurate the information they use to plan ahead, there is always the possibility that fashions, tastes or laws will change and cause the business to collapse.

If a firm is successful, it can grow and gain from economies of scale: but there are natural limits to the amount of growth that can – or should – take place for any firm.

# 7 THE STRUCTURE OF ORGANIZATIONS

## 7.1 Introduction

Unit 4 described the range of organizations found in the UK economy. There is usually a link between their business objectives and their internal organization, because how a business is organized tends to reflect its objectives.

Firms which provide public services may be organized differently to those firms that have been formed to make profits for their owners. Both types of business organization often have departments or **functions** as the basis of their internal structure: departments such as Production, Personnel, Sales and Accounts are typically found.

Some firms – often the larger companies which manufacture and sell a range of products – may be organized on a **product** basis, their different product lines being the main influence on their structure. They may operate as a series of 'Divisions' or groups. Courtaulds plc, for example, organizes its operations under the business sectors, business groups and activities shown in fig. 7.1.

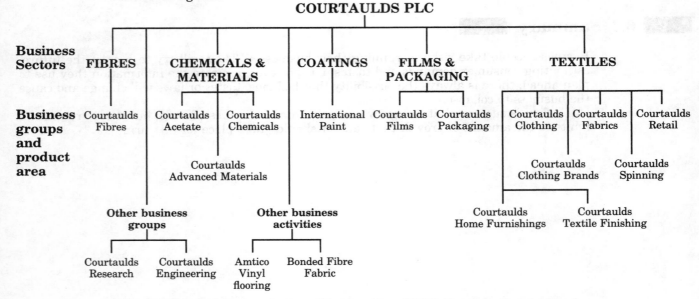

**Fig. 7.1** Courtaulds: organization of its operations (1988) Courtesy: *Courtaulds plc*

If firms such as multinationals are based in a number of countries and are trading in different markets, they may be organized on a **market** basis, having different structures for their various home and overseas markets or bases.

Finally, managers of some firms may decide to organize themselves using a **project-based** approach. This is becoming an increasingly popular form of organization and is sometimes called a **matrix** structure. Firms which are planning to launch new products, or involved in large, 'one-off' contracts, may develop their organizational structure around these products or projects, each product/project having a manager and a specialist workforce.

## 7.2 Organization Charts

The function of an organization chart is to show the **internal structure** of a firm. Fig. 7.2, at the top of the next page, shows the organization chart of a typical medium-sized manufacturing company.

The departmental structure of the firm can be seen clearly. The chart will show the **status** of each manager and the **communication lines** within the company. The Board of Directors and the Managing Director are at the top of this 'tree' and the different functions – each of which has its own internal structures – are then listed under the titles of the individual managers.

Organization charts can be presented in other forms, which give less emphasis to the idea of status. A popular alternative is the **horizontal** chart shown in fig. 7.3.

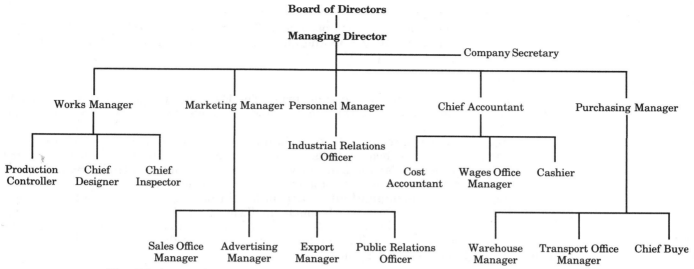

**Fig. 7.2** A typical organization chart for a manufacturing company

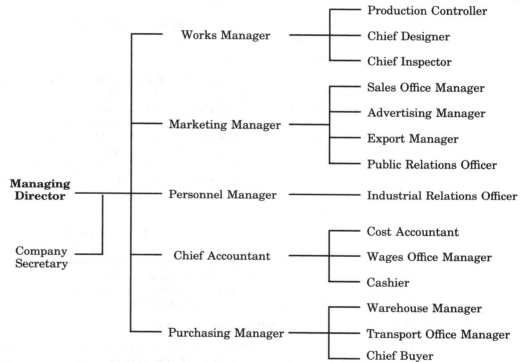

**Fig. 7.3** Horizontal organization chart layout

## 7.3 Functional Organization

Functional organization is the method most widely used by firms. They divide their operations into a series of key **departments**, which allows specialization to take place. Specialist managers and other staff, and specialist equipment can be employed by the firm to increase output and efficiency.

The more important functions are now outlined.

### Production

This is an important department for those firms engaged in manufacturing. It is responsible for turning the raw materials into the finished goods. **Services** are also produced by many firms in the economy.

### Accounting

The accounting function – sometimes called the **finance** function – has the responsibility of obtaining, recording, controlling and analysing the funds of the firm. Its efficient operation is vital to the firm's survival, e.g. by making sure that there are sufficient funds available for the firm to pay its debts.

*Marketing*

This function is responsible for such aspects as selling, market research, packaging design, advertising and distribution. It acts as the all-important 'bridge' between the firm and its customers.

*Other functions*

There are many other key functions in most firms. The **Personnel** department is responsible for 'hiring and firing'. It controls the number and – through its selection procedures – the quality of the firm's staff.

The **Buying** function ensures that the firm obtains the correct number and standard of raw materials, components or finished products to resell, at the correct times. This stock, together with the stocks of stationery, and finished goods for despatch, will be controlled by the **Stock Control** department, to guard against problems such as deterioration or theft.

These functions are **interdependent**. It is pointless in having a very efficient accounting function if the firm's marketing is extremely inefficient; similarly, a firm may have an excellent marketing organization but sell few products because of low standards of production. The design, manufacture and selling of new and existing products will involve all these functions working very closely together.

## 7.4　Organizational Terms

There are a number of terms used when a company's organization is analysed. The important terms are as follows:

### Span of control

A 'span of control' is measured by **the number of workers directly controlled by one person**. As fig. 7.3 shows, the span of control of the Managing Director is the five managers directly under his control; the Works Manager has a span of control of three people; and so on.

The span of control of an individual depends on a number of factors. The **nature of the employee's work**, i.e. the amount of supervision that he or she requires, is a major factor: highly skilled work will need quite intensive supervision and so the supervisor's span of control is likely to be limited to a few workers. If a person's span of control is too wide, supervision and control become inefficient, and this is likely to be reflected in the quality of the output.

### Chain of command

A firm's chain of command derives from its **hierarchical** structure. The chain runs typically from the Board to the Managing Director, then to the managers of the different departments, through these managers to the section heads and supervisors, and finally down to the shop floor and office staff. The chain of command highlights the **status** of the various employees, indicating who takes decisions and to whom these decisions are passed. It is an indication of the formal communication structure of the firm.

### Delegation, responsibility and authority

The Board and Managing Director will not take all the decisions required by the firm. Their role is to make the more long-term, **strategic policy** decisions. They will **delegate** – pass on – the responsibility of making the day-to-day decisions to the various managers and supervisors of the firm. In turn, these managers will delegate certain tasks to their own staff: for example, the Purchasing Manager may ask the Warehouse Manager to examine alternative layouts for the warehouse, or the Chief Accountant might ask the Wages Office Manager to carry out an analysis of wages costs.

The delegation of duties must be accompanied by the appropriate **authority** to do those duties. If the Warehouse Manager is to have the **responsibility** of checking how the warehouse could be reorganized, his own boss, the Purchasing Manager, must give him that authority. The normal source of people's authority to act comes from their job description (Unit 13).

If managers do not delegate properly, this can mean that they carry out routine tasks which their subordinates could easily do, and the time of these managers is therefore less efficiently used than it should be. The other extreme would be for the manager to delegate too much responsibility to subordinates, who may then be carrying out tasks for which they should not be responsible.

### Centralization and decentralization

These terms are closely linked to the idea of authority and the amount of delegation taking place. Where there is a lot of delegation in a firm, decisions are made at various levels of the firm, which is said to be **decentralized**. Firms which do not practise much delegation have authority **centralized**, with the higher levels of management keeping control of the decision-making.

### Line and Staff organization

The traditional organizational chart shows the chains of command as a series of lines. **Line** authority is found within the various departments, with the line of command linking the Managing Director to the departmental managers, and finally to the shop floor and office workers.

The 'line managers' may be supported by various specialists who are not directly in this line of command. For example, the Warehouse Manager may be advised by a specialist in factory layout, or the Purchasing Manager may be helped by a member of the Personnel Department in drawing up a job description for a new post in the Purchasing Department. These **staff** roles advise line management and whole departments – such as Personnel – may work on a staff basis.

## 7.5 Summary

Most organizations are structured along departmental lines. The management of a firm, when examining its internal structure, must consider the range of alternatives available, because in many cases a departmental structure may not be the most appropriate form of organization.

Whatever organizational structure is used, an organization chart can be drawn up to display the spans of control and chains of command. This chart has its limitations: it will not show the degree, or the effects, of delegation actually taking place: and the efficiency of the organization will depend as much on the motivation of its workforce as on its structure shown by the chart.

# 8 PRODUCTION

## 8.1 Introduction

Where a firm locates its production function will depend on a number of factors (Unit 2). Once located, this function will try to make the firm's goods as efficiently as possible. The Production Department of a manufacturing firm will be organized to produce the right **quantity**, at the correct **quality** and for the lowest possible **cost**. To do this, it needs to work very closely with other functions, in particular Marketing (Unit 11), Accounting (Unit 10) and Purchasing (Unit 9).

The term 'Production' includes services, as well as the manufacture of goods. Although services are not physically 'made', they must still be provided as and when required and will be costed and analysed in much the same way as the products of a typical manufacturing company.

## 8.2 Costs of Production

Efficient, large-scale production can bring a range of economies of scale (Unit 6) to a company. However efficient production may be, the company will still have to meet **various costs of** producing the goods. These costs include:

1 Wages of employees.
2 Raw material costs.
3 Expenses of lighting, heating and power (e.g. running the machinery).
4 Costs of servicing and repairing equipment.
5 The expense of transporting the raw materials to the factory.

These different costs can be classified under a series of headings, to help the business to analyse and control them. One type of cost already considered is **Opportunity Cost** (Unit 1), where the cost of doing something is measured by what else has had to be given up in order to do it. For example, the opportunity cost for a manufacturer of toys, who is bringing out a new battery-powered car, might be a new range of toy furniture for a doll's house. There are not enough resources for the manufacturer to produce both, so one has to be abandoned for the other to be produced.

### Fixed and variable costs

The total costs of a firm can be separated into those which are fixed and those which are variable. One reason for classifying costs as fixed and variable is to carry out **breakeven analysis**, which is explained later in the Unit.

#### Fixed costs do not change as output changes

Examples of fixed costs include factory and office rent; office salaries (which do not depend on the number of items produced); insurance premiums, e.g. for fire or vehicle insurance; and the road tax paid on company vehicles. These costs do not alter, whether the factory is working to capacity or whether it is producing nothing.

Fixed costs are, therefore, literally fixed (in the short-term). They will change over a period of time: road tax and insurance premiums will increase, and the rent of the factory will rise. These changes in fixed costs do not, however, arise from changes in the firm's output.

#### Variable costs change as output changes

These costs result from a firm's output and will change as the output level changes. Examples include the costs of raw materials used in producing the items and 'piece-work' wages, where workers are paid on the basis of the number of products they make.

In reality, the distinction between these two costs is not always clear. Many costs are **semi-variable**: they contain both fixed and variable elements, and therefore vary partly according to how many items are produced. For example, a factory which is planning to double its output will face increased labour, power and transport costs; but although these costs will increase, they will not double in size.

### Direct and indirect costs

A firm's **direct costs** are those costs that can be **directly linked to particular product lines**. Examples include the costs of running the machinery which is used to manufacture specific products; the cost of raw materials used for a particular product; and the wages of production workers who are directly involved with making particular products. Direct costs are usually variable in nature.

**Indirect costs** are shared between the different product lines: they **do not relate to one particular product**. Examples include the cost of company stationery, which is used for all the company's products and services; the salaries of the management staff who are involved with all aspects of the company; and office and factory rent. Indirect costs are likely to be fixed in nature; the term **overheads** is often used to describe these costs.

The classification of costs into direct and indirect is also important to a firm. The firm's management will need to know not only the total costs but also the costs of making individual product lines. This enables the profitability of these individual product lines to be calculated and so decisions can be made about what prices to charge, and further levels of production can be determined.

In practice, a firm's accountant may try to allocate all the indirect costs to the different product lines. Factory rent, for instance, could be **apportioned** – shared out – on the basis of the floor space taken by each product line.

### Average and Marginal Costs

The benefits that economies of scale bring to a company result in lower unit costs: the cost per item made is lower. This **average cost of production** is found by dividing total output by total cost: this can be calculated at different levels of output, to see whether economies or diseconomies of scale are taking place. As output starts to rise, a firm's total costs will increase but its average costs will typically fall: this is because the same amount of fixed costs – which do not increase as output increases – are spread over a greater level of output. When diseconomies of scale (Unit 6) start, the average costs of the firm will rise as production rises.

Calculating, or estimating, a firm's average costs at different levels of production gives more information to its management, who can again use the information for pricing and other decisions.

The **marginal cost** of a product represents the **cost of making that individual product**. It is measured by finding the increase in the total costs to a firm which comes from producing one more item.

For example, if total costs of producing 99 items are £499, and the total costs increase to £500 when the hundredth item is made, the average cost is:

$$£500 \text{ (total costs)}$$
$$\div$$
$$100 \text{ (total output)}$$
$$=$$
$$£5.00$$

The marginal cost of the hundredth unit is:

$$£500 \text{ (total cost of 100 units)}$$
$$-$$
$$£499 \text{ (total cost of 99 units)}$$
$$=$$
$$£1.00$$

This is an important item of information for a firm's managers: they can use this information, for example, in deciding whether or not to accept a new order for goods. Using the figures above, this firm's management knows that the firm must charge £5 per item to cover the total cost of meeting an initial order of 100 items. It realizes, though, that if it could accept further orders, it could charge a lower price for its product (because £1 is likely to be the marginal cost of these further items).

### Standard costs

The use of standard costs is an attempt by firms to calculate what it should cost to produce items. The firm's accountant will try to establish the **standard labour cost** of producing one item: techniques such as work study (see page 62) can be used to calculate how much labour is involved in producing something. In addition to labour costs, **standard material costs** can be set: these are the costs of the materials that are needed for the product. Finally, a **standard cost of overheads** per item produced can be calculated and included in the total standard cost.

The standard cost is therefore a target to be aimed at by the firm. However, because these standards are estimates, there will be **variances** between the standard cost and the actual cost of production. For example, the raw materials may increase or reduce in price, or poor quality control may result in higher wastage of materials than anticipated; or labour costs may rise through higher-than-expected pay deals. The analysis of these variances gives management information which can be used in the bid to **control** the firm's costs and profitability.

## 8.3 Breakeven Analysis

The breakeven point for a firm is found where total costs equal total revenues. At this point, **the firm is making neither a profit nor a loss**. The breakeven point is particularly important to a firm, because it is at this point of output at which it begins to make a profit. If the firm is producing and selling an output below this point, it will be making a loss; if the firm can produce and sell above this point, it will be in profit.

Breakeven analysis uses fixed and variable costs as the basis for calculating the breakeven point: this calculation can be shown on a graph, or it can be done numerically.

### CONSTRUCTING THE BREAKEVEN CHART

To construct a breakeven chart or graph, information on a firm's fixed costs, variable costs and sales (number and price) must be obtained. This information is plotted on a graph, with a horizontal axis of quantity produced, and a vertical axis of costs and revenue (£).

#### Fixed and Variable Cost lines

If a company's fixed costs – factory and office rent, administration salaries, etc – total £10 000, this fixed cost line is plotted as a straight line which starts at the £10 000 point on the vertical axis and runs parallel to the horizontal axis (fixed costs are constant at £10 000). Fig. 8.1 shows this breakeven chart, and the fixed cost line is labelled.

The firm's variable costs – raw materials, production wages etc. – are 50p per unit. If output is planned at 5000 units, the total variable costs will be £2500 (5000 × 50p). This line is also plotted on the graph (see fig. 8.1). The line starts where the fixed cost line meets the vertical axis: at this, zero, output the variable cost is also zero. At the other end of the line (the 5000 output point), the gap between the fixed costs and the variable costs is £2500, i.e. the total variable costs at this output.

The firm's **total costs** consist of these two costs:

#### Total Costs = Fixed Costs + Variable Costs

The Variable Cost line in fig. 8.1 therefore also represents the firm's Total Cost line. Total costs at the maximum output of 5000 units are £12 500: £10 000 fixed cost plus £2500 variable cost. The **total cost at each level of output** can be clearly seen from the total cost line.

#### The Total Revenue line

The Total Revenue line can then be plotted (see fig. 8.1). If the firm's selling price for its product is £3.00, the total revenue at the maximum output of 5000 will be £15 000 (£3 × 5000). If this point on the graph is joined to the zero point where the two axes meet (at an output of zero, sales revenue will also be zero), the total revenue line will be drawn.

The firm's breakeven point is where the total revenue and total cost lines intersect. A line drawn from this point down to the Output axis shows that 4000 units represents the

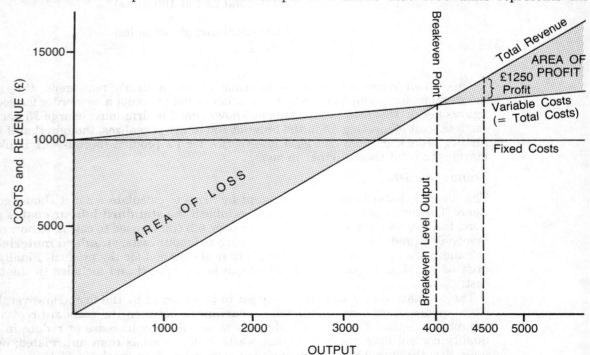

Fixed costs £10,000, Variable costs 50p per unit, Sales price £3 per unit.

**Fig. 8.1** Breakeven chart

**breakeven level of output**. Sales of over 4000 will give the firm a profit: the triangle below it – representing output and sales under 4000 – is the area of loss. If the firm anticipates making and selling all 5000, then its **margin of safety** is the area between 5000 and the breakeven point: it knows that production and sales can fall to 4000 before it fails to make a profit.

The profit or loss at all levels of output can be read from the graph. For example, at output and sales of 4500, the firm's total revenue line shows £13 500 and the total cost line reads £12 250. The gap between the two lines – the firm's profit, since total revenue is, literally, above total cost – is £1250.

## CALCULATING THE BREAKEVEN POINT

A firm's management is interested in the amount of **contribution** that a product makes to its fixed costs. These fixed costs have to be met, regardless of whatever level of output the firm is producing and selling. The contribution that a product makes towards the fixed costs is calculated as follows:

$$\frac{\begin{array}{r}\text{Sales price} \\ -\text{ Variable cost}\end{array}}{\text{CONTRIBUTION}}$$

The contribution is towards paying the firm's fixed costs. When sufficient 'contributions' have been made, the fixed costs will be covered by the firm: this is its breakeven point.

Using the information in fig. 8.1, the sales price is £3.00 and the variable cost £0.50 per unit. The contribution is therefore:

$$£3.00 - £0.50 = £2.50$$

Each item sold contributes £2.50 towards the firm's fixed costs. A firm's breakeven point can then be calculated by **dividing the contribution into the fixed costs**. The company's fixed costs from fig. 8.1 are £10 000: dividing this by £2.50 (2.5) gives 4000 as the breakeven output.

The amount of profit or loss at each level of production can also be calculated with this method. For example, output and sales of 3000 would produce a total contribution of £7500 (3000 × £2.50): since fixed costs are constant at £10 000, the company must make a loss of £2500 here:

| | |
|---|---:|
| Total costs | £10 000 |
| − Total revenue | £7500 |
| Loss | £2500 |

At a level of output and sales of 4200, the contribution would be 4200 × £2.50, i.e. £10 500: profit is £500 (contribution £10 500 less fixed costs £10 000).

## 8.4 Methods of Production

The production of different types of goods will be organized in different ways.

### Job production

Also known as 'unit' production, this is where a **single unique product** is made from start to finish. Its characteristics are:

1 It is based on the **individual specification** of a customer.
2 Skilled labour is often used, and labour costs tend to be high since the work is **labour-intensive**.

Examples of job production include large 'one-off' construction orders for ships, by-passes, individually designed houses, bridges etc; and 'made-to-measure' suits and clothes.

### Mass production

Also known as 'flow-line' production, the products that are being made pass from one stage of production straight to the next stage. **Large numbers of identical products** are made, as cheaply as possible (economies of scale are likely with mass production).

When the final products are in liquid form, their mass production is often referred to as 'continuous-flow' or 'process' production.

The characteristics of mass production are:

1 There is a **mass market** for the finished product.
2 The firm is usually **capital-intensive**, employing specialist machinery and employees skilled in its operation.

Fig. 8.2 Job production: construction of a single factory building

Fig. 8.3 Mass production of chocolate bars Courtesy: *Cadbury Ltd*

3 The process may be almost completely **automated**, with relatively unskilled labour being employed.

4 The production lines are operated as **continuously** as possible (e.g. by shift-work), to keep the costs as low as possible.

Examples of mass-produced products include manufactured goods such as cars and consumer durables, books, light bulbs, milk bottles and toys; and manufactured liquids and 'semi-liquids' such as jams, milk, medicines, oil and beer.

### Batch production

In batch production, similar products are made in 'blocks', or **batches**: it therefore falls somewhere between Job and Mass production. The Production Department's tasks with batch production include deciding **how many** to make in a batch ('economic runs' are required, to keep costs under control) and **in what order** the various batches of the different designs or products should be made.

Examples of batch production include the construction of similar houses on a new estate, or similar factory units on a new industrial estate. Many manufactured goods (e.g. producing different knitwear sizes and designs, or different designs of furniture) are made in batches.

## 8.5 Work in the Production Department

The **Works Manager**, or **Production Manager**, has the responsibility of the overall management of the production process. The key functions under the control of the Works Manager are as follows.

### Production Engineering

The firm's management has to decide what is to be produced. Once this decision has been taken, it is the role of Production Engineering to plan **how the product is made**. The decisions to be taken include:

1 Which processes are to be used in making the product.
2 What standard of material is required.
3 What special tools and equipment are to be used and if any purpose-built tools need making.
4 Production planning, i.e. planning when production will take place, for how long it will take place and when the raw materials are to be ordered and delivered.

### Production Control

Production control follows on logically from production engineering. The purpose of production control is to **ensure that the production plans are being followed** by, for example, checking that production is taking place on time and making sure that agreed standards of quality are being kept to.

### Quality Control

The Production Department is often responsible for **inspection**, even if the company has a separate Inspection Department. Inspection is a part of **quality control**, which attempts to ensure that there is as little waste as possible from the production process.

**Fig. 8.4**
Quality control: inspection of a turbine rotor
Courtesy: *GEC Turbine Generators Ltd*

### Research and development

A company's Research and Development unit or department has the function of examining possible new manufacturing processes and products and, if any new ideas seem worth developing, of testing them out. The research and development staff often work closely with Production, for example in testing out the quality of new designs or new materials which are to be used in the production process.

Production is probably the function most affected by the speed of modern technological change. Many new important developments are taking place in production, through research and development successes: these are outlined in Unit 20.

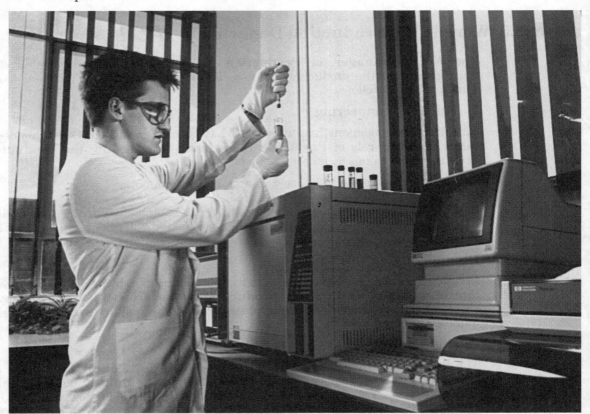

**Fig. 8.5** RTZ Chemicals – ISC Division, research analytical laboratory. Gas chromatography/mass spectroscopy being used  Courtesy: *RTZ Ltd*

### Work study

The Production Department often employs work study experts. Their role is to **assess the ways in which work is carried out**: this helps the firm's managers to introduce more efficient (and less physically tiring) methods of work for the staff. It also – through techniques such as **time and motion study** – gives management information on how long jobs take to do. This information can then be used to calculate standard costs (see page 57).

## 8.6 Summary

There are different production methods in use today. The major development this century has been the use of **mass production** techniques, which allow identical products to be made at extremely low costs. Mass production has brought cars, washing machines, videos and other consumer durables within the reach of many, and has led to wide consumer choice in washing powder, jam, records and hundreds of other products.

Whatever method of production – mass, unit or batch – is used, a firm will need to analyse and control the **costs** of production. Costs can be classified under a number of different headings: for example, **breakeven analysis** can take place if they are grouped as either fixed or variable costs. Production must be efficiently carried out for costs to be kept as low as possible, to allow a profit to be made by the firm.

# 9 PURCHASING

## 9.1 Introduction

Both manufacturing and non-manufacturing firms will have to make all sorts of **purchases**. Those involved in manufacturing will need to buy their raw materials, or components for assembly, before production can take place; others will purchase specially printed stationery (letter-headed paper, blank memo forms, blank invoices, etc) from suppliers; and office furniture, new delivery vans and factory equipment must be bought. The range of responsibility of a typical purchasing department is shown in fig. 9.1.

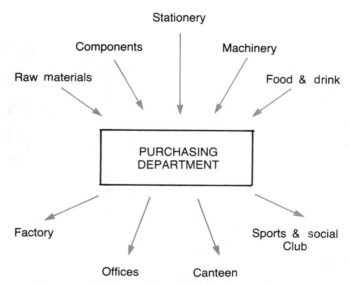

**Fig. 9.1** Work of a typical Purchasing Department

## 9.2 The Role of the Purchasing Department

The main role of the Purchasing Department can be described as **materials management**. Production—especially mass production—is often a very complex process, requiring many different items to be supplied at different points in time. If the Purchasing Department fails to obtain the correct stock, production lines can slow down or even come to a halt.

The items to be supplied by Purchasing must be 'correct' in many ways: they must be bought at the correct **price**, at the correct **quality level** and in the correct **quantities**; and they must be delivered at the correct **time** and to the correct **place**.

## 9.3 Stock Control

The function of **Stock Control** is, as its names suggests, to control the firm's stocks. There are conflicting 'pulls' in the firm, which influence buying and stock control policy. Fig. 9.2 (overleaf) summarizes the situations that can occur when either too much or too little stock is held.

Purchasing departments have therefore to achieve a 'balancing act'. A firm which, for example, buys its goods in large quantities will receive discounts which lower the unit price of the items bought: but it will also lead to an increase in storage costs for the firm and more money being 'tied up' in stocks than if fewer had been bought.

Similarly, if the Purchasing Department buys raw materials which are of a slightly lower quality than before, cheaper prices are paid, but the reduced quality of these materials could cause higher wastage costs when they are used in production.

Important influences are, firstly, the **security** of the stock against both theft and deterioration (by the weather, by handling or by age); secondly, there is the **obsolescence** factor, making sure that stock does not become out-of-date through changes in fashion or in the production process; and, lastly, there will be the influence of **cashflow**, ensuring that stocks are used efficiently, that not too much capital is kept in stocks, and that competitive terms are obtained when buying the stocks.

The HIGHER the stock level, the more stock available for production

*BUT*

increased risks of stock becoming out-of-date, deteriorating or being stolen; and increased costs of storage

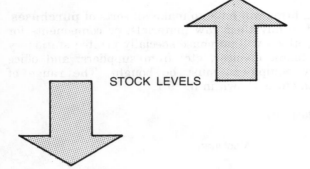

STOCK LEVELS

The LOWER the stock level, the lower the storage and holding costs

*BUT*

increased risk of running out of stock and halting production

**Fig. 9.2** The 'pulls' in stock control

**Fig. 9.3** Stock control at work Courtesy: *British Shoe Corp Ltd*

**Fig. 9.4** Work in a modern buying department  Courtesy: *British Shoe Corp Ltd*

**Methods of stock control**

Efficient stock control is normally based on establishing **correct stock levels**. The Purchasing Department will establish the following levels:

1 **Maximum stock:** the highest level of an item's stock to be held.
2 **Minimum stock:** the lowest level at which a new order must be placed.
3 **Economic Order Quantity** level (EOQ): the number of items the firm will reorder, once the minimum stock level has been reached. The EOQ is calculated by comparing the costs the firm would face by holding a lot of stock with the savings it gets from buying this stock in bulk (i.e. price discounts).

## 9.4 Purchasing and Technology

Purchasing departments have been affected by the increased use of **information technology** systems in business. Stockholding lends itself to computerized control. **Computer databases** can be used to record the receipts and movements of a firm's stock; the 'point-of-sale' terminals in many large stores will record a product's sale and at the same time update its stock record and – if necessary – create an order for more of the stock.

## 9.5 Summary

Without efficient buying, a manufacturing firm cannot produce the goods that it must sell to make its profit. Successful purchasing is based on buying in the right quantities and at the right quality so that costs of buying and of storage can be controlled. The items bought must also be obtained at the right time and delivered to the right place, otherwise there is a risk of production having to stop.

# 10 THE ACCOUNTING FUNCTION

## 10.1 Introduction

Information on the financial position of a firm must be collected and acted upon. This will allow **financial control** to take place. Financial control is vitally important to all organizations, whether they set out to make a profit or to provide a service to the community.

The accountant is the person most closely associated with controlling the finances of an organization. He or she will have at least two key roles to carry out:

The accountant will **study the various alternatives** open to the firm; for example, through working out the various costs of obtaining new machinery. This involves applying the 'opportunity cost' idea from Unit 1.

The accountant will then **recommend the best financial course of action** on the basis of these alternatives; e.g. by presenting figures to show whether it is cheaper to buy the machinery outright, to buy it on credit, or to lease it from the manufacturer.

## 10.2 Purposes of Accounting

It is the purpose of the accounting function to:

$$\left.\begin{array}{l} \text{OBTAIN} \\ \text{RECORD} \\ \text{ANALYSE} \\ \text{PRESENT} \end{array}\right\} \begin{array}{l} \text{financial} \\ \text{information} \end{array}$$

### Obtaining information

The accounts department of any firm will obtain its information or data from a wide variety of sources. For example, the sales department will send copies of its sales invoices to accounts, from which the quantity and value of the firm's sales will be seen: and the firm's incoming mail will contain cheques from debtors which need to be recorded and banked, and statements from creditors which have to be paid.

### Recording information

Recording information in the firm's accounts is a well-known accounting activity and forms the **book-keeping** element of accounting. The collection of accounts kept by a firm is often known as its **Ledger**. These accounts may be grouped together under certain headings:

The **Sales Ledger**, containing customer accounts.

The **Bought Ledger**, which holds the accounts of the firm's suppliers.

The **Cash Book**, which will contain details of the firm's cash and bank accounts.

The **General Ledger**, keeping all the other accounts.

### Analysing information

Recording the details of the various transactions in these accounts allows the accountant to analyse and interpret this information. This is carried out by using a variety of **accounting ratios**, to identify and highlight any trends.

Other managers are also involved in 'advance planning', by being required to produce **budgets** which plan the future performance of their own departments.

### Presenting information

The accountant has a key role as a **communicator**, in presenting financial information to the rest of the management team. Appropriate non-technical language must be used, for the benefit of those to whom this information is communicated.

The people who are interested in this financial information include other managers, owners of − or potential investors in − the firm, and the firm's creditors (who supply it with goods on credit).

### Modern systems

Developments which have taken place in computerized accounting systems have led to a widespread use of microcomputers and specialist accounting packages by accountants. The computer has become an important tool of the accountant, allowing financial information to be collected, analysed and presented very quickly and accurately.

## 10.3 Profitability and Liquidity

When checking a firm's financial performance, the accountant will examine its profitability and its liquidity. Not all organizations are created with the objective of making a profit – most sports and social clubs, for instance, do not have this objective – but even these non-profitmaking organizations have to 'account' for their financial surpluses or deficits.

*Profitability*

One reason for keeping accounts is to record the firm's **revenues** (income) and **expenses**, from which the profit can be calculated. The amount of profit which has been made can then be compared to other important totals, such as the total sales or the total value of capital invested. This gives a guide to the firm's profitability.

Profit acts as both a reward for risk-taking and as an internal source of funds for a business (see Unit 5 and later in this unit).

*Liquidity*

Unit 5 also introduced 'Working Capital'. This is the best-known measure of a firm's **liquidity**, that is, its ability to meet its debts as they fall due. The firm's working capital is the difference between its **current assets** (cash or 'near-cash' items such as short-term debts owed by its customers) and its **current liabilities** (its own short-term debts, such as the money it owes to its creditors). Fig. 10.1 shows a firm's current assets, current liabilities and working capital.

|  |  | £000 | £000 |
|---|---|---|---|
| **Current assets** |  |  |  |
|  | Closing Stock |  | 250 |
|  | Debtors |  | 490 |
|  | Cash in Hand |  | 10 |
|  |  |  | 750 |
| **Current liabilities** |  |  |  |
|  | Creditors | 370 |  |
|  | Bank Overdraft | 30 |  |
|  |  |  | 400 |
| **Working capital** |  |  | 350 |

Fig. 10.1 A company's working capital

The working capital ratio is covered later in the Unit, together with the 'Acid Test' ratio, which is a further measure of a firm's liquidity.

## 10.4 Accounting Entries

Different firms will keep their accounts using different systems. Some firms will use a **computerized system**, where the accounts are recorded on computer disks or tape, while other firms will operate non-computerized, **manual systems**.

The layout of the accounts themselves will also differ from system to system. Fig. 10.2 shows a typical layout.

SALES LEDGER:

| *A. Lee and Co Ltd* | *Debit* £ | *Credit* £ | *Balance* £ |
|---|---|---|---|
| May  1  Balance |  |  | 140 |
| May  9  Sales | 120 |  | 260 |
| May 17  Returns |  | 20 | 240 |
| May 24  Bank |  | 140 | 100 |

Fig. 10.2 The account of A. Lee & Co Ltd

This is an illustration of a debtor account. Lee & Co is a customer, buying goods on credit and paying for them at a later date. The information in the account tells us that:

1 On May 1 Lee & Co owed £140 to the business;

2 on May 9 the company sold Lee & Co £120 worth of goods on credit, increasing the total owed to £260;

3 on May 17 goods worth £20 were returned by Lee & Co to the business, possibly because they were faulty;

**4** on May 24 Lee & Co paid the business the amount owed (the opening balance);

**5** the debtor, Lee & Co, still owes £100 to the business at the end of the month.

*Debiting and crediting*

Regardless of the style of layout or of the method of recording, all accounts basically follow the same book-keeping methods. This involves making 'debits' and 'credits', entries in one or other of the account columns.

### Classifying accounts

The accounts of a firm can be grouped under various headings. This classification is important when the nature and purpose of the final accounts of a business is considered later in the unit.

*Expenses*

These are costs of running the business, such as the rent payable for the factory, the wages of its workforce, the cost of advertising and money paid for raw materials used in making its finished products.

*Revenues*

A firm's revenues are the sources of its income and its profit: the most common illustration is sales income, from the firm selling its goods or its services.

*Assets*

These are items which are owned by the firm, being used to help it to earn its revenue: common examples are delivery vans, machinery and stock.

*Liabilities*

A firm's liabilities are the amounts which it owes, for example in the form of bank loans and overdrafts.

## 10.5  External Control: Auditors

A firm exists either to make a profit, or to provide some form of service. Profit is made for the benefit of the owner or owners, and the service is provided either for its members (such as the members of a local sports club) or for the community at large (e.g. the public services of education and health).

In all cases, an **investment** has to be made before either profit can be earned or the service can be provided. The shareholders of a limited company have to invest in their shares; a bank may invest some of its depositors' money in businesses; members of a sports or social club invest their subscriptions in that club; and salaried and waged adults pay contributions (taxes and national insurance) towards the cost of the public services. Some **guarantee** needs to be given to the investors that the organization is conducting its affairs honestly and that it is presenting these investors with **accurate and truthful financial information**.

There are many ways of protecting members of the public. For example, the various laws outlined in Unit 18, the 'watchdogs' helping to control the public sector (Unit 4), and the forms of internal check that firms use to protect themselves against fraud. **Auditors** have an important role to play here. They provide an **independent check** on the operations of a firm: this independent check gives a guarantee that the financial information presented by the firm is fair and accurate. Potential investors in a company, for instance, can use this information to judge whether to invest, knowing that the financial information gives a 'true and fair view' of the company.

## 10.6  Internal Control

*Credit control*

Businesses carry out a range of internal controls and checks. One widely used form of control is **credit control**. Any business which allows its goods or services to be sold on credit will need to check the following:

**1** Its potential customers are credit-worthy and so likely to be able to pay their debts to the business.

**2** Its debtors keep within their maximum credit limits.

**3** The debtors pay the amounts they owe within the agreed time period.

*Internal check*

To try to limit the amount of fraud that takes place, systems can be set up so that the work of one person is checked independently by another. For example, at least two people should be involved with recording and issuing cash and with preparing invoices: the work of one person acts as a check on the work of the other.

## BUDGETING

The use of budgeting techniques is another important form of control. Budgeting exists to help managers to **plan ahead in financial terms**. A firm's budget is a detailed forecast of future plans and action for the business, measured in money, in the same way that a household budget plans an individual's or family's income and expenditure.

By budgeting, the managers will be in a position to compare the **actual future performance** of their department with their **planned (budgeted) performance**.

### The need for budgeting

A firm's management must do the following:

*Plan for the future*

By comparing budgeted and actual performances, managers are given information which helps them to control the firm by controlling their own departments.

*Set performance targets*

Managers must consult with, and delegate responsibility to, their own staff (Unit 7). All staff can be involved in preparing the budgets, which will encourage them to think ahead and to take on further responsibilities.

*Take prompt action*

Comparing budgeted (planned) and actual performance will produce **variances**, or differences. These variances can be analysed and acted upon by the managers concerned.

### Budget preparation

A typical manufacturing company would prepare budgets along the lines suggested in fig. 10.3.

| *Budget* | *Meaning* |
|---|---|
| SALES | Planned future sales: number and price of each product to be sold |
| PRODUCTION | Output per item and per week |
| FIXED ASSET | Cost of, and when to buy, new machinery and equipment |
| DEPARTMENTAL | Various department or function budgets, such as Transport or Advertising |
| FINAL ACCOUNTS | Forecast profit or loss for the budgeted period |
| CASH | Cash inflows and outflows in the period, and when they are to take place |

**Fig. 10.3** Budgets

Preparation of the Sales Budget may involve the Sales Manager in having to answer the following questions:

1 How many units are to be sold?
2 Of which products/lines?
3 In which sales areas?
4 At home or overseas?

The preparation of budgets by the various managers should not be done completely in isolation: the budgets need to be **integrated**. From the Sales Budget, for example, other budgets such as the Advertising Budget would be prepared. Another budget that will follow logically from the preparation of the Sales Budget is the Production Budget. Production runs can be planned and budgets related to other areas such as the purchase of extra machinery and the employment of additional staff can then also be prepared.

## 10.7 Cash Budgeting and Forecasting

All businesses need adequate working capital so that they can meet their debts as they become due for payment. Lack of working capital may mean the following:

1 The business cannot pay its staff on time.
2 It cannot take advantage of cash discounts offered by its creditors for prompt payment.
3 It cannot pay its creditors at all, which could lead to legal action by creditors to recover their debts; this in turn could force the business to close down.

### Working capital and cash budgeting

Accountants must, therefore, calculate future flows of working capital. In particular, **cash forecasts** need to be prepared as part of a cash budgeting exercise.

*The reasons for cash budgets*

By preparing forecasts of cash coming in and going out of the business, the accountant can identify times of the year when there will be **shortfalls** of cash, so an overdraft can be arranged with the bank. **Surpluses** of cash can also be seen, which could be invested by the business on a short-term basis. Cash Budgets can be drawn up following the construction of all the other budgets. It becomes possible to forecast the movement of cash, by identifying:

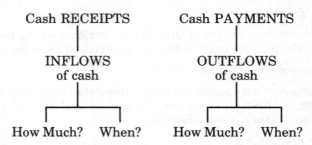

The layout of a typical cash flow budget is shown below in fig. 10.4.

**Cash Flow Budget**

|  | January £000 | February £000 | March £000 |
|---|---|---|---|
| **INFLOWS** | | | |
| Sales | 450 | 420 | 470 |
| Other Income | 50 | 30 | 40 |
| **TOTAL INFLOWS** | 500 | 450 | 510 |
| **OUTFLOWS** | | | |
| Raw Materials | 60 | 80 | 110 |
| Wages | 80 | 80 | 90 |
| Selling Expenses | 10 | 20 | 25 |
| Rent and Rates | 5 | 5 | 5 |
| Light and Heat | 5 | 5 | 5 |
| Buying Assets | | 300 | 50 |
| Other Outflows | 25 | 10 | 30 |
| **TOTAL OUTFLOWS** | 185 | 500 | 315 |
| **NET CASH SURPLUS OR DEFICIT** | 315 | (50) | 195 |
| **BALANCE FROM LAST MONTH** | 25 | 340 | 290 |
| **CASH BALANCE TO CARRY FORWARD** | 340 | 290 | 485 |

**Fig. 10.4** A Cash Flow Budget

The planned future cash movements – how much and when – are therefore anticipated, and managers can see the cash effects of their plans.

## 10.8 Profit and its Calculation

Private sector businesses are set up to make a profit. Profit is:

1 A **reward** to the entrepreneur for taking the risk of running the business.
2 An important **internal source of funds**, which allows further development of the business.
3 A **source of cash**, which helps the business to meet its debts.

Profit is calculated as follows:

**Sales and other revenues**
less
**Various expenses**

## 10.9 Final Accounts

### TRADING and PROFIT and LOSS ACCOUNTS
#### for the Year Ended 31 December

|  | £000 | £000 |
|---|---|---|
| Turnover |  | 1000 |
| less: Cost of Sales |  |  |
| Opening Stock | 40 |  |
| Purchases | 620 |  |
|  | 660 |  |
| Closing Stock | 60 |  |
|  |  | 600 |
| Gross Profit |  | 400 |
| less: Expenses |  |  |
| Rent and Rates | 20 |  |
| Light and Heat | 10 |  |
| Advertising | 25 |  |
| Wages and Salaries | 70 |  |
| Office Expenses | 125 |  |
| Depreciation | 45 |  |
| Bad Debts | 5 |  |
|  |  | 300 |
| Net Profit |  | 100 |

### BALANCE SHEET as at 31 December

|  | £000 | £000 | £000 |
|---|---|---|---|
| FIXED ASSETS |  |  |  |
| Premises |  |  | 200 |
| Machinery |  |  | 60 |
| Vehicles |  |  | 40 |
|  |  |  | 300 |
| CURRENT ASSETS |  |  |  |
| Closing Stock |  | 60 |  |
| Debtors |  | 100 |  |
| Cash at Bank |  | 20 |  |
|  |  | 180 |  |
| CURRENT LIABILITIES |  |  |  |
| Creditors | 60 |  |  |
| Proposed Dividend | 20 |  |  |
| Unpaid Corporation Tax | 40 | 120 |  |
| NET CURRENT ASSETS |  |  | 60 |
| NET ASSETS |  |  | 360 |
| Financed by: |  |  |  |
| SHARE CAPITAL |  |  |  |
| 200 000 £1 Ordinary Shares |  |  | 200 |
| RESERVES |  |  |  |
| Fixed Asset Replacement Reserve |  | 70 |  |
| Undistributed Profits |  | 30 | 100 |
| LOAN CAPITAL |  |  |  |
| Debentures |  |  | 60 |
|  |  |  | 360 |

**Fig. 10.5** Final accounts

## THE TRADING AND PROFIT AND LOSS ACCOUNTS

A firm will produce a set of final accounts to calculate its profit and to list its assets and liabilities. The purpose of the **Trading and Profit and Loss accounts** is to calculate and display the gross and net profits.

**Gross Profit** is shown in the first account, the Trading account, and is the difference between sales revenue and the cost price of these sales.

**Net Profit** is calculated in the Profit and Loss account; it is the balance left after all other expenses have been subtracted from the gross profit.

These final accounts record the business expenses and revenues. Payments of business expenses, such as payments for rent and rates, are known as **revenue expenditure**. The amount of revenue expenditure will affect the amount of profit made by the business.

### Content of the accounts

Items shown in the Trading and Profit and Loss accounts above are fairly typical examples. They include:

1 **Turnover:** items sold at selling price (sales less any returns from customers).
2 **Cost of sales:** items that have been sold by the business, valued here at their cost price: either the cost of producing them (for manufacturing firms), or the cost of the goods that have been bought for resale by firms such as those 'high street' stores which buy in the finished articles and then 'mark up' the prices to make their profits.
3 An adjustment for opening and closing **stocks** is made, so that the 'Cost of sales' figure represents the same number of items sold – at cost price – as the 'Turnover' figure (the number of items which have been sold at the higher, selling price).
4 **Expenses:** these are the various costs of running the business, such as rent and rates, lighting and heating, selling and distribution costs, and wages and salaries. Business expenses usually include two items:
  (a) **depreciation,** which is the cost of 'using up' the major assets of the business, for example through the wear and tear of delivery vehicles, furniture, and machinery;
  (b) **bad debts,** which are costs of selling on credit. When a debtor firm cannot pay the debt it owes to the company, the company will have to write off the debtor as an expense.

## THE BALANCE SHEET

The Balance Sheet will show what the business owns and what it owes. Following the same classification of accounts used on page 68, the Balance Sheet displays the business **assets and liabilities**. The payments for business assets, such as the purchase of a new delivery vehicle or a new machine, are referred to as **capital expenditure**. This type of expenditure, unlike revenue expenditure, will not affect the calculation of the business profit.

### Content of the Balance Sheet

Items in the Balance Sheet are usually classified under the following headings:

1 **Fixed assets:** these are assets that have a long life and are not bought by the firm to resell to others; for example, its premises, machinery, furniture and delivery vehicles.
2 **Current assets:** these include cash and money in the bank, together with 'near-cash' assets such as stock-in-hand and debtors.
3 **Current liabilities:** amounts owed by the firm which have to be paid in the near future. They are often shown as a deduction from the firm's current assets (as in the illustration above), so that the amount of working capital can easily be seen. Typical examples are creditors (suppliers of goods on credit), bank overdraft, unpaid Corporation Tax, and one other:
    **Proposed dividends,** which are part of the profits to be paid out in the near future to the shareholders (as their reward for investing in the firm).
4 **Share capital:** the total value of the investment made by the various shareholders (see Unit 5).
5 **Reserves:** undistributed profits which may be held back as a general reserve or for a specific purpose such as replacing fixed assets as they depreciate (a Fixed Asset Replacement Reserve).
6 **Loan capital:** debentures are an important source of long-term loans to businesses. Unit 5 explains the difference between shares and debentures.

## THE APPROPRIATION OF PROFIT

Partnerships and limited companies face the problem of sharing one net profit between more than one partner or shareholder. Their profit and loss accounts therefore contain an 'appropriation' section, which shows how the net profit is to be appropriated, or shared out. This section will include its distribution to the various partners or, for a limited company, any proposed dividends for the shareholders. Corporation tax (which limited companies must pay on their profits) will be deducted from profits here, as well as any transfers to the reserves of the limited company and the balance of undistributed profit (again, for a limited company).

## 10.10 Interpretation of Accounts

Part of the accountant's work is to analyse the financial performance of the firm. The Government will be interested in the company's performance, because companies provide a source of revenue (Corporation tax). Other people who will be interested include:

1 **Owners,** who wish to assess the value of their investment in the firm.
2 **Managers,** who need to check the efficiency of their departments.

3 **Creditors,** to see whether it appears to be safe to allow credit to the firm.
4 **Other lenders,** such as banks or debenture holders, who are interested in how easily the firm can meet its debts to them.

## AREAS OF ANALYSIS

The accountant will analyse the firm's profitability, its liquidity and how efficiently it is using its assets (such as its stock). To do this, a series of **ratios** can be calculated.

### Profitability ratios

| Name | Calculation | Purpose |
|---|---|---|
| GROSS PROFIT MARGIN (%) | $\dfrac{\text{Gross Profit}}{\text{Turnover}} \times 100$ | To show what percentage of turnover is represented by gross profit (how many pence out of every £1 sales is gross profit). |

If this percentage is increasing, the business is receiving a higher gross profit for every £1 of sales than before; and vice versa.

| Name | Calculation | Purpose |
|---|---|---|
| NET PROFIT MARGIN (%) | $\dfrac{\text{Net Profit}}{\text{Turnover}} \times 100$ | To show what percentage of turnover is represented by net profit. |

An increase in this percentage means that the business is making a higher net profit per £1 of sales than before – this may be because the gross profit percentage has also increased by about the same amount, or that the expenses (as a percentage of turnover) have fallen. As with the gross profit percentage, this percentage could be compared with that of other firms in the same industry, to see whether the business is more profitable or less profitable than its competitors.

| Name | Calculation | Purpose |
|---|---|---|
| RETURN ON CAPITAL EMPLOYED ('ROCE') | $\dfrac{\text{Net Profit}}{\text{Capital Employed}} \times 100$ | To show how profitable the owners' investment is by calculating the percentage return. |

This percentage return – how many pence net profit out of every £1 capital employed – can then be compared to the rate of return the owners would be likely to receive if they invested in other areas: to see whether it is worthwhile their continuing to invest in this business.

### Liquidity ratios

| Name | Calculation | Purpose |
|---|---|---|
| WORKING CAPITAL RATIO | Current Assets to Current Liabilities (as a ratio) | To check the ability of the business to pay its short-term debts. |
| LIQUID CAPITAL ('ACID TEST') RATIO | Current Assets less Stock, to Current Liabilities (as a ratio) | To see whether the business can meet its short-term debts without having to sell any stock. |

### Use of asset ratios

| Name | Calculation | Purpose |
|---|---|---|
| RATE OF STOCK TURNOVER ('STOCKTURN') | Cost of Sales/Average Stock | To give the number of times per period that the average stock is sold. |

Average stock is often calculated as Opening Stock + Closing Stock, this total then being halved. If the stockturn is increasing it is likely that the business is holding lower average stocks than before and is operating more efficiently; and vice versa.

| Name | Calculation | Purpose |
|---|---|---|
| DEBTORS' COLLECTION PERIOD | $\dfrac{\text{Debtors}}{\text{Turnover}} \times 365$ | To show the length of time (number of days) on average that it takes debtors to pay their debts to the business. |

This indicates how efficient the business is at collecting its debts.

| Name | Calculation | Purpose |
|---|---|---|
| CREDITORS' COLLECTION PERIOD | $\dfrac{\text{Creditors}}{\text{Cost of Sales}} \times 365$ | To show the average length of time, in days, that the business takes to pay its creditors. |

### Using ratios

Using the figures from the final accounts in fig. 10.5 (page 71), the ratios produced, together with their calculation, are shown below.

*Gross profit margin:*

$400/1000 = 0.4 \times 100 = 40\%$

Gross Profit is 40p for every £1 of sales: therefore, the remaining 60p in the pound represents Cost of Sales.

*Net profit margin:*

$100/1000 = 0.1 \times 100 = 10\%$

Every £1 of sales realises 10p net profit: the difference between the 40p gross profit and 10p net profit is the expenses (30p of every £1 sales).

*Return on capital employed:*

$100/300 = 0.33 \times 100 = 33.3\%$

Every £1 of their capital employed in the business – that is, capital invested plus their reserves – earns about 33p net profit for the shareholders.

*Working capital ratio:*

$180:120 =$ a ratio of 3 to 2 (or 1.5 to 1) current assets to current liabilities.
The business has £1.50 cash or 'near cash' with which to pay every £1 of its short-term debts.

*Liquid assets ratio:*

$(180 - 60 \text{ stock} =) 120:120$, giving a ratio of 1:1 liquid assets to current liabilities.
The business, without selling any stock, can meet its short-term debts from its liquid assets.

*Rate of stock turnover:*

$600/50 = 12$ times a year.

The business takes a month, on average, to 'turn over' (buy and sell) its stock.

*Debtors' collection period:*

$100/1000 = 0.1 \times 365 = 36.5$ days.

Debtors take about 36 days, on average, to pay their debts to the business.

*Creditors' collection period:*

$60/600 = 0.1 \times 365 = 36.5$ days.

The business takes about 36 days' credit, on average, from its creditors.

### Applying the ratios

Many of these ratios mean little as they stand. They need to be compared with:

**The ratios of other firms in the same industry,** so that this firm's performance and efficiency can be compared to others.
**The same firm's ratios from previous years,** to see whether the firm is increasing its efficiency.

## ▮ 10.11 Published accounts ▮

Public limited companies (Unit 4) must publish their final accounts. People and other organizations interested in buying some of the shares of the PLC are therefore able to study the financial information included in these published accounts.

The document published by the PLC will contain not only the company's final accounts for the year, but also a range of other information. The following areas are normally covered:

1 Brief details of the PLC (e.g. its products and its subsidiary companies).
2 A summary of the financial highlights for the year.
3 The Chairman's statement which summarizes the company's performance during the year and the hopes for the future.
4 Brief details of the Board of Directors.
5 The Directors' Report, which may cover aspects such as the share dividend awarded, the level of employment in the company, share option schemes, and matters of health and safety.
6 The PLCs final accounts.
7 Notes to these accounts, which help explain how the figures are arrived at.

**8** A fund flow (cashflow) statement, to illustrate the liquidity position.

**9** A five-year financial summary of progress.

---

The year 1987/88 was a good one for Courtaulds. The results were comfortably ahead of those for 1986/87, which was itself by far the best year the Group had had in the 1980s up to that time. The advance in 1987/88 was achieved despite severe adverse effects, between them totalling some £40m, from a cyclical downturn in Courtelle and from the translation effects of changes in year-end exchange rates. Indeed the combined operating profits of the businesses other than Courtelle, translated at the same exchange rates as last year, increased by well over 30%.

Particularly notable performances came from Films & Packaging, from Coatings and from the acetyl-based businesses – yarns, cigarette filter tow and speciality plastics. Films & Packaging and Coatings have become substantial and successful businesses in their own right, making significant progress in highly competitive markets and opening up many opportunities as a result. Mention must be made of the Textiles group, which now has sales approaching £1bn and which has performed outstandingly in imparting coherence and momentum to Courtaulds formidable range of textile activities since they were put together into a single group in 1985.

C. A. Hogg, *Chairman*

---

**Fig. 10.6** Extracts from the Chairman's statement  Courtesy: *Courtaulds plc*

| YEAR ENDED 31 MARCH | 1988 £m | 1987 £m |
|---|---|---|
| **Turnover** | **2,421.2** | 2,261.9 |
| Cost of sales | **(1,776.5)** | (1,656.9) |
| **Gross profit** | **644.7** | 605.0 |
| Selling and distribution expenses | **(244.9)** | (231.6) |
| Administrative expenses | **(183.4)** | (169.5) |
| **Operating profit** | **216.4** | 203.9 |
| Share of profits of related companies | **16.4** | 9.7 |
| | **232.8** | 213.6 |
| Interest payable net of investment income | **(12.2)** | (12.5) |
| **Profit on ordinary activities before taxation** | **220.6** | 201.1 |
| Taxation | **(50.9)** | (46.6) |
| **Profit on ordinary activities after taxation** | **169.7** | 154.5 |
| Minority interests | **(10.5)** | (9.2) |
| | **159.2** | 145.3 |
| Extraordinary Items | **(15.8)** | (11.4) |
| **Profit attributable to Courtaulds plc** | **143.4** | 133.9 |
| Preference dividends | **(0.1)** | (0.1) |
| **Profit attributable to ordinary shareholders** | **143.3** | 133.8 |
| Ordinary dividends | **(47.0)** | (36.6) |
| **Transferred to reserves** | **96.3** | 97.2 |
| **Earnings per ordinary share** | **40.9p** | 38.2p |

**Fig. 10.7** Extracts from the Group Profit and Loss Account  Courtesy: *Courtaulds plc*

| 31 MARCH | 1988 £m | 1987 £m |
|---|---:|---:|
| **Fixed assets** | | |
| Tangible assets | 579.7 | 495.5 |
| Investments | 32.0 | 29.2 |
| | 611.7 | 524.7 |
| **Current assets** | | |
| Stocks | 420.5 | 397.0 |
| Debtors | 404.0 | 375.6 |
| Cash and deposits | 184.8 | 247.3 |
| | 1,009.3 | 1,019.9 |
| **Creditors** | | |
| (amounts falling due within one year) | | |
| Loans and overdrafts | (65.7) | (80.1) |
| Other | (596.2) | (534.3) |
| | (661.9) | (614.4) |
| **Net current assets** | 347.4 | 405.5 |
| **Total assets less current liabilities** | 959.1 | 930.2 |
| **Creditors** | | |
| (amounts falling due after more than one year) | | |
| Loans | (274.2) | (187.1) |
| Other | (22.2) | (31.0) |
| | (296.4) | (218.1) |
| **Provisions for liabilities and charges** | (23.6) | (34.6) |
| | 639.1 | 677.5 |
| **Capital and reserves** | | |
| Called up share capital | 101.1 | 100.3 |
| Share premium account | 117.5 | 115.0 |
| Profit and loss account | 395.5 | 444.3 |
| | 614.1 | 659.6 |
| **Minority interests** | 25.0 | 17.9 |
| | 639.1 | 677.5 |

**Fig. 10.8** Extracts from the Group Balance Sheet  Courtesy: *Courtaulds plc*

## 10.12 Summary

All firms are separate from the people who own or run them. A firm needs funds to operate: its owners must obtain these funds, and its managers must manage them. The accounting function is most closely involved with the **profits**, the **liquidity** and the **general finances** of the firm and the accountant is employed to obtain information about these aspects. There will be a need to calculate current profit levels (or the cost of various services provided), to budget for future income and expenditure, and to record and analyse present and future financial performance.

# 11 MARKETING

## 11.1 Introduction

Unit 1 described a 'market' as a place where buyers and sellers met and where goods and services could be bought and sold. It also classified markets under headings such as 'consumer' and 'industrial'.

Firms in both sectors of the economy will have their own markets: markets for health services and health-food products; public transport and private transport; and industrial cleaning and domestic window-cleaning. There is a **labour market** – firms demand work and employees supply work. Unit 5 explained the **capital market**, much of which is centred on the workings of the London Stock Exchange.

'The market' to a firm consists of its actual or potential customers, who can afford to buy the firm's goods or services. It is the role of the firm's **Marketing Department** to examine the market and to provide information on it. The Marketing Department will be interested in the needs of the firm's customers: the firm can then design its goods and services to satisfy these needs. By doing this, the firm should be successful, i.e. it will make profits and survive.

## 11.2 The Marketing Mix

Marketing is one of the most varied activities in modern firms. In the last 20 years, people in business have realized that it is not good enough simply to produce a product or service and then hope that it will sell. **Market research** must be carried out, to see what sort of product – what design, what colours, what size, what price, etc – is demanded; the product must be attractively **packaged**; it must be brought to people's attention through **advertising and sales promotion**; and it must be made available through efficient **distribution**.

'Marketing mix' is a term which is used to describe these various marketing activities. They are often summarized as 'the four Ps', as in fig. 11.1

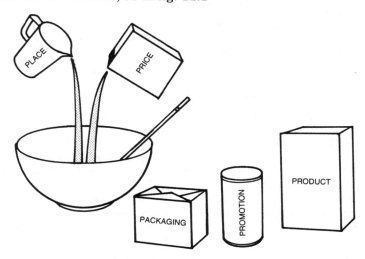

**Fig. 11.1** The marketing mix

**Product:** this refers to the nature of the product itself, e.g. its design and quality, how it compares with competitors' products and whether different models are to be made.
**Price:** this is the price at which it is to be sold and includes how its price compares with the prices of its competitors.
**Place:** this is concerned with the forms and channels of distribution (Unit 12) that are to be used in getting the product onto the market.
**Promotion:** this means how it is to be advertised, whether any discounts are to be offered and what other types of sales promotion are to be used.

Sometimes, a fifth 'P' is identified: **Packaging**, because of its great influence and importance, even though it is one of the elements in the fourth 'P' (advertising and promoting the product).

## 11.3 Markets and Segmentation

The 'market' for a product can sometimes be broken down into different **segments**. For example, the car market in the UK consists of a number of segments: fig. 11.2 summarizes some of the segments and their different needs.

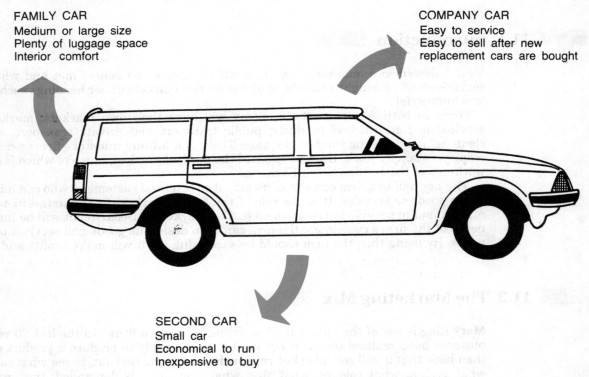

**FAMILY CAR**
Medium or large size
Plenty of luggage space
Interior comfort

**COMPANY CAR**
Easy to service
Easy to sell after new
replacement cars are bought

**SECOND CAR**
Small car
Economical to run
Inexpensive to buy

**Fig. 11.2** Market segments

Car firms can therefore develop particular models for particular markets, such as the 'fleet' (company car) market, and plan their advertising campaigns accordingly. Some firms specialize in one or two segments only: Rolls Royce is an example of a car manufacturer specializing in the luxury car segment.

Each market segment will have its own unique requirements and therefore will need a different 'mix' of marketing resources. Market segments – and markets in general – vary in their make-up. Consumers in these markets and segments will differ in the following ways:

1 **Age.** This is an important influence on fashion and therefore on the style of clothes that a clothing manufacturer may decide to market.
2 **Population.** The total size of the population is important when marketing, as well as its regional distribution, e.g. when deciding on where to advertise and how to distribute the products.
3 **Groupings.** Companies are interested in the various groups making up their markets. Different religious and cultural groups will have their own specialist demands for goods and services, and the number and size of family groups is important to those firms marketing such products as baby clothes and toys.
4 **Income.** The size of disposable income will help determine, for example, the quality of the products marketed and how many models ('standard' and 'super', etc) a firm decides to make and market.

## 11.4 Market Research

Market research will provide the Marketing Department of a firm with information about the elements of the marketing mix. The research will be into factors such as the market itself, the likely demand for the product, the variety of models that the customers appear to want (this leads to **product development**), the best price to charge and how best to advertise and distribute the product.

### METHODS OF MARKET RESEARCH

The management of a firm involved in market research has the choice of using its own marketing department or employing a specialist market research organization.

The methods of market research available are often grouped under two headings. There is, firstly, **Desk research**: this uses **existing sources** of information to research into the market.

Secondly there is **Field research** which involves obtaining **new information** about the market by going 'into the field' and asking people.

### Desk research

A company planning to use desk research may decide to use **its own sales statistics** to identify trends or customer requests for changes in existing products or requests for new models. It can also **investigate competitors' products** already on the market, discovering their popular and unpopular points to help it design a new, more popular, product at a competitive price. Finally, the company may use **government and other sources of statistics** (e.g. on population and on spending patterns) to assess trends that are taking place. Typical sources include the various government publications (Unit 19), trade association publications and the 'quality' newspapers and periodicals such as *The Financial Times*.

Desk research has two major advantages over field research. Firstly, it is less expensive; secondly, the information is already available and is therefore quicker to obtain.

### Field research

There are various methods of field research available to a firm. Each method involves using one or more of the following investigation techniques:

1 **Questionnaires**, designed specifically for the task, and completed by holding interviews with potential consumers (either face-to-face in the street, over the telephone, or through the post).
2 **Test marketing**, where a potential new product is marketed in one area of the country only and the reactions to it studied to see whether it should be launched nationally or abandoned.
3 Using **consumer panels**, where selected people are given the product and asked to comment in detail on it.

The major advantage that field research has over desk research is that it is done specifically for the new (or existing) product in question. Desk research is done for other purposes and therefore the information collected is not always fully relevant to the product being researched.

## █ 11.5 The Product Life-Cycle █

Products have a limited life, not only from the consumer's viewpoint, but also as far as the producer is concerned. For example, a particular car model might last 5 or 10 – or, in the case of the Mini, over 25 – years before it is phased out and replaced by a completely new model. New inventions and technology make many products obsolete. Fashion can be another major influence on the life of a product.

Some products survive because they now sell in different segments of their original markets: e.g. fountain pens, becoming far less important in the popular pen market due to the success of the biro, compete successfully in the 'quality pen' market; and black and white TVs still sell in reasonable volumes – but now mainly in the 'second TV' market.

Products, with their limited lives, have a **life-cycle**. Different products last for different lengths of times but their life-cycles have certain common elements. Fig. 11.3 illustrates these elements.

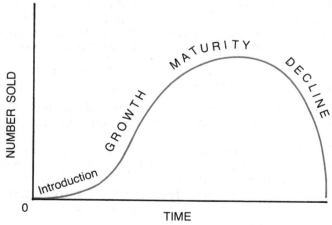

**Fig. 11.3** Stages of the product life-cycle

Following its development (using market research techniques), which can take a long time, the product is introduced onto the market. This **Introduction** stage is supported by heavy advertising and promotion – initial sales will be low until people get to know of the product and buy it. At this point, the costs of production – which include massive costs of development – far exceed the revenue from its sales.

The **Growth** stage occurs as more and more people buy the product. It establishes a 'brand loyalty' among its users, who will deliberately choose this product rather than a competing brand. Sales rise and the product becomes more profitable as the sales revenue starts to pay off the early high costs.

At the **Maturity** stage, the product has reached its peak of sales. It is fully established in the market and at its most profitable for the company. It may have reached 'market saturation' and the firm's competitors will probably have modified their own products, or brought new ones out, to compete with it.

The actions of the firm's competitors, changes in tastes and fashion or in technology, and other influences bring the product into the stage of **Decline**. Sales fall as its market share reduces and it eventually stops being made and sold.

### Extending the life

The length of the product's life-cycle can often be extended by modifying the product in some way. Companies often use a 'new, improved' style of modification, linked to changes in packaging, an advertising campaign and sales promotion (e.g. the 'free gift' approach) to keep their products on the market for a longer period.

## 11.6  Pricing Decisions

Price is one of the elements in the marketing mix. The price that a firm decides to set for its product will depend on both **internal factors** – i.e. the costs of production (Unit 8) – and on **external factors**, for example the prices of competing products on the market.

A firm's costs will influence the pricing formulas that it uses to set a selling price for its products. **Cost-plus pricing** may be used: the firm will add a profit mark-up onto its unit costs of production. If unit costs are, for example, £1.00, a mark-up of 50 per cent would give the firm a selling price of £1.50. Cost-plus pricing has its limitations, since it is not easy to work out accurately the unit costs of production in advance – it also ignores the prices of competitors' products. The use of **breakeven analysis** and **marginal costing** techniques (Unit 8) can also be used in setting a suitable price.

The firm's management can use different **price strategies** for their products. These strategies can be 'high-price' or 'low-price'.

### High-price strategies

With a **Skimming** strategy, a firm launches a new and unique product and decides to charge a high price to 'skim' the market. Some people will buy the new product at this high price, because of its 'status symbol' appeal. As the status appeal dies down, the firm reduces the price so that more are sold.

A **Maximizing** strategy may be used: where there is great demand for a product or service which has a short life-cycle, the manufacturer will try to maximize profits by charging very high prices.

### Low-price strategies

Using a **Penetration** policy, a low price is set to enable the firm to capture a large market share. Prices can be increased later, to earn profits.

A **Capturing** strategy can be used if a company is making a range of products which are linked in some way. If, for example, a company is producing items of equipment and also the 'software' (such as some form of refill) used by that equipment, it may sell the equipment at low prices and then charge high prices for the software.

### Other strategies

There are a number of other pricing strategies that can be used.

1 **Odd pricing:** using prices that end in odd numbers, e.g. £1.99, 95p.
2 **Psychological pricing:** making the item look cheaper by pricing it at, say £9.95 and not £10.00.
3 **Discrimination pricing:** using different prices in the different market segments. For instance, where the use of public transport can cost students and senior citizens less than it does commuters.
4 **Market pricing:** the item is priced at the current market price, to avoid price wars.

## 11.7  Promotion

Promotion is one of the four 'Ps' in the marketing mix. It consists of three main elements: advertising, personal selling and sales promotion.

1 **Advertising** involves a sponsor paying for the non-personal presentation of a message. Advertising is therefore **paid for**, which distinguishes it from publicity which is not paid for

by the sponsor. It is **non-personal**, being directed to a mass audience and not to an individual; this distinguishes it from personal selling, which is directed at an individual. Advertising has a **sponsor**, unlike most publicity; producers pay for their products to be advertised.

2 **Personal selling** provides the special, individual information and contact which advertising (being non-personal) cannot. It is often used to support advertising.

3 **Sales promotion** 'pushes' a product through activities such as displays, exhibitions, demonstrations and shows.

In order to promote a product, there must be something about that product which allows it to be promoted. The packaging and branding of products (see page 85) helps a **brand image** to become established, which in turn helps with advertising and promotion.

**Product differentiation** – making your product different from those of your competitors – is often created by aspects such as the product's branding and packaging. Once a product becomes differentiated from other similar products, advertising, personal selling and sales promotion can be used effectively.

### Types of promotion

There are two types, or forms, of promotion: they are often treated as distinct but advertising and sales promotion campaigns often contain elements of both.

1 **Persuasive:** the objective of persuasive advertising and promotion is to convince the customer that he or she needs and should buy the firm's product. It also includes persuading the public to choose this product rather than rival firms' products. Persuasive promotion is supported by the use of branding, packaging and other forms of product differentiation.

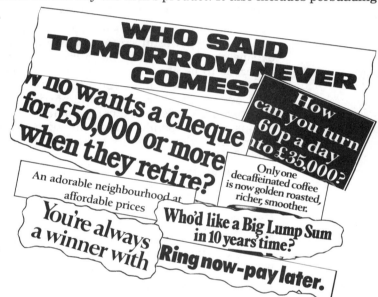

Fig. 11.4 'Persuasive' and 'Informative'

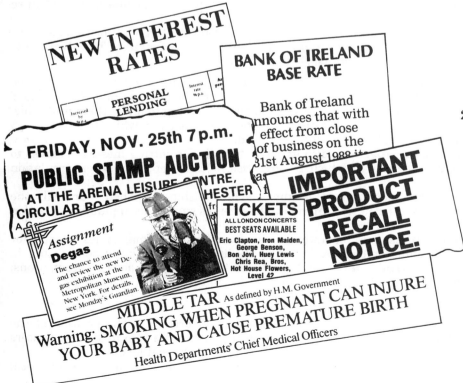

2 **Informative:** here, the emphasis of the advertisement or sales promotion is to give full information (e.g. technical information) about the product. Informative advertising and promotion is often used by public services, for example in Yellow Pages, by British Rail publishing train timetables and by the Government telling people about the likely harmful effects of smoking (although there is also an element of persuasion with this last example).

Fig. 11.4 shows how advertisements can persuade and inform.

## 11.8 Advertising

Firms which advertise their goods and services may do so for a number of reasons:

1 To **introduce new products** onto the market. Advertising can be used to reach a mass audience, who may otherwise not hear about the new product.
2 To **increase sales** of existing products, e.g. by pushing the product in a new segment of the market.
3 To **compete with others**. This 'competitive' advertising often occurs where products are substitutes: butter and margarine manufacturers, for example, use competitive advertising. Other advertising may involve attacking competitors' products, e.g. the advertising battles between rival lawn mower manufacturers.
4 To **cooperate with others**, such as where a washing machine producer and a washing powder supplier join forces in an advertisement.
5 To **improve company image**: the advertising of some multinational companies may concentrate on the company name and image, rather than on its products.

### ADVERTISING MEDIA

The **message** of the advertisement may be persuasive, informative or both. The **medium** is the method used to communicate that message. There are many different media from which to choose. Typical examples of media which are used are summarized below.

#### Commercial television and radio

**Television advertising** is used by large firms which sell consumer goods: it can be persuasive and is very powerful since it can reach millions of potential customers. The adverts are expensive both to make and to broadcast (the cost here depends on the time of day that the advert is to be shown: certain times are 'peak viewing' and therefore more expensive). The advertisement will have the benefits of colour, sound, vision and movement and it can be tailored to particular groups and particular times of broadcasting, such as the advertising of new toys for Christmas during children's TV programmes.

This is an expanding field for advertising, with the impact of breakfast television, the extension of viewing hours by the major ITV companies and the development in satellite and cable TV stations.

**Commercial radio** is a newer medium. It is much less expensive to make and to broadcast the sound-only advert. However, commercial radio reaches fewer people per station than commercial TV.

#### Papers and periodicals

Many companies choose to advertise in papers, either instead of, or as well as, advertising on TV and radio. Advertising in papers differs from TV and radio advertising in the following ways:

1 It has the advantage of being **permanent**: the advert can be cut out and kept for future reference.
2 The advert can provide the reader with **far more information** than a TV or radio advert.
3 The advert will suffer from a **lack of impact**, especially when compared to TV advertising. There is also no guarantee that it will be read.

**Daily and Sunday national newspapers** are often grouped into the 'qualities' (e.g. *The Financial Times, The Guardian, The Times, The Independent, Observer*) and the 'tabloids' such as *The Mirror* and *The Star*. Both groups depend on advertising to make them profitable: the tabloids, with their higher sales figures, tend to be more expensive in which to advertise. A wide range of consumer products is normally advertised.

**Regional and local newspapers** are also important media for getting messages across to large numbers. They are cheaper in which to advertise, because of their lower circulation figures.

**Free newspapers** ('free-sheets') rely totally on advertising for their survival: the advertising tends to be more informative, from local businesses such as local plumbers, garden centres and garages.

**Periodicals and magazines** are often 'interest' based, such as those magazines catering for runners, hi-fi 'buffs' or computer enthusiasts. Adverts are from businesses specializing in these areas. There are also **trade periodicals**, devoted to particular trades or occupations; again, the advertising is of a specialist, often informative, nature.

#### Other media

**Posters** are widely used by many firms selling mass-appeal products. The position of the large, permanent poster sites affects how much the poster will cost the firm to display. Posters are also a valuable medium to advertise forthcoming events, at a local level.

**Cinemas** can be a useful form of (often informative) advertising for national and local business; advertisers need to aim their adverts at the relevant age-ranges attending the cinemas.

**Leaflets** are delivered or posted to houses on a large scale. Direct mailing, often known as 'mail shots', has grown in popularity: firms can buy mailing lists from various sources and the accompanying letters can be personalized by using modern technology. People are often tempted by offers, for example by a 'gift' or the offer of a 'free' weekend's holiday.

**Viewdata and teletext** agencies include Prestel, which operates a viewdata system, and commercial TV's Oracle teletext service. Advertisers can purchase electronic 'pages' and provide information about their products or services.

Other advertising media used include **illuminated signs** and printing on **carrier bags**.

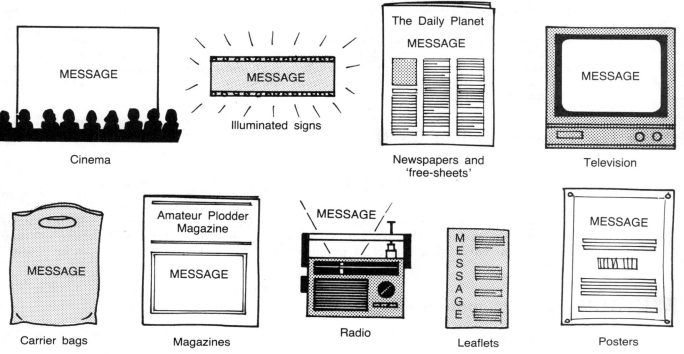

**Fig. 11.5** The main advertising media

### Influences on the advertisement

The advertisement content, style and medium will be influenced by a number of factors.

1 The **nature of the product**. Industrial-market products are often advertised in trade magazines, in an informative way: consumer-based products and services often use more persuasive techniques, in the mass-market forms (e.g. television).
2 Where the product stands in its **life-cycle**. Advertising tends to be more informative in the early days of the product's life and increasingly persuasive as the product reaches the stages of maturity and decline.
3 The **advertising budget** will determine which media can be afforded for the campaign.

The two major influences which help to decide which advertising medium is used are the **cost** of the different media and the nature of the **target group**. When examining 'media cost', the Marketing Department must include not only the cost of using the various media but also the expense involved in creating the advertisement. Television adverts in particular are very expensive, both to write and to film.

If the target group is a national one, then a national form of advertising will probably be used. The target group may be a specialist-interest one, in which case a specialist magazine would be a suitable medium. Where the advertisement is to be informative in style, perhaps inviting the audience to respond in some way, press advertising is likely to be used rather than television or radio advertising.

## THE ADVERTISING AGENCY

Designing a professional, persuasive or informative advertisement is a specialist activity. For large-scale national advertising, many firms use an **advertising agency**. Advertising agencies may provide a range of marketing expertise for interested firms: as well as carrying out advertising, the agency may also offer to undertake other work, such as market research, for the firm.

The agency's advertising work consists of selecting the medium to be used, writing the advert, designing its overall appearance and style, and arranging for its display or broadcast. The agency may also obtain feedback for the firm on the advert's success.

## ARGUMENTS FOR AND AGAINST ADVERTISING

1 Advertising provides **information** to consumers who may not otherwise discover the product. This increases the consumers' standard of living.
2 It **increases sales**, which leads to higher production and possibly more jobs; also **economies of scale** leading to cheaper prices for consumers.
3 **Competition** is encouraged through advertising, which should again result in lower prices.
4 **TV and newspapers are subsidized** through their advertising revenue.
5 **Employment** is created in the advertising industry.

But:

1 **Higher prices** can be the result if advertising is unsuccessful, because increased sales revenue does not cover advertising costs.
2 It can lead to **exploitation**. Advertising can tempt people to buy what they do not need or cannot afford, or encourage them to buy products that may be harmful (e.g. alcohol) but which have a tempting, advertising-created image and appeal. It can also encourage people to want more and more material possessions, and its appeal may be an emotional one, rather than a rational one.

## 11.9 Personal Selling

Advertising is impersonal: it is directed at a mass audience and so it tends to be very generalized. The use of **personal selling** allows the firm's message to be personally tailored to the individual buyer. In this way, personal selling can be an important supporting activity to advertising.

Sales staff will have the responsibility of liaising with the customer. They will deliver the product to the customer; they can provide demonstrations and technical information; and they can pass on advertising and sales promotion materials, such as free samples or product leaflets.

## 11.10 Sales Promotion

**Sales promotion** is also used to support advertising in attracting customers. Sales promotion techniques include the following:

1 **Free samples.** These have the great advantage of getting potential consumers to actually try the product.

**Fig. 11.6** Forms of sales promotion

2 **Price reductions.** Consumers are encouraged to buy the product at, say, 10p off; or there may be a coupon attached (or mailed direct to the consumer) which offers a discount off the next purchase.

3 **Premium offers.** Customers may be offered:
   (a) **free gifts;** contained in the package itself, such as free gifts in packets of breakfast cereals, or offered at the point of sale (e.g. at petrol stations);
   (b) **send-away gifts,** where customers receive the gift after sending away a number of product labels to obtain it;
   (c) **low-price purchases** of goods, for example where a product is offered for sale at a greatly reduced price if the customer also sends off a number of labels or special coupons.

4 **Competitions.** Consumers may be encouraged to buy the product if it is accompanied by a competition offering a major prize such as a free holiday.

5 **Point of sale demonstrations and displays.** The product is demonstrated at major exhibitions and shows for consumers to see its potential; it may also be attractively displayed using purpose-built displays.

6 **After-sales service.** Customers may be tempted to buy products – particularly expensive ones – if the after-sales service is clearly linked with the product at the point of sale. A firm's **guarantee** relating to after-sale use of the product is often used as a sales promotion technique.

7 **Sponsorship.** This is sometimes used by firms to promote their image and products. For example, tobacco sponsorship exists in some areas of sport, partly because tobacco companies are not allowed to advertise cigarettes on television.

## 11.11 Packaging and Branding

**Packaging** has to do more than simply protect a product. It is now recognized as being an important element in the marketing mix, with a product's package being used in product differentiation (see page 81). Different colours, sizes or shapes – such as the shape of the bottle

**Fig. 11.7** Packaging the 'Wispa' brand chocolate bars  Courtesy: *Cadbury Ltd*

that the product comes in – can be used effectively by manufacturers in helping to promote their products through their packaging.

The package will normally display the product's **brand name**. Branding of products has developed this century: its advantage to consumers is that they know that the next item carrying the same brand name that they buy will be virtually identical in quality to the last one bought.

Branding brings other benefits to a company. The company's name, when established with one brand, can encourage consumers to buy new, different brands bearing that same name (e.g. a new Kellogg's cereal or a new Marks and Spencer style of jacket). The brand name also acts as the basis for advertising and sales promotion, and it allows brand loyalties to become established: consumers will buy the same brand of soap, shampoo, etc, next time they need these items.

## 11.12 Summary

More and more firms are becoming market-oriented in outlook. Instead of making a product that it hopes will sell, the management of a market-oriented firm will first of all examine the potential market for that product. To do this, it uses market research techniques, either involving desk research or field research.

The firm's management will be aware of the elements of the marketing mix, when considering whether to launch a new product. The product itself is only one element: the place (the market), the price at which it is to be sold and the methods of promotion to be used are the other important elements. Unless all are closely considered, it is probable that the firm's new product will fail in the marketplace.

# 12 TRANSPORT AND DISTRIBUTION

## 12.1 Introduction

The marketing mix (Unit 11) includes 'place' as one of its main elements. Firms making products for a particular market have to decide how their products are to reach that market. In doing this, they will make decisions about the method of **transport** to use and about the **channels of distribution** through which the product will pass.

## 12.2 Channels of Distribution

Manufacturers must be able to sell their goods to consumers: this is achieved by sending these goods through various channels of distribution. The channels shown in fig. 12.1 represent the main ways that manufactured goods are passed from manufacturer to consumer.

Each channel includes the same activities: as well as the act of buying and selling, the product will be **promoted** at the various stages of distribution, **stored** for a time, then **transported** to the next stage.

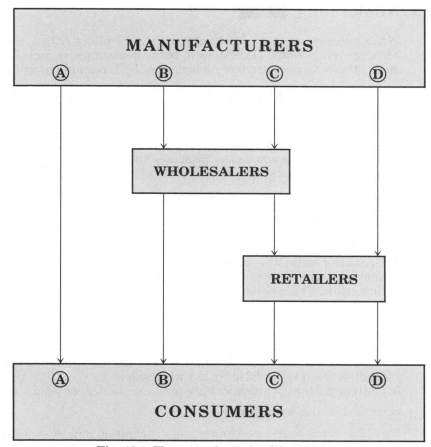

Fig. 12.1 The main channels of distribution

A manufacturer may sell direct to the consumer, as shown in channel A, and omit both wholesaler and retailer. Some manufacturers – for example, many china producers in the Potteries area – run factory shops from which their products can be bought. Variations on the 'manufacturer-direct-to-consumer' channel include the door-to-door selling of products (Avon cosmetics and Betterwear products are well-known examples) and mail order selling through agents (who carry out some of the retailer's duties).

In channel B, the retailer is omitted, the wholesaler receiving the goods from the manufacturer and then selling them direct to the final consumer. These wholesalers are usually based in densely populated areas and often sell consumer durables at low prices.

Channel C shows the traditional pattern. The manufacturer sells in bulk to wholesalers, who then resell in smaller quantities to retailers: the retailers sell single items to consumers.

Many foodstuffs and finished goods are still sold through this traditional channel.

The wholesaler may be omitted by a manufacturer, who then sells direct to large retailers (channel D). These retailers, because of their size, can also carry out the function of a wholesaler, e.g. by being able to store large quantities of the goods. One popular development related to this channel is where manufacturers set up their own retail outlets through vertical forwards integration (Unit 6). The franchising of retail outlets (Unit 4) illustrates another important variation of this channel.

### Selecting the channel

The choice of channel is largely determined by the product to be distributed. **Consumer goods** use the channels outlined above. The channel's cost and the amount of control the manufacturer wants over distribution, are two important influences in deciding which channel will be used. The influences of **cost** and **control** also affect the choice of channel for:

1 **Raw materials and foodstuffs.** Raw materials are often distributed through a number of commodity exchanges: an example is The London Metal Exchange, which grades and sells a range of metals. Some foodstuffs are also sold either through a commodity exchange such as The Baltic Exchange, through wholesale markets for fresh produce such as Smithfield (meat) and Billingsgate (fish), or through specialist marketing boards such as The Milk Marketing Board.
2 A number of different channels are also used to sell **industrial goods**. There may be direct selling to the final user; wholesalers or manufacturer's agents may also be used to distribute items, such as farm machinery and steel (e.g. through steel stockholders).

## 12.3 Wholesaling

Wholesalers trade in a variety of markets, handling either raw materials or finished goods. They provide a range of services to both their suppliers and their customers: with consumer goods, these services are for the benefit of both manufacturers and retailers.

### THE WHOLESALER'S SERVICES FOR MANUFACTURERS

1 **Bulk buying.** It is easier and cheaper for a manufacturer to deal with a few large orders rather than with many small orders.
2 **Storage.** The manufacturer's own warehousing costs are reduced.
3 **Promotion.** The wholesaler promotes the product and advertises for the manufacturer.
4 **Advice.** Feedback on the success of the goods is given by the wholesaler to the manufacturer.
5 **Risk-bearing.** The wholesaler acts as the manufacturer's market, therefore taking on the risk of not being able to sell the goods.

### THE WHOLESALER'S SERVICES FOR RETAILERS

1 **Breaking bulk.** The wholesaler buys in large quantities but sells to the retailer in smaller amounts, which saves the retailer the costs of holding large amounts of stock.
2 **Selection.** The wholesaler typically has a range of manufacturers' goods from which the retailer can choose.
3 **Credit.** By granting credit, the wholesaler helps the retailer to finance the purchase of goods. Some wholesalers operate as 'Cash and Carry' outlets, where retailers gain lower prices if they pay cash for, and collect, their purchases.
4 **Information.** Product information (e.g. technical information, or information about new product lines) is provided by the wholesaler.
5 **Delivery.** Many wholesalers are prepared to deliver goods to the retailer.

### Survival of the wholesaler

Fig. 12.1 shows that some channels of distribution now miss out the wholesaler. The growth of large-scale retail outlets has led to these organizations carrying out the wholesaler's traditional functions, such as warehousing and breaking bulk, so eliminating the need for a separate wholesaler. More and more manufacturers are also carrying out some of the wholesaler's traditional functions. As large-scale retailing has grown, the number of small retailers has reduced, which in turn has led to a reduction in demand for independent wholesalers.

Wholesalers have adapted to cope with these changing conditions. To make the small shops more competitive, **voluntary chains** such as Spar and VG have been set up: wholesalers run the voluntary chain, supplying a large number of independent retailers with their goods. National advertising, cheaper prices through bulk buying, and 'own-brand' goods are examples of the benefits available to the retailers in these chains.

By providing a **cash-and-carry** service (see above), wholesalers have helped both themselves and the small independent retailer to survive.

## 12.4 Retailing

Retailers form another link in the chain of distribution from manufacturer to consumer. Like wholesalers, these retailers also offer **services to manufacturers**, such as giving information on product performance, storing the manufacturer's products and providing manufacturers with a ready market for their goods.

A retailer also provides **services for consumers**. Advice about products is given by the retailer; the retailer provides consumers with a wide range of similar products to choose from; and the retailer provides a convenient, local outlet for consumers, which often offers credit and delivery facilities and after-sales service.

There are a number of different forms of retail outlet: the main ones are summarized below.

### Independent retailers

Small retail shops are still widely found. They are often sole trader organizations (Unit 4) which specialize in one product or service, such as a local butcher or hairdresser. Normally supplied by wholesalers, their overall importance in retailing has declined because many of them cannot compete with the larger retail organizations.

### Department stores

A department store is normally run as a PLC (Unit 4); it may exist as a single store, or as a 'multiple' department store such as Debenhams, which is found in a number of towns. These stores consist of various departments which sell a wide range of products such as foodstuffs, toys, furniture, clothing and footwear, offering quality goods supported by a high level of service.

### Multiple stores, discount stores and superstores

Multiple stores are also known as **chain** stores. These PLCs have a head office and at least 10 branches throughout the country. They may be **specialist multiples**, such as Burtons which specializes in clothes; or they may operate as **variety multiples** (e.g. British Home Stores and Littlewoods) which sell a wide range of goods. Food **supermarkets** are a type of specialist multiple store.

Outlets such as Comet or Kwik-Fit are often classed as **discount stores**. These stores buy centrally in bulk; they are based near centres of population (normally at out-of-town–not in costly city centre–locations); they advertise on national TV and in local papers, control their display and service costs very carefully and sell their goods at a discount.

With the trend towards establishing out-of-town shopping sites, there has been a growth of **retail superstores** at these sites. Many of these superstores have developed from discount

**Fig. 12.2** Modern technology in retailing: point-of-sale control  Courtesy: *British Shoe Corp Ltd*

stores and the traditional foods supermarkets. Shops such as Sainsburys, Tesco and MFI can often gain greater economies of scale by setting up superstores in out-of-town locations, and they may then decide to close down some of their more expensive city centre outlets.

*Other types of retail outlet*

**Franchising** (Unit 4) is becoming an increasingly popular form of retail outlet. **Cooperative retail societies** (Unit 4), **mail order** firms such as Littlewoods, the use of automatic **vending machines** and the creation of **voluntary chains** (see page 88) are other major types of outlets through which products are sold.

## TRENDS IN RETAILING

There is a widespread use of **self-service** in retailing, where customers select the items they wish to buy and take them to a cash desk. More recent trends are mentioned above: they include the development of town centre and out-of-town shopping precincts and the growth in the number and importance of large-scale retail outlets.

Many retailers are also **diversifying**, by extending their range of product lines. Superstores are a good example of this. A specific example is Boots plc, which used to be popularly called 'Boots the chemists' but now operates as a variety multiple selling a wide range of consumer products.

Fig. 12.3 gives an indication of the relative importance of the different retail outlets.

| Size of Outlet | Number of Businesses | 1984 | | | |
| --- | --- | --- | --- | --- | --- |
| | | Number of Outlets | Number of Employees | Turnover (£ million) | Growth in Turnover since 1980 |
| Single outlet retailers | 201 633 | 201 633 | 813 000 | 24 268 | 38% |
| Small multiples (between 2 and 9 outlets) | 28 207 | 73 670 | 349 000 | 10 604 | 26% |
| Large multiples (10 and more outlets) | 949 | 67 850 | 1 164 000 | 47 469 | 45% |

**Fig. 12.3** Retail outlets Source: *Business Statistics Office, CSO 'Blue Book' 1988 edition*

## 12.5 Transport

Transport is an essential element in a channel of distribution, in getting the goods to the final consumer. Firms often have a choice of which form of transport to use. Fig. 12.4 illustrates the main internal forms of goods transport used in Great Britain.

| Total (million tonnes) | 1981 | 1986 |
| --- | --- | --- |
| Road | 1286 | 1455 |
| Rail | 154 | 140 |
| Water | 119 | 133 |
| Pipelines | 75 | 79 |

**Fig. 12.4** Goods transport in Great Britain
Source: *Department of Transport, CSO 'Blue Book' 1988 edition*

The factors which determine the form of transport used are as follows:

1 The **cost** of transport: for example, road transport is usually cheaper than rail transport over short distances.
2 The **product**: different forms may be used depending on whether the product is fragile, very heavy or bulky, perishable, very expensive, in liquid form, etc.
3 The **speed** required: products needed urgently will use different forms of transport to those products that are not so urgently required.

### Road haulage

Road haulage is the most frequently used form of inland transport in the UK. It is typically cheap and fast, compared to rail: it can also deliver door-to-door and is more flexible because it is not subject to strict timetables.

Some companies will employ specialist local or national haulage firms to move their products. Other companies will run their own transport fleet: a bakery may deliver its own products to grocers, or a large retail organization can use its own fleet of lorries to move goods from its warehouses to its shops (it may also own delivery vans which are used to **deliver** its goods to customers).

By running its own transport, a company can gain from **free advertising** on the vehicles and delivery is **quicker and cheaper** than through using a specialist road haulier. The company will have to ensure that its transport staff and vehicles are fully used, to gain from having its own transport.

### Railways

British Rail is road transport's major inland competitor. Its strength is in moving bulky goods over long distances: it is also often used to transport some urgently-required or dangerous items such as nuclear waste.

In recent years, British Rail has struggled to keep some of its freight business: for example, distribution of daily newspapers has recently been lost to road transport. Attempts to modernize its range of services, e.g. the **Red Star** fast delivery service and the **Freightliner** container service, have helped BR to remain competitive.

### Air and sea transport

Both these forms of freight transport are largely – but not exclusively – used for international trade. **Air transport** of freight, though expensive, is extremely fast over long distances. It tends to be used for items which are urgently-required, highly expensive, or perishable.

Many forms of **sea transport** exist, including cargo liners, tankers and container ships. Although slow when compared to air transport, these ships can move bulky items more cheaply. The discovery and exploitation of North Sea oil, for example, led to an increase in sea transport around our shores.

### Recent developments in transport

The use of **containers** has grown in the last 20 years. The 'container' is a fixed-size, large box which has its contents sealed inside: it can be moved by crane from one form of transport to another (e.g. from a container ship to a container lorry), or a 'roll-on, roll-off' system can be used, for example on cross-Channel ferries. Containerization leads to quicker delivery and better security since the goods are sealed in the containers.

**Pipelines** are another important development. They are used to carry liquids or gases, for example from North Sea rigs to inland refineries.

## 12.6 Summary

Firms use various methods to get their products to their customers. A number of channels of distribution can be employed, which may make use of the specialist functions (such as storage) offered by wholesalers. Developments in retailing – such as in the scale of the retailers – have meant that, increasingly, specialist wholesalers may not be used by a manufacturer.

The **cost** of a channel of distribution is one of the factors which helps to determine whether it will be used by a manufacturer. Cost is also important when firms decide on the form of transport to use. For moving goods inland, the major competition is between the use of road or rail transport. Either or both of these forms may also be used when a firm exports or imports goods, in conjunction with air or sea transport.

# 13 THE PERSONNEL FUNCTION

## 13.1 Introduction

The role of the personnel function in a firm is to deal with the people who work – or who would like to work – in that firm. Larger organizations will have a specialist Personnel Department, which will be involved in 'hiring and firing': recruiting, selecting and training of staff, considering their welfare, keeping their records and handling their voluntary leaving, retirement or dismissal.

## 13.2 Work of the Personnel Department

The range of work done by a Personnel Department is shown in fig. 13.1. As this diagram shows, Personnel may calculate and organize the payment of employees' wages and salaries (Unit 14), and it will certainly include industrial relations work (Unit 15).

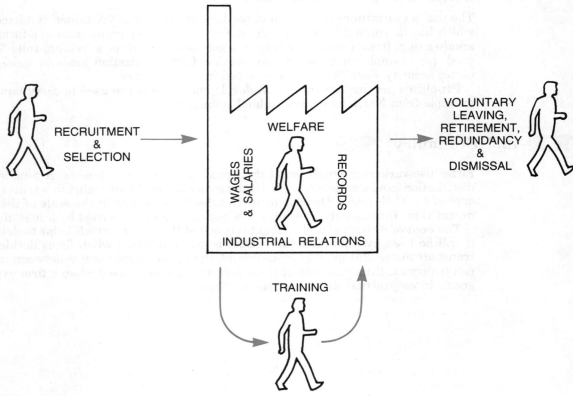

RECRUITMENT & SELECTION

WAGES & SALARIES

WELFARE

RECORDS

INDUSTRIAL RELATIONS

TRAINING

VOLUNTARY LEAVING, RETIREMENT, REDUNDANCY & DISMISSAL

**Fig. 13.1** The work of a personnel department

As the firm expands or as its employees retire or leave for other jobs, new staff will have to be recruited. The role of Personnel in **recruitment** is to inform potential employees that there are vacancies available, for example through newspaper advertisements.

Following the advertising of the vacancies, Personnel Department staff – working with the departments which have the job vacancies – have the task of selection, deciding who is the best applicant for each job.

All employees can benefit from **training**. New staff will be given a special, induction, training: the Personnel Department must also provide training opportunities for existing members of staff, to improve their present levels of knowledge and skills and to learn new skills.

Personnel work is also concerned with **staff welfare**. High levels of motivation (Unit 14) lead to a happy and contented workforce, which in turn should lead to high-quality output being produced. All firms must meet minimum health, safety and other standards (Unit 18); and the Personnel Department staff may be asked to help those employees who are experiencing personal problems.

Details of employees will be kept by Personnel, as **staff records**. These details will typically include personal data such as the home address and marital status of the employee, together with details of wage or salary rates, training courses attended and promotions received.

Since Personnel deals with employee records, it will also – in many organizations – be responsible for calculating and distributing the **wages and salaries** and for negotiating and developing the pay structure in the firm.

One of the key roles of Personnel staff lies in the field of **industrial relations**. Disputes between the organized groups of management and workforce – and between individual employees – can occur in all firms. The Personnel Department has a vital role to play in helping to resolve these disputes.

## 13.3 Recruitment

Recruitment involves Personnel Department staff in **assessing the nature of the post** to be filled and in **advertising the post**. All firms must recruit new staff from time to time, for the following reasons:

1 To replace staff who have left for another job, or staff who have retired, been dismissed, or promoted to new posts within the firm.
2 To bring in staff with new skills required (e.g. where computer specialists are employed following the computerization of accounts or wages).
3 To employ additional staff when business is expanding.

The main stages in recruitment involve drawing up a job description and job specification, preparing the advertisement and advertising the post.

### JOB DESCRIPTION AND JOB SPECIFICATION

The specialist department – such as Accounts, Purchasing or Sales – which has a vacancy will consider both the **type of work** that the post involves and the **type of employee** who would be best suited to do the work. It is the role of a job description to give details of the work, and the role of a job specification to outline the qualities and skills of the person that would be an ideal employee.

The **job description** will state the job title and its location and will explain in detail the duties of the post, together with any special features of the job, or special equipment that is needed to carry it out. The job description details will form the basis of the advertisement drawn up for the post (fig. 13.2).

The **job specification** outlines the personal qualities that the firm is looking for in the new member of staff. It will therefore contain details of expected qualifications and work experience, what physical and/or mental abilities the employees must possess and what sort of judgment or initiative he or she will need to use in the job. Like the job description, some of the details given in the specification will be included in the job advertisement.

### JOB ADVERTISEMENTS

Fig. 13.2 (overleaf) shows typical job advertisements. They contain details of both the job and the person required to fill the job. The information taken from the job description will be the job title and location, the pay and the conditions of work: the age, qualifications and experience required by applicants come from the job specification. Further details are normally given, such as to how to get an application form, or how otherwise to apply for the post.

Job advertisements are **informative** rather than persuasive (Unit 11) and are subject to laws which ensure that they do not discriminate in a racial or sexist manner: these legal controls are covered in Unit 18.

A firm may decide to advertise the post **internally**. Advertisements would be displayed on noticeboards and could be published in the firm's magazine. The post would be filled from the present staff, which can be quicker and less expensive than looking outside for new staff: it can also improve morale, because the staff realize that promotion is possible. With internal appointments, however, no 'new blood' is introduced, which could lead to fewer new ideas being present.

Where the post is to be advertised **externally**, Personnel staff must decide on the location of the advert. Possible places for advertising include the following:

1 **Jobcentres.** Run by the Department of Employment, they are located throughout the country, advertising those local vacancies supplied to them by companies (see fig. 13.3).
2 **Employment agencies.** A good example is the Professional and Executive Recruitment Agency (PER), which specializes in professional, managerial, scientific and technical recruitment. A firm may send details of a job vacancy to this, or another local or national agency, such as Brook Street Bureau or Pertemps: these agencies then check their records and provide potential employees for interview, and are paid a fee by the employer if the person is appointed.

**Fig. 13.2** Job advertisements

**3 Newspapers and magazines.** Many professional and managerial vacancies are advertised in the 'quality' newspapers, or in specialist magazines or journals, e.g. *The Administrator*, which are sent to members of professional bodies. Local papers are also used, for managerial, clerical and manual vacancies.

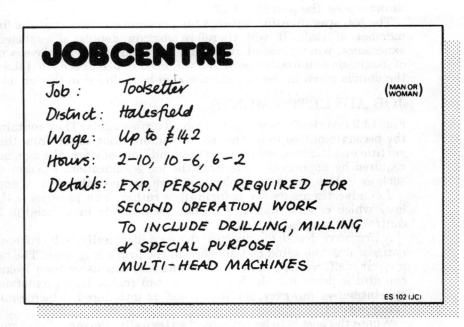

**Fig. 13.3** Jobcentre advertisement

### Application forms

Interested applicants will normally have to complete a **job application form**. This form requires applicants to give various personal details about education and experience. It also asks for **references** to support the application. The persons providing the references – the referees – will be asked to give their opinions on the applicant's suitability for the post.

As an alternative to sending out a standard application form, the Personnel Department might ask applicants to submit a **curriculum vitae:** this 'CV' will contain basically the same information as that requested by a typical application form.

## 13.4 Selection

Following the advertising of the vacancy, the Personnel Department will receive the applications for the post. A decision must then be made as to which of the applicants are to be put on the **short list**. The short list is drawn up by eliminating those applicants who do not meet the job specification; they may be regarded as being too inexperienced, too old, overqualified, etc. The requirements of the Race Relations and Sex Discrimination Acts (Unit 18) must be observed so that applicants are not discriminated against on the basis of sex or race.

### THE INTERVIEW

The interview gives the firm's interviewers the opportunity to find out more about the shortlisted candidates: it also gives the candidates the chance to discover more about the vacancy and the firm in general. It therefore has a dual purpose.

*The interviewer can assess:*

1 The interviewee's **verbal communication skills** and **social skills**.
2 The interviewee's **physical appearance** (often thought to be particularly important for posts in selling, or working as a receptionist).
3 The interviewee's **confidence** in handling questions and stressful situations.
4 The **accuracy** and completeness of information on the application form.
5 The likely **compatability** of the interviewee with his or her future colleagues.

*The interviewee can assess:*

1 Likely **promotion** prospects.
2 **Working conditions.**
3 The possibility of further **training**.
4 The apparent friendliness or otherwise of **existing staff**.
5 The general **facilities** available.

### Selection tests

Some firms may run a series of tests to help them decide which of the shortlisted applicants is most suitable for the post. These tests may be designed to assess a candidate's intelligence, personality or aptitude (suitability) for the post.

**Intelligence tests** are designed to check an applicant's general mental and reasoning abilities and may involve testing verbal and numerical reasoning.

**Personality tests** set out to discover an applicant's personality, attitudes and beliefs, in an attempt to find out whether he or she fits in with the general style, philosophy and 'ethos' of the company.

**Aptitude tests** are set where the employer wants to see the applicant actually carrying out similar tasks to those involved in doing the job. For example, an applicant for a secretary's post may be required to take down shorthand, or type a memo, at some stage during the selection process.

## 13.5 Appointment

Once the applicant has been selected by the interview panel and has accepted the position offered, a **contract of employment** is drawn up. This contains the following information:

1 Names and addresses of both parties.
2 Job title.
3 The date that employment begins.
4 Scale or rate of pay and pay intervals.
5 Hours of work.
6 Holidays and holiday pay.
7 Sickness or injury; how to notify and rates of pay.
8 Pension schemes.
9 Length of notice required.
10 Disciplinary rules of the firm.
11 Grievance procedures used.

### Terminating the appointment

Employees may be made **redundant**. Redundancy occurs when their jobs are no longer required by the firm, for example due to a change in work practices or production methods, or changes in demand for the firm's goods or services. Employees may be eligible for redundancy pay, the amount of pay being based on factors such as the length of their service with the firm, their age and their rate of pay. The Government provides a redundancy fund and many firms have their own redundancy agreements (which would provide better redundancy pay than the minimum required under law).

Employees can be **dismissed** where there is good cause to do so. Typical situations where employees could be dismissed include where they have stolen the firm's goods; where they cannot do the job; where their continued employment would be illegal (e.g. where a lorry driver has been banned from driving due to a drink-driving offence); and where their conduct at work deserves dismissal (such as continued drunkenness, or violent behaviour). An employee is often given verbal warnings, which are then followed by written warnings, before being dismissed. All employees have protection against **unfair dismissal** (Unit 18).

## 13.6 Training

The Personnel Department will have the task of making sure that new employees start working efficiently as soon as possible. This means that an **induction** training programme needs to be established and operated by Personnel.

As employees become settled into their jobs, they may find that the nature of their jobs is changing, or that they have to develop additional skills to stand a chance of getting promoted. In these situations, further training will be provided, or organized, by the Personnel Department. This training may be **internal** – run within the firm itself – or **external** (taking place outside the firm).

### Induction training

The purpose of induction training is to get the new employees to feel 'at home' as quickly as possible, so that they can start making a contribution to the work of the company. It also provides new employees with a feeling of 'being wanted' and so improves levels of morale.

A typical induction programme will include the following:

1 A talk on the firm's history and products.
2 A tour of the firm.
3 Introductions to, and brief talks by, departmental heads or their deputies.
4 Introduction to colleagues.
5 Discussion about any immediate training needs.

### Internal training

Also known as 'on-the-job' training, this is the most common form of training provided by firms. The employees learn as they work, the 'teacher' being the person currently doing the job, or possibly an instructor employed by Personnel. Short courses may also be organized by Personnel and run on the premises, as 'off-the-job' support.

Internal training is very popular. Because it runs in the employee's normal working environment, it is **fully related to the firm's needs** and it is **quick and inexpensive to organize**. It does have the disadvantage, however, that the training is only as good as the trainers, who may not do their own work efficiently, or who may possess poor demonstration or communication skills. Bad working practices may therefore be taught.

**Fig. 13.4** Off-the-job training on a computer lathe

**External training**

External, 'off-the-job', training may involve employees attending local colleges and studying for various qualifications, to improve their manual, clerical, supervisory or managerial skills. Since specialists are involved in the training, it should be of a **high quality**. It will also introduce **more new ideas and techniques**, 'from outside', into the firm; and it is likely to be **regarded more highly by the trainees**, e.g. through their studying for a nationally recognized qualification. It may, however, be more expensive (although firms do not have to take their own staff from production to act as trainers) and will not normally be devoted exclusively to the needs of any one firm.

*Government training schemes*

Much external training is nowadays organized through the Department of Employment. The **Youth Training Scheme** (YTS) is an important national training scheme. It is a two-year training programme involving 16-year-old school leavers being placed in organizations and receiving on-the-job training there. They also receive off-the-job training, leading to nationally recognized qualifications, often taken at a local college. Many employers now use the YTS as a basis for selecting and employing some of their future staff, although they are not obliged to take on any trainees once these trainees have finished the Scheme.

The Adult Training Programme's **Employment Training** (ET) scheme is another national Government training scheme. It provides training for the long-term unemployed, and started by offering 300 000 off-the-job training places, at an initial cost of over £1 billion.

## 13.7 Summary

The personnel function is important in all businesses, because it is directly involved with the **people** working in those businesses. If all employees are highly motivated and happy, a firm's output and efficiency should both be high: but a discontented workforce can lead to disruptions in production and possibly even closure of the firm.

One way that the Personnel Department can help a firm to achieve a satisfied workforce is to ensure that suitable people are recruited, selected and trained. In order to do this, recruitment procedures must be used which are suitable for the job in question: the most appropriate form of advertising, for example, should be used. Selection procedures – which may involve some testing of the shortlisted applicants – must also be efficiently carried out.

Once the new employees are in post, they will want to settle down as quickly as possible: efficient induction will help this to take place. As time progresses, and procedures and processes change, further training may be required to ensure that employees are using the most modern methods: here again, the Personnel Department will make a valuable contribution.

# 14 WORK AND ITS REWARDS

## 14.1 Introduction

There are many different occupations in the United Kingdom. These occupations can be classified according to the sector of the economy into which they fall. Farmers, miners and fishermen will work in the primary sector; manufacturing and construction jobs are found in the secondary sector; and the tertiary sector's occupants include accountants, greengrocers, catering staff and long-distance lorry drivers.

Regardless of the sector in which they are employed, each person has to go through a recruitment process (Unit 13) before starting work. When appointed to a post, the new employee will hope to achieve some form of **job satisfaction** from that post.

## 14.2 Human Needs and Work

People seek employment for a number of reasons. Pay is an important 'motivator' for most employees: but people also appear to want to work for a number of other reasons, in the hope of getting job satisfaction. Motivation is important in business, since it identifies how contented or satisfied a firm's employees are. Workers who are highly motivated tend to work efficiently: if they have a low level of motivation, output will suffer and industrial disputes (Unit 15) can result.

### MOTIVATION THEORIES

#### Maslow

There have been many theories put forward in an attempt to explain why people want to work. An American psychologist, Abraham Maslow, identified a range of **human needs** which, he argued, people tried to satisfy. As one type of need became satisfied, another type of need would then present itself: these needs are in a 'hierarchy', i.e. an order of importance, as shown in fig. 14.1.

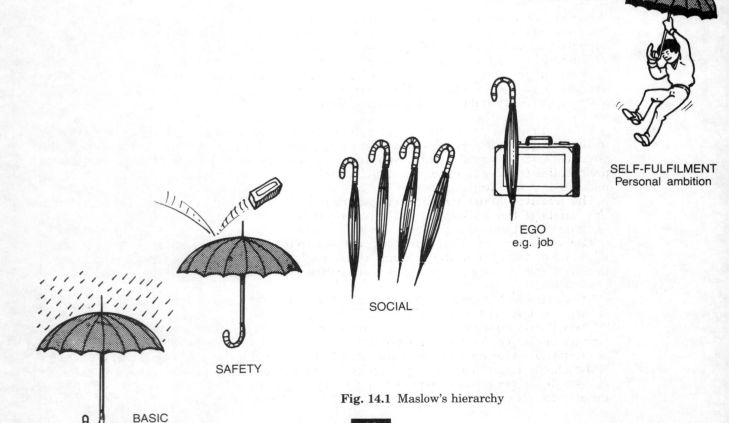

SELF-FULFILMENT
Personal ambition

EGO
e.g. job

SOCIAL

SAFETY

BASIC
e.g. shelter

**Fig. 14.1** Maslow's hierarchy

This shows us that Maslow believed that five groups of needs exist. The first, **basic** needs are to do with survival and include the need for clothing, warmth and shelter. In a business environment, people will want these basic needs to be met. Once the basic needs are satisfied, people's **safety** needs have to be met. A person will need to be safe from physical harm, whether at home or at work; a safe (i.e. secure) job is also a factor here. An individual's **social** needs are unimportant when basic and safety needs are not being met. Once these are met, however, people will want the companionship and friendship that comes from being part of a group, such as a group of workmates.

Once these three types of needs are being satisfied, the need to achieve something personal then arises. The final needs in the hierarchy are often called 'higher needs', since they arise when the 'lower needs' – basic, safety and social needs – are being achieved.

People may have **ego** needs to satisfy. These needs arise from a desire for self-esteem, linked to having a job and to making some sort of contribution to the community. The highest needs are the **self-fulfilment** ones. These involve some form of personal ambition: in the work context, this could refer to finding great job satisfaction through doing work that includes a lot of responsibility or which is highly creative and where there is a wide recognition of its quality and importance.

Maslow's theory highlights the importance of work to individuals and offers some explanation why unemployment is such a major problem for all societies where employment is regarded as 'the norm'. According to him – and to many other theorists – employers should recognize that there are a range of needs that work must meet and they should therefore provide their employees with jobs that are satisfying, in order for output to be at its most efficient.

### Herzberg

Another American psychologist, Frederick Herzberg, identified what he called **hygiene factors** in work. These hygiene factors are the basic, essential factors such as acceptable working conditions (safety, cleanliness, adequate rest breaks, control of noise, etc) which form the foundation for having happy and well motivated employees. If they are ignored or neglected, these factors will cause morale and motivation to fall, leading to lower output and a discontented workforce. They need to be present but they do not, by themselves, motivate the employees.

The 'motivators' for employees, according to Herzberg, include **recognition** (having your efforts at work recognized), **achievement** (the feeling of 'a job well done'), possible or actual **advancement** or promotion, and being given more **responsibility**. These are therefore the factors that employers need to take into account when they consider how best to motivate their employees.

## 14.3 Job Satisfaction

Different people have different ideas as to what makes a job 'satisfying'. The general ideas of theorists such as Maslow and Herzberg give some clues to the factors which lead to people enjoying their work. Major influences on job satisfaction include the following:

**The pay level** for a job is clearly important to most people. High levels of pay allow workers to obtain more material possessions: a high wage can also compensate for uncomfortable or dangerous working conditions. Many employees are, however, willing to accept pay levels lower than they could earn elsewhere, since pay is only one of several factors in job satisfaction.

**Fringe benefits,** or 'perks', can also influence the level of job satisfaction. Popular perks include company cars, luncheon vouchers and subsidized travel or holidays. Employees are often entitled to buy the company's goods at discount or to benefit from its services at preferential rates. For example, staff in banks and building societies are able to obtain mortgages at favourable rates.

**The working hours** may be unattractive and 'antisocial', with shift-work being involved. The length of the working day, the number of holidays and the convenience of 'flexitime' working can all influence the level of job satisfaction.

**The environment** also influences job satisfaction. This includes the levels of noise, vibration or dust; the availability and appearance of canteen, changing, cleaning and other facilities; and the degree and quality of heating and ventilation (e.g. the existence of air-conditioning).

Other factors influencing job satisfaction include the degree of **job security** and the existence of **friendly colleagues**.

These factors do not operate in isolation but combine to give an overall level of satisfaction for a particular job. A person may decide to take a career in one of the 'caring' professions such as nursing or social work – which tend not to be highly paid in the UK – because of the content of the job, the status given to it by the public and the level of responsibility involved. However, pay is still a major consideration and many people regard pay levels as the most important of these factors.

## 14.4 Wages and Salaries

A firm's employees will normally earn either **wages** or **salaries** as a reward for their labour. Fig. 14.2 explains the typical difference between a 'waged' employee and a 'salaried' employee.

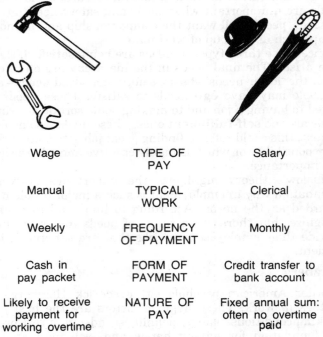

| Wage | TYPE OF PAY | Salary |
| --- | --- | --- |
| Manual | TYPICAL WORK | Clerical |
| Weekly | FREQUENCY OF PAYMENT | Monthly |
| Cash in pay packet | FORM OF PAYMENT | Credit transfer to bank account |
| Likely to receive payment for working overtime | NATURE OF PAY | Fixed annual sum: often no overtime paid |

**Fig. 14.2** Wages and salaries

Different groups of workers in the same firm – and different occupations in general – will have different pay levels. Accountants, lawyers and other well qualified professionals will normally receive high salaries: workers in occupations where lower qualifications are needed to do the job, tend to receive lower wages and salaries. These **wage differentials** arise because jobs differ, in the following ways:

1 The level of qualifications (e.g. accountants) or amount of training (doctors) required.
2 The degree of danger or discomfort involved (offshore oil-rig workers).
3 The amount of natural ability required (world-class professional sportsmen and women).
4 The level of fringe benefits (e.g. a company car) available.
5 The location of the work (higher pay in south-east England).
6 Union influences (many non-unionized occupations receiving low rates of pay).

## 14.5 Payments Systems

There are a number of ways that the employee's wage can be calculated.

### Flat rate

The payment of salaries usually involves a **fixed rate** (one-twelfth of the employee's annual salary) being transferred at the end of each month into a bank account. Many wages are also paid at a weekly set rate, the amount of pay not depending on the employee's output. The advantage to the firm is that the individual's pay – and therefore the total wage bill – is easily calculated; the disadvantage is that there is no financial incentive for employees to work longer or harder, so that more can be produced.

### Time rate

Employees are paid a **set amount per hour**, for each hour worked. All employees doing similar jobs receive the same hourly rate; after a number of hours have been worked during the week, a higher, **overtime rate** is used to pay employees for the extra hours worked. An example of how an employee's wage would be calculated using a time rate system is given in fig. 14.3.

The advantage of a time rate system to the company is that extra work (overtime) is encouraged through extra pay, when output needs to be increased; the drawbacks are that the total wages bill is less easy to calculate and there must be a 'clocking-on and off' timekeeping system which can cause administrative problems.

### Piece rate

Employees producing items are **paid an agreed amount for each item made**: the items produced must be of an acceptable quality for payment to be received. Employees may receive

```
NAME  Lee.A      STANDARD RATE £ 8:00.

WORKS NO. YL 48.   STANDARD HOURS  38

                   OVERTIME RATE £ 12:00


HOURS WORKED

Monday         8

Tuesday        8:5

Wednesday      8:5

Thursday       7:5

Friday         7:5

Saturday

TOTAL HOURS    40·00


38.  at standard rate £ 8:00.  Total £ 304:00

2.  at overtime rate £ 12:00  Total £  24:00

                   GROSS PAY £ 328:00
```

**Fig. 14.3** Time rate calculation

part of their wages as flat rate, with the rest of their wages on a piece rate basis. A popular variation on this is where sales staff receive **commission** for each sale that they make.

A firm can gain from using a piece rate system because employees are encouraged to work hard, since higher output means higher pay. It can also be regarded as a fairer system of payment than flat rate and time rate systems, because efficient and hard-working employees receive higher pay than inefficient or lazy ones. The disadvantages are that the quality of the output may suffer, with employees rushing their work; more quality control supervision is needed; and fixing the amount of piece rate payment can be difficult and can lead to disputes.

### Bonuses

The firm may award bonuses to employees at particular times of the year. This is often done at Christmas and/or just before the annual summer holiday period. There may be a **merit bonus** scheme, which involves staff in a grading exercise. Staff who have exceeded production or (in the case of salespersons) sales targets, or those office staff regarded as being most efficient and hard-working during the year, will receive a bonus or a higher-than-average pay increase.

Bonuses can be used by a firm to encourage loyalty amongst staff, as well as to improve production and sales by setting targets for which there is a financial reward. A bonus system can cause disputes, however, between those individuals or groups that receive them and those that do not; also, the level of bonus to award to an individual can be difficult to calculate.

### Profit-sharing schemes

Some firms may have an agreement with the workforce to **share out part of their profits** between the employees as a form of bonus. Shares in the firm may also be distributed, according to the size of profits, to employees. These schemes have the advantage of making the

| INDUSTRY | PERCENTAGE OF COMPANIES WITH: | |
| --- | --- | --- |
| | *An employee scheme* | *No scheme* |
| Manufacturing | 32 | 68 |
| Retail distribution | 21 | 79 |
| Finance | 56 | 44 |
| Services | 43 | 57 |
| Other (mainly construction) | 25 | 75 |
| ALL COMPANIES | 30 | 70 |

**Fig. 14.4** Companies with profit-sharing and employee share ownership schemes, 1985 Source: *Department of Employment, 'Social Trends' No 18, 1988*

employees feel a part of the firm, because they are sharing directly in the profits which they have played a part in creating.

Fig. 14.4 illustrates the current popularity of these schemes: it is based on a Department of Employment survey of over one thousand large companies. Nearly three quarters of the larger public companies surveyed had a scheme of some sort, although fewer than 20 per cent of private companies operated such a scheme.

## 14.6 Fringe Benefits

Some employees may receive fringe benefits in addition to their pay. There are many examples of these 'perks'; they can be used to encourage people to work in low-paid jobs, and they have also been created either to get round government pay restraints or as a means of avoiding paying income tax. Examples of 'perks' are shown below.

### Free or subsidized meals

Many companies run canteens which offer meals to employees at low prices; other firms may give luncheon vouchers which employees can use to obtain food during their lunch or other breaks.

### Sports and social clubs

Larger companies often provide a range of sporting and other facilities for the benefit of employees and their families.

### Company cars

These are often supplied to managers and certain other staff (e.g. the sales force). Although staff now have to declare the use of a company car, which affects their income tax liability, this is still one of the most important perks offered by firms.

### Subsidized travel

Certain firms, particularly public transport organizations such as British Rail, offer their staff free or subsidized travel. Other perks of this type include travel agents allowing staff subsidized travel or holidays abroad and local authorities which give a petrol allowance to employees who have to use their own cars in the course of their work.

### Discounts on purchases

Many manufacturing firms allow staff to buy their finished goods – cars, tyres, clothes, etc – at below market price. Retailers may also allow their employees to buy certain goods (e.g. surplus food which has reached the 'sell-by' date) at a substantial discount.

### Savings on loans, mortgages, pensions and life assurance

Some local authorities allow certain employees to take out low-interest loans so that they can buy cars; other organizations such as commercial banks may offer low-interest loans or mortgages to their staff. A firm could offer its employees a free private pension scheme. Free life assurance is another fringe benefit available to some staff.

### Private health and education

Membership of BUPA or a similar private health scheme can be a perk in some jobs. If a job involves a lot of overseas work and travel, a firm may offer to pay the fees for the employee's children to attend a private school.

### Removal costs

Many firms which require staff to move round the country will assist them by paying their removal costs and the legal fees involved in buying and selling houses.

## 14.7 Gross Pay and Net Pay

Fig. 14.3 on page 101 shows how a person's pay is calculated on a time rate basis. The total wage of £328.00 is that employee's **gross pay** – but this will not be the amount that is actually taken home. There are a series of **deductions** – some voluntary, some compulsory – before the employee receives his or her **net pay**.

Members of staff will each receive a **payslip**, which notifies them of their gross pay, the various deductions made and their net pay. Fig. 14.5 is an example of the typical items shown on a payslip.

| CODE NO. | PAY NO. | NAME | N. I. NO. | Month | PAY ADVICE |
|---|---|---|---|---|---|
| 274L | 0113611 | V. HODGSON | YL324892A | DEC. | |

| CUMULATIVE INFORMATION | | PAY | | DEDUCTIONS | |
|---|---|---|---|---|---|
| PAY TO DATE | SUP'N to DATE | BASIC | 925.00 | INCOME TAX | 174.50 |
| 8471.25 | 540.75 | OVERTIME | 14.00 | NAT. INS. | 61.50 |
| TAX TO DATE | N. I. TO DATE | OTHER | | SUPERAN. | 58.00 |
| 1566.50 | 576.60 | | | OTHER | 2.00 |

| | | | | |
|---|---|---|---|---|
| GROSS PAY | 939.00 | | | |
| TOTAL DEDUCTIONS | 296.00 | | | |
| NET PAY | 643.00 | TOTAL | 939.00 | TOTAL | 296.00 |

**Fig. 14.5** A payslip

## INFORMATION ON THE PAYSLIP

The pay advice will be dated: in this example, the month is shown. The employee's name, pay number and National Insurance number are also typically shown. All people who pay National Insurance contributions (see below) are given an identification number, against which their payment of contributions is recorded.

### Tax code number

The most common method of collecting income tax is the **Pay As You Earn** (PAYE) method. All people in employment are allowed to earn a certain amount every year before they have to start paying income tax (on the rest of their income). The amount that they can earn free of tax varies according to their circumstances; for example, allowances can be received for children or dependent relatives.

As an illustration, if a person is allowed to earn £4800 a year without paying tax and she earns £6800 in that year, she only has to pay tax on the amount earned over £4800 (i.e. she pays tax on £2000). In the PAYE system, her **tax-free allowance** of £4800 is spread over the tax year. If she is paid monthly, she can earn £400 each month – £4800 divided by 12 – before paying tax. Her **code number** would be 480, which is found by taking the last digit off the tax-free amount (£4800). In the payslip example above, the code number is 274 and so the total tax-free pay in the year would be £2740.

A letter follows the tax code number: in this case, it is 'L', which signifies that the employee receives the Lower, single person's, allowance.

The PAYE system operates throughout the tax year. This means that 'Cumulative Information' on the total 'Pay To Date', together with the other totals of 'Superannuation To Date', 'Tax to Date' and 'National Insurance To Date' are kept to make sure that total deductions are correct.

### Deductions from pay

Deductions may be compulsory – being enforced by law – or voluntary. The main compulsory deduction is **Income Tax**, collected in this example under the PAYE scheme. The other compulsory deduction is **National Insurance**: payments made by the employee (the employer also making a contribution) which go towards the cost of the State retirement pension and the National Health Service. The amount paid depends on the size of the employee's income.

**Superannuation** payments may be made towards a pension scheme: many employees nowadays 'contract out' of company schemes and enter private pension schemes, deductions again being made from their pay. Other voluntary deductions may be made for items such as **Trade Union Subscriptions** and **Save As You Earn** (SAYE) schemes.

### Gross and net pay

The employee's gross pay is calculated by adding together the amounts received as basic and overtime pay, together with any other payments such as the payment of travelling expenses, to which the employee is entitled.

The 'Gross Pay' box displays the employee's gross pay for the month: 'Total Deductions' are then subtracted and the net pay is transferred to the employee's bank account.

## 14.8 Summary

There are many factors which can influence people's choice of career. Most people want jobs that are interesting or challenging in some way and they may place little emphasis on the level of pay for such work. To them, the amount that they earn has little to do with 'job satisfaction'.

Different jobs receive greatly differing scales of pay for a variety of reasons, such as the different levels of qualifications or natural aptitude required to do them. The methods of payment used for these jobs can also vary: employees may be paid a fixed sum weekly or monthly, or their earnings may vary according to how long they are at work, how many items they make or sell, or how profitable the company has been over the past year. The calculation of wages and salaries is often under the control of a Wages Section in the Personnel Department; some firms may run an entirely separate Wages Department. All employees will be notified of their gross pay, deductions from pay and net pay through some form of pay advice issued by the wages staff.

# 15 INDUSTRIAL RELATIONS

## 15.1 Introduction

The relationship between the employer and the employee is sometimes described as that of 'master and servant'. An employer is normally in a much more powerful position than an employee, even though workers are protected by a range of laws (Unit 18). Although the employer probably has financial and other resources which are not available to individual workers, these employees can act together as a single unit – as a **union** – to protect themselves and to improve aspects of their work, such as their pay or working conditions.

Trade unions have received a great deal of 'bad press' in the 1980s: this bad publicity may sometimes be justified, but is often quite inaccurate and ignores the valuable work that unions have done, and continue to do, for their members. Employers, too, can link together effectively in organizations such as the Confederation of British Industry (the CBI) and gain similar benefits from membership.

## 15.2 Trade Unions

The trend in the 1980s has been for trade union membership to fall, both in total and as a percentage of the total working population. This trend is seen in fig. 15.1, which shows that the number of people belonging to a trade union fell by about 20 per cent between the end of 1979 and the end of 1985.

| Year | Number of Unions | Membership (millions) | Percentage of Working Population |
|------|------------------|------------------------|-----------------------------------|
| 1979 | 454 | 13.3 | 51.1 |
| 1982 | 408 | 11.6 | 44.8 |
| 1985 | 373 | 10.7 | 38.4 |

**Fig. 15.1** Trade unions: numbers and membership
Source: *'Social Trends' No 18, 1988*

Historically, the modern trade union developed as a result of the Industrial Revolution in the last century. There are different types of trade union, although they will have common aims. Many of these unions are relatively small, with over a half of the 1985 total having fewer than 1000 members each. In 1985, nearly 60 per cent of all union members belonged to the 10 largest unions, such as the Transport and General Workers' Union (approximately 1¼ million members in 1988) and MSF (Manufacturing, Science and Finance: a 'white collar' union, having approximately 650 000 members in 1988).

### TYPES OF TRADE UNIONS

The 'blue-collar' unions are normally separated into three types: craft unions, industrial unions and general unions. A fourth group also exists, separated from these three by the status of the occupations that it contains: these are the 'white-collar' unions.

#### Craft unions

These were the first unions established, being set up to control the number of new entrants to the craft they represented. They consist of a group of skilled workers, or a group of skilled occupations. Some of these unions are quite small and one company may have a number of them representing its workers. This can make it difficult for management in negotiations, and sometimes demarcation ('who does what') disputes arise between the unions.

Examples of craft unions include the National Graphical Association, the National Union of Journalists and the AUEW (Amalgamated Union of Engineering Workers).

#### Industrial unions

An industrial union includes most of the workers in that industry. Negotiations tend to be more straightforward for managers, since they are often dealing with only one union.

The majority of miners are in the National Union of Mineworkers. USDAW – the Union of Shop, Distributive and Allied Workers – is the major industrial union for the retail trade. Another example is COHSE, the Confederation of Health Service Employees, which is an important industrial union in the National Health Service.

### General unions

These tend to be very large unions, which contain high proportions of semi-skilled and unskilled workers. Their members are drawn from a number of different industries. The large size of the union and the wide range of interests it can represent, can cause the union some difficulties.

Examples of general unions include GMBATU (the General Municipal and Boilermakers' Union) and the TGWU, the Transport and General Workers Union.

### White-collar unions

These unions contain non-manual, clerical and professional workers. Although total union membership has declined in the 1980s, white-collar unions have grown in size and in importance.

Examples of white-collar unions are MSF, which represents workers in scientific and financial occupations, and the National Union of Teachers.

These groupings are not always precise and are affected by changing circumstances. One development in this field is the **company union**: popular in Japan, this is where a company has its own union. Another development is the **single-union agreement**: often linked to a no-strike agreement, this is found where a company sets up a new factory and agrees with one union that this union shall represent all the workers at that factory.

## 15.3 Aims of Trade Unions

All trade unions will involve themselves in activities which benefit their members. In carrying out their aims and activities, they are subject to legal controls (Unit 18). Their main aims can be summarized as follows:

1 To **negotiate with employers**. This bargaining will be about pay and allowances, hours to be worked, working conditions and pension and retirement arrangements. Unions will also negotiate with employers concerning job satisfaction and job security, e.g. where there is a threat of redundancy for their members.
2 To **protect their members**, against unfair dismissal or disciplinary action and against possible lay-offs or redundancy (through negotiation, as in 1 above). Part-time workers can be protected; a union may also have to fight for equal pay and treatment for women and protect some members against racial discrimination.
3 To **give their members the rights to which they are entitled**, such as sick pay, maternity leave and pay and appropriate safety standards.
4 To **advise and represent their members**: they may provide personal advice and legal advice on problems at work. Members having accidents, or facing difficulties, at work can be represented by union officials; and unions provide representation at industrial tribunals.
5 To **influence others** – notably individual employers, employers' organizations and the Government – to benefit their members and workers in general.

### BENEFITS OF UNION MEMBERSHIP

Workers who join a trade union will pay a weekly, monthly or annual subscription. For this, they receive a number of benefits from their union membership, which are summarized in fig. 15.2.

Training and
education programmes

Financial and
insurance services

Legal and
technical advice

Improved
pay

Protection
against
exploitation

Sports and
social facilities

Better working
conditions

Representation with employers
and other organizations

**Fig. 15.2** Benefits of trade union membership

## 15.4 Trade Union Organization

### Head office and areas

The structure of the larger unions is often based on a series of district or area offices, which are staffed by full-time union officials, such as an **area organizer**.

The head offices of these unions – normally situated in London – are where **specialist staff** are based, such as experts in labour law: they provide specialist advice to branches and individuals. The union **president** and **general secretary** (who is usually the spokesperson for the union) work at the head office.

### Workplace organization

The most important union official found in many workplaces is the **shop steward**. The steward works part-time for the union and is typically elected from among the workers that he or she represents. The leading shop steward in a factory is called a **convener**: the convener and stewards act as the link between the union members at the company and the area and national officials. The following are typical functions of a shop steward:

1 Collecting subscriptions from current members and distributing union information to them.
2 Recruiting new members.
3 Negotiating agreements and checking that these management-union agreements are being carried out.
4 Taking part in Safety Committees and similar management-worker committees.
5 Representing individual members, or groups of members, who believe they have grievances.

## THE TRADES UNION CONGRESS (TUC)

Although each union is independent from the others and will have its own set of rules and regulations, it will also have aims which are similar to those of the other unions. It can be in their joint interests to get together and agree common policies and approaches.

**The TUC** is the central body where unions get together to discuss matters and most trade unions are affiliated to it. It is the 'voice' of the unions: the TUC will promote the general aims of its member unions and will seek to influence the Government, as well as to negotiate with employers. Like its member unions, the TUC has its own full-time organization and the TUC **General Secretary** is seen as the figurehead of the union movement.

## 15.5 Employers' Organizations

Unions were formed originally so that groups of workers could compete more equally with powerful employers. Some small firms regard large unions as being too powerful and so they, too, group together to match union power and to protect their individual and joint interests. There are various **employers' associations** found, which act as the employers' equivalent of trade unions.

## THE CONFEDERATION OF BRITISH INDUSTRY (CBI)

**The CBI** is the major employers' association in Britain and fulfils the same role for employers as the TUC does for unions. It represents all levels and types of industry, in both the private and public sectors. The CBI will negotiate with the TUC on many issues on which there may be disagreement. It will also attempt to persuade the Government to carry out policies that are in the interests of its member employers.

Like the TUC, the CBI is an influential pressure group on business matters. It also has a permanent full-time organization and its **Director General** acts as its figurehead.

### Other employers' associations

The CBI, since it represents approximately a quarter of a million firms, tends to promote general business policies. Various **trade associations** and other employers' associations (usually members of the CBI) exist to meet the needs of the smaller companies in their specialist fields. Examples of these are the Road Haulage Association, the National Farmers Union and the Society of Motor Manufacturers and Traders.

Local **Chambers of Commerce** help local business, for example by providing advice, assistance and overseas contacts for exporting firms. They act as an important link between the individual firms and local and central governments.

## 15.6 Collective Bargaining

Most union members would regard their union's main role as improving their pay and working conditions. **Collective bargaining** is the normal way in which pay and conditions are agreed. Union officials, representing various groups of workers, will attempt to **negotiate** a pay deal or a settlement on new working conditions. These negotiations take place at different levels, either on an individual employer basis, or nationally with a group of employers. There may be national agreements which lay down minimum wage levels, holidays, etc: in some industries, these national agreements may then be improved by various local agreements.

## 15.7 Industrial Disputes

Analysis by the Department of Employment (published in 'Social Trends 18', 1988) showed that just under 2 million working days were lost in the UK during 1986 due to work stoppages. This was a relatively low total, the yearly average for the period 1976–85 being approximately 11 million working days. Fig. 15.3 shows the main causes of these stoppages in both 1986 and 1987.

| Cause of Stoppage | Percentage of Working Days Lost 1987 | 1986 |
|---|---|---|
| Pay disputes | 82 | 59 |
| Disputes over manning and work allocation | 5 | 13 |
| Disputes over redundancy | 5 | 15 |

**Fig. 15.3** Main causes of work stoppages in the UK, 1986 and 1987
Source: *Department of Employment, 'Employment Gazette', July 1988*

Collective bargaining therefore does not always succeed. The union may insist on demanding a higher pay rise than the management side will accept and if the parties cannot agree an industrial dispute will occur. Methods used by unions in times of industrial action include the use of overtime bans, work-to-rule and go-slows, sit-ins, 'blackings' and strikes.

With **overtime bans**, the union will instruct its members not to work overtime: this can lead to falling levels of production and will put pressure on the employer to agree to the union's demands. In a **work-to-rule**, employees will follow the rule book very closely, which will slow down or even halt production. A **go-slow** occurs when employees carry out their jobs more slowly than normal, again reducing output.

Employees may resort to **sit-ins**, by refusing to leave the premises and occupying them in an attempt to make sure that goods neither enter nor leave the firm. Most sit-ins occur when there is a threat of closure, with the workers continuing to produce the firm's products, possibly eventually running the firm as a workers' cooperative (Unit 4). Workers may also 'black' products: in **blacking**, a union refuses to handle goods which have been made by workers from another union, in an attempt to support that other union in its disputes with management.

### Strikes

A strike involves the workers in withdrawing their labour. The United Kingdom economy has sometimes been described as 'strike-prone' but this is far from the truth: the number of days lost through industrial action compares very favourably with many industrialized competitors. Many more days are lost to production through absences due to illness and injury than through strike action.

Strikes are viewed by unions as a last-resort strategy, since their members also suffer as the employers suffer. There are various types of strike action that may occur.

#### Token and selective strikes

A **token** strike – where workers may withdraw their labour for, say, a day or half a day – will be organized by the union to warn management of the possibility of future, more serious action if negotiations are not successful. A **selective** strike is an alternative approach, where certain workers only – often selected by area – come out on strike, with their colleagues giving financial or other support.

#### Sympathetic strikes

Although less frequently found nowadays, these occur when groups of workers decide to strike 'in sympathy' with others who are involved in the major strike.

#### All-out strikes and picketing

An all-out strike is usually **official**, being supported by the union which must have balloted its members (a secret ballot) to obtain majority support for the strike. It may be an **unofficial**, or 'wildcat', strike, which happens when the union members at a company cease working without first getting official union backing.

To make the strike more effective, groups of workers on strike will act as **pickets** at the company's entrances: informing other workers of the strike and persuading them to support it through not 'crossing the picket line' and entering work.

## 15.8 Resolving the dispute

Where a major dispute has started, it may be resolved by the action of either of the parties: the employers may offer improved terms, or the strike may collapse with the union accepting what is 'on the table'. The Government may also bring pressure to bear on either side, to try to break the deadlock.

If the deadlock persists, the employers or unions involved can call on the services of the **Advisory Conciliation and Arbitration Service** (ACAS). ACAS was established in 1975 to improve industrial relations. It acts independently of both employers and unions and offers the following services:

1 **Conciliation** services. An ACAS official will talk to both sides, to find areas of 'common ground' which then form the basis for further negotiations between the parties.
2 **Arbitration** services. If both sides agree, their dispute can be put 'to arbitration'. ACAS will provide an independent third party to listen to arguments presented by both sides and will offer what this third party sees as a fair settlement. The employer and the union will previously have agreed to accept the results of this arbitration.
3 **Other** services, such as publishing guidelines and 'codes of practice' on industrial relations.

## 15.9 Summary

Following the enclosure of land and the start of the Industrial Revolution in the 19th century, many workers were forced to live and work in the most appalling conditions. Gradually, unions were established which provided their members with some protection against this exploitation. Union power has grown, although there has been a reaction against this, notably by the Conservative Governments of the 1980s.

'Them and us' attitudes still exist and the valuable work done by both trade unions and employers' associations may be overlooked. There are many benefits for an employee from joining a trade union; and an employer also gains much from membership of a trade or employers' association. The TUC and the CBI, although holding different views on many aspects of the economy, often try to work together to improve the economy: this in turn should lead to improvements for both employer and employee. If specific conflicts arise, the parties can call on ACAS, an independent organization, in an attempt to resolve this conflict.

# 16 BUSINESS DOCUMENTS

## 16.1 Introduction

During the 1980s, much has been written about 'the new technology' and the 'paperless, electronic office'. In reality, paper is still the most important medium found in offices and much office work revolves round handling letters, memos and other **business documents**.

Firms involved in trading – buying and selling items – will enter a number of transactions. These transactions are supported by **trading documents** such as invoices and delivery notes. The various business documents act as a **record** of events. This allows firms to work out how much they are owed, how much they owe other firms, their VAT liability, etc. Documents also act as **proof** that a transaction has taken place, should any dispute arise between buyer and seller.

## 16.2 The Main Trading Documents

A flow of documents takes place between buyer and seller. This flow is shown in fig. 16.1.

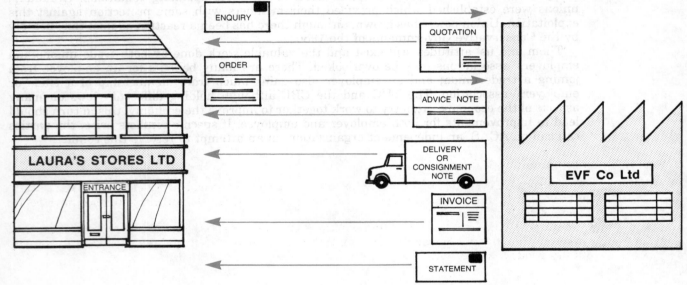

**Fig. 16.1** Document flow

The buying company sends **Letters of Enquiry** to potential suppliers, to check details of prices, delivery, discounts and credit terms, etc. From the information received, one supplier will be selected by the buyer.

On receiving the enquiry, suppliers will forward product details to the buyer. These **Quotations** are often supported by trade catalogues and price lists and will clarify details of prices, discounts, delivery times and costs.

If the buying department wishes to take advantage of a quotation, it will raise an **Order** which tells the seller:

1 The number of items ordered.
2 Their description, catalogue number and price.
3 Where and when they are to be delivered.

The supplier may acknowledge receipt of this order by issuing an **Acknowledgement** to say that the requirements of the order can be met. The seller may then forward an **Advice Note** separately from the goods, to inform the buyer that they have been despatched.

A **Delivery Note** is sent when the supplier's transport is used to deliver the goods. It will be signed and returned by the buyer as proof of receipt. If the supplier's own transport is not used, a **Consignment Note** will be issued to the carrier of the goods, to provide the carrier with details of the goods and delivery address.

Fig. 16.2 shows an **Invoice**. It will contain details of the goods despatched, their description, quantity, unit and total prices. The overall invoice total is shown, less any trade discount and plus the cost of VAT. Details of any costs of transporting the goods, and of any cash discounts offered for prompt payment, are also shown. Invoices normally have the abbreviation 'E & O E' included. This stands for 'Errors and Omissions Excepted': it protects the supplier against any errors that are contained on the invoice and allows corrections to be made.

Where goods are expensive, or the buyer is not known to the seller, the seller may issue a **Pro-forma Invoice**, which requests the buyer to pay for the goods before they are sent. These invoices can also be used where goods are sent on a 'sale-or-return' basis.

If the buyer is a regular customer, the seller may send a **Statement of Account**. This summarizes the trading that has taken place and shows the amount still owed by the buyer, as well as details of any discounts that are available for prompt payment.

*ΕＵf*

**EVF Co Ltd**
Highbridge Road, Wellington, Somerset TA1 2ER
Telephone (0952) 459741   Fax (0952) 459842

To: Laura's Stores Ltd
Taunton Road          Date: 19.8.89
Burnham-on-Sea
Somerset  LS7 8EF    Order No.: 160180

| PROD. CODE | QUANTITY AND DESCRIPTION | UNIT PRICE £ p | | TOTAL £ p | |
|---|---|---|---|---|---|
| EV8 | 10  'Foxy' cuddly toys | 2 | 50 | 25 | 00 |
| TD2 | 12 'Tina' dolls | 12 | 00 | 144 | 00 |
| | | | | 169 | 00 |
| | Less: Trade discount 10% | | | 16 | 90 |
| | | | | 152 | 10 |
| | Value Added Tax 15% | | | 22 | 81 |
| | | TOTAL DUE | | 174 | 91 |

Terms: 2½% 28 days
E&OE                      VAT Reg. 403-8871-988

**Fig. 16.2** An invoice

*Debit and Credit Notes*

The purpose of a **Debit Note** is to increase the invoice total owed by the seller. It will be issued if the buyer has been undercharged, or if more goods than are shown on the invoice have been sent to the buyer.

A **Credit Note** is issued by the supplier if the buyer has to pay less than stated on the invoice. This may be due to an error on the invoice, or because the buyer has had to return faulty goods to the seller.

## 16.3 Documents Used in Foreign Trade

UK firms engaged in international trade use a variety of documents when exporting and importing goods. The following are the main documents involved:

1 **Bill of Lading.** This is used when goods are shipped and shows their details and destination. It acts as a receipt and also as evidence of ownership of the goods. If goods are to be sent by air, an **Air Waybill** will be used.

2 **Certificate of Origin.** This document states the country of origin of the goods. It is needed for the importing country to identify the rate of any tariffs to charge, or to apply any embargoes that are in operation.

3 **Export and Import Licences.** An Export Licence may be needed by a firm before it is allowed to export its products (e.g. armaments). A government importing goods may have a policy of issuing Import Licences, for example to control the number of imports of a particular product (through quotas).

*The European Community*

The start of 1988 saw the introduction of the EC's 'Single Administrative Document' (SAD). It has replaced many forms which were previously used to record movement of goods between the UK and the other Member States. This means that all EC members use the same documentation (and operate the same external tariff: Unit 3). Different copies of the SAD are used to cover despatch, entry and transit requirements.

# 17 BUSINESS COMMUNICATION

## 17.1 Introduction

Businesses employ, and are owned and run by, various groups of people. Workers, directors and shareholders are three important groups closely involved with a business: other influential groups include customers, suppliers and the Government. **Communication** will take place both between these groups and between the individuals who make up the groups. Effective communication is one of the key elements – together with **control** and **coordination**, the 'three Cs' – which lead to efficient management of a firm.

The elements that make up the process of communication are:

1 The transmitter (the sender).
2 The message being transmitted.
3 The medium by which it is sent.
4 The receiver of the message.

## 17.2 Internal and External Communications

Within an individual firm, **internal communication** will take place at, and between, the various levels. Directors communicate with one another concerning the firm's overall strategy; they inform managers of these plans, who will in turn communicate with other employees. Negotiations will take place over pay and working conditions; managers will communicate instructions and orders and will seek to improve morale and motivation through effective communication. Employees will also communicate with each other, for example over production, wages, and health and safety matters.

**External communication** occurs when a firm's directors or employees communicate with those individuals and groups who deal with, but are outside, the firm. Shareholders will receive copies of the firm's annual accounts, together with the reports of the Chairman and Directors; government departments will require statistical and financial information from the firm, for taxation and other purposes; an advertising agency will be consulted over the firm's advertising policies; customers need informing that goods have been despatched or that their orders cannot be met; and suppliers will be contacted if their goods are not up to standard, or if delivery of goods has not taken place.

Communication – both internal and external – can take place in a number of different ways. It can be in a **written** or a **verbal** form, it may be in a **pictorial** format, or it could use **electronic** means to get its message across.

## 17.3 Written Communication

Written communication is an important internal and external medium in business.

### Internal written forms

**Letters,** although more often associated with external communications, are sometimes used internally. Specific examples include using them to give warnings to an employee over behaviour likely to lead to dismissal; and informing new employees of their contract terms, or existing employees of promotion. Letters will also be sent between different sites or divisions of the same company.

**The memorandum** (or 'memo') is the most widely used internal written communication. It is more concise and less formal than a business letter (e.g. by being neither signed nor fully addressed) and is used at all levels to provide a written record of information. Fig. 17.1 is an example of a memo.

**Notices** and **company journals** are used in business to provide various written details, for example of company health and safety rules, or of sports and social club activities. They are also used to internally advertise jobs. The journal may contain items such as articles written by employees, details of discounts on the firm's products available to employees, and developments taking place within the organization.

Various formal meetings will take place in a firm. Each meeting will have a written **agenda**, which acts as a summary of the main business to be conducted at that meeting. **Minutes** of meetings will be kept in a written form: these act as records of what has been agreed at the meetings.

```
┌─────────────────────────────────────────┐
│                                          │
│  Internal memorandum     [G] GABRIEL'S of│
│                          WOLVERHAMPTON   │
│  From  Sales Manager                     │
│                                          │
│  To  Sales Staff        date: 18 October │
│                                          │
│            MOTOR INSURANCE               │
│                                          │
│                                          │
│   Following the opening of our Walsall   │
│   branch, please ensure that your car    │
│   motor  insurance  covers  you  for     │
│   personal business use in addition to the│
│   normal Social, domestic and pleasure   │
│   Cover.                                  │
│                                          │
│                                          │
└─────────────────────────────────────────┘
```

**Fig. 17.1** A memo

**Reports** are drawn up by individuals or members of company committees. They are formal written documents and can be on anything, such as the progress of a new product, possible understaffing in a particular department, or the effects of computerizing certain operations.

### External written forms

**Trading documents** such as invoices and statements are important examples of written communication which takes place between firms (Unit 16).

**Business letters** are sent to customers, suppliers and many other people and organizations: the most frequently used form of external communication, they are much more formal than the internal memo and again may act as written evidence.

The **Annual Report and Accounts** of a limited company must be sent, by law, to all its shareholders. This document contains a Directors' Report outlining the company's progress and plans, and the Final Accounts (Unit 10). Companies often present summaries of this information in the form of diagrams, charts or graphs (see figs. 17.2, 17.3 and 17.4).

## 17.4 Verbal Communication

The two main forms of verbal, or oral, communication are the telephone and meetings.

**The telephone** is used as both an internal and an external form of verbal communication. It has the advantage over business letters and memos that it is faster and more flexible (the message can be adapted if necessary, unlike letters and memos). A 'phone call, however, does not give the permanent record of the communication that letters and memos provide and it can be more expensive.

**Meetings** of all types involve face-to-face oral communication. Many informal meetings, for instance between a departmental head and section heads, take place. Examples of formal meetings – usually supported by an agenda and minutes (see above) – include management-union negotiations, safety committees and employment interviews. Probably the most important formal meeting for a limited company is its **Annual General Meeting**, where the directors outline their plans to the company shareholders, the company's performance is discussed and some of the directors stand for re-election.

## 17.5 Visual Communication

The purpose of visual communication is to **summarize and simplify** complicated information. Important information is highlighted and unimportant information will be excluded. Visual communication is also used where **impact** is required to 'get the message across', for example through using a picture which has been printed as a poster to publicize some aspect of safety.

Many of these pictorial forms are produced nowadays using computer programs. The following are the main forms of visual communication:

1 Various kinds of **charts and graphs**.

2 **Pictures** and **photographs**.

3 **Flowcharts** and other diagrams.

4 **Maps** and plans.

Fig. 17.2 is an illustration of both a pie chart (on consumers' spending) and a graph (showing total personal gross and net income, savings and spending).

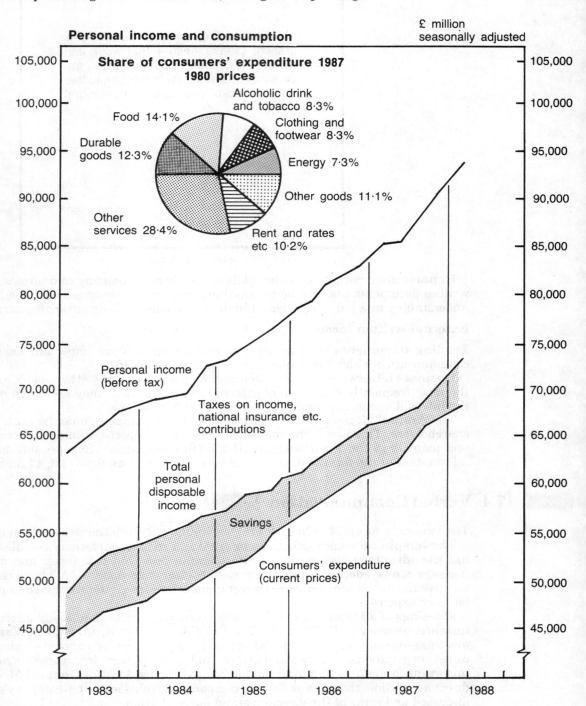

**Fig. 17.2** Pie chart and graph: personal income and consumption details
Source: *'Economic Trends', July 1988*

Figs. 17.3 and 17.4 illustrate different bar charts, used by companies as summaries in their published accounts. Fig. 17.3 provides a summary of Courtaulds turnover (sales) and profits, for each business sector 1987–88. They are percentage bar charts, used as alternatives to pie charts. Fig. 17.4 is another type of bar chart. It summarizes the growth in the **earning and dividends per share of BICC plc, 1983–87.**

**Turnover and profit by business sector 1987/88**

TURNOVER          OPERATING PROFIT

18%
£453m                                          21%
                                               £48m

FIBRES

4%
£103m

WOODPULP                                       15%
11%                                            £33m
£281m

CHEMICALS
&
MATERIALS                                      9%
15%                                            £19m
£385m

COATINGS

13%                                            13%
£333m                                          £28m

FILMS
&
PACKAGING                                      13%
                                               £30m

39%
£982m

TEXTILES

                                               29%
                                               £66m

TOTAL                                          TOTAL
£2,537m                                        £224m

**Fig. 17.3** Bar charts Courtesy: *Courtaulds plc*

**Earnings and dividends per share**

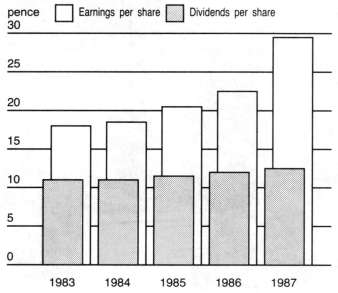

**Fig. 17.4** Bar chart Courtesy: *BICC plc*

## 17.6 Electronic Means of Communication

Computers, word processors, video-conferencing, 'fax' and other machines are increasingly used to:

1 **Prepare**
2 **Transmit**
3 **Store**

communications between businesses.

### Computers

Computers can communicate with other, similar, computers, for example to transfer or 'download' data. This is often done using a telephone line to transmit the data, supported by appropriate computer software and a **modem**. Companies can obtain information electronically from computer **databases** – large information stores – both at home (such as Prestel) and overseas. Interested firms may become information providers on these electronic databases.

### Word processors

These are used by firms in preparing written communications such as business letters. They also store the letters electronically, on computer discs.

### Video-conferencing

This uses electronic means to allow face-to-face meetings to take place when people are in different parts of the country. The people involved will visit studios (either specially constructed for companies at their individual branches, or through British Telecom's **Confravision** service) and will have their picture and words transmitted to the others who are at different locations. In this way, the meeting can take place as if all were in the same room. Although expensive at the present time, improvements in the technology used are likely to make video-conferencing more popular, since a firm's employees could be saved the time, expense and inconvenience of travelling great distances to attend meetings.

### Facsimile transmission (Fax)

Fax machines are becoming popular in business. One machine, linked to a telephone line, will transmit letters and pictures to another machine at the end of the 'phone line: this other machine may be at another branch of the company either in the UK or overseas, or owned by a different firm. Firms not owning or renting fax machines can use the **Intelpost** fax service of the Post Office. Transmission is almost instantaneous – the communication is received by the one machine as it is transmitted by the other – and charts, diagrams and maps, as well as written information, can be sent.

**Fig. 17.5** Verbal, written and electronic communication  Courtesy: *Beecham plc*

## 17.7 Storing and Retrieving Information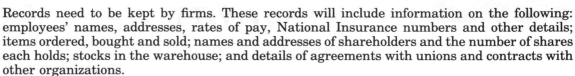

Records need to be kept by firms. These records will include information on the following: employees' names, addresses, rates of pay, National Insurance numbers and other details; items ordered, bought and sold; names and addresses of shareholders and the number of shares each holds; stocks in the warehouse; and details of agreements with unions and contracts with other organizations.

A system of record-keeping involves **storing** and **retrieving** the information. To be efficient, the record-keeping system must have the following qualities:

1 It must be capable of being **expanded** when necessary.
2 It must be **easily understood** by all who have to use it.
3 The information must be **easily and quickly accessible** to those requiring it.
4 It must be **secure** from those who are not entitled to use it.
5 The information must be kept **safe from deterioration**.

**Paper-based** records will be kept by all firms. A filing and retrieval system for paper records is easy to establish: copies of the documents can be made and filed, for example in alphabetical, date or other relevant order. These filing systems can, however, take up an increasing amount of space, and mis-filing of information leads to delays and inefficiency.

Some firms **microfilm** various documents. One piece of microfilm will store many hundreds of pages of information and eliminates much of the need to store the paper documents, thereby saving space. The microfilm is also more durable than paper and once the record has been microfilmed it becomes tamper-proof. Special equipment such as a microfilm reader is, however, required to operate a microfilm system.

**Computerized record-keeping** is becoming more popular with firms. Computer databases, once set up, provide quick access to vast amounts of information: this information can also be transferred from one database or terminal to another quickly, and it can easily be converted into paper or microfilm forms. The dangers of computerized record-keeping include the risk of 'hackers' gaining access to confidential information and, if the system breaks down, stored information cannot be retrieved and may be lost. The recent Data Protection Act provides, in certain circumstances, people with a certain amount of protection, allowing them the right to see what information about them is stored on computerized records.

## 17.8 Summary

Communication is a two-way process. Each element of the communication process must work effectively for communication to be effective.

The **transmitter** must use an appropriate level of language and show a positive attitude when making the communication; the **message** must not be too distorted by noise or other factors; a suitable written or other **medium** must be selected; and the **receiver** must also display a positive attitude and possess the level of knowledge required to understand the communication.

# 18 CONTROLLING BUSINESS ACTIVITY

## 18.1 Introduction

All businesses – whether they are run to make profits for their owners, or to provide a service for the public – will be influenced by the environment within which they have to operate. The activities of firms, just like those of people, are affected by a wide range of laws and regulations. Some of these laws are created to **control** business activity; other regulations will **aid** business activity (Unit 19).

There are a number of different organizations which either assist or control business and influence its environment. The major influences on firms are shown in fig. 18.1 below.

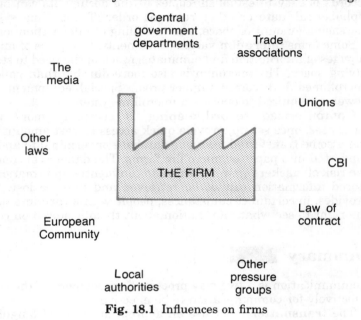

Central government departments

Trade associations

The media

Other laws

Unions

THE FIRM

CBI

European Community

Law of contract

Local authorities

Other pressure groups

**Fig. 18.1** Influences on firms

## 18.2 Central Government

The Government of the United Kingdom will aid business, as well as control it. Its main areas of control, described in detail later in the Unit, are as follows:

1 Control of a firm's **location and development**, for example through planning permission laws and regional policy.
2 Controlling the firm's **relationship with its workers**, e.g. by protecting workers through health and safety regulations.
3 Controlling the **relationships between firms**, through monopolies and mergers legislation (laws) and the law of contract.
4 Control of the **relationship between firms and consumers** by, for example, passing consumer legislation.
5 Controlling firms through **taxation and other financial policies**.
6 Controlling the activities of **trade unions**, through legislation.
7 Control of **international trade** through using, for example, tariffs or quotas.

### Reasons for government control and assistance

All governments take steps to influence the workings of their country's economy. In trying to improve people's standards of living, governments encourage **economic growth** in the economy, by adopting policies they believe will help firms to produce more and to become more efficient.

The main economic goals of a government include the **control of inflation** (i.e. control of prices), providing **full employment** (Unit 2) and keeping a stable **balance of payments** (Unit 3). Sometimes these goals conflict with one another. Increased production levels in the economy may lead, for example, to a fall in the level of unemployment: but this may also 'suck in' a lot of imported raw materials which can cause balance of payments problems. In addition, higher employment levels will lead to more money in the economy (because more people are earning), which in turn may raise prices (increasing inflation) or cause imports of finished goods to rise, leading to further problems with the balance of payments.

Governments must also balance the benefits that come from an increased standard of living – such as more material possessions – with possible reductions in the 'quality of life'. Certain industrial processes, whilst they may make goods more cheaply, could cause high levels of pollution. Also, firms which are allowed to start up in south-east England may benefit the local and national economy, but also add to the congestion levels in that region and do little to help solve problems of unemployment in other parts of the country.

A government will attempt to balance the financial and social **costs** with the financial and social **benefits** that arise from the actions of firms. This **cost-benefit analysis** can be used to decide how a government should best use its resources: for example, whether it should help to finance the building of a new underground line in London, or whether more investment should take place in the nation's motorway system.

## 18.3 Control and the European Community

In carrying out its control, the UK Government is influenced by its membership of the **European Community** (Unit 3). It has to ensure that EC rules and regulations – often called **Directives** – on pollution, levels of production, the free movement of labour, tariffs etc, are applied. These regulations must also be taken into account when the Government frames new laws which it wants to pass through Parliament.

Examples of EC Directives are given later in the Unit.

## 18.4 Controlling Business Location and Development

The **planning regulations** of central (and local) governments will help to determine where firms can set up in business and whether they can expand on their present sites. The **regional policy** of central governments will also influence the location of industry (Unit 2).

Development will also be controlled through laws which are passed to protect the environment. Pressure groups (page 123) play an important role here and firms also have to obey European Community and UK Government laws. There are over one hundred EC environmental directives which include controlling the discharge of dangerous substances by companies, and also controlling the noise level of new motorcycles and the level of exhaust emissions from vehicles in general.

## 18.5 Controlling the Firm's Relationship with its Workers

### The contract of employment

A firm's workers are employed under this contract. It follows the normal rules of contract law outlined in section 18.6 and must contain certain information (Unit 13).

The **Employment Protection (Consolidation) Act** of 1978 draws together earlier Acts which provided protection to employees, for example in stating minimum lengths of notice to be given to them. Employees (other than those in special occupations, such as the army or the police) are now protected against **unfair dismissal**.

An employee who wants to pursue a claim for unfair dismissal can, with union help, involve ACAS (Unit 15) in the dispute. If this fails, an **industrial tribunal** will decide whether the dismissal was fair. If it is a case of unfair dismissal, the employee will be entitled to compensation, reinstatement (to the original job) or re-engagement (to a new job).

### Pay

Pay agreements for public sector employees are partly controlled by government expenditure levels. In the private sector, most pay agreements are negotiated. The Government may also attempt to influence general pay levels, to control the level of inflation.

The **Equal Pay Act** 1970 forces employers to pay men and women who are doing similar work equal rates of pay for their work.

### Discrimination

The Equal Pay Act is one form of protection against sexual discrimination. Further protection is given by the **Sex Discrimination Acts** 1975 and 1987. The conditions of these Acts make it unlawful for an employer to discriminate on the grounds of sex when advertising a job, employing a person or setting a retirement date. People who believe that they have been discriminated against can approach the Equal Opportunities Commission for advice; they may then pursue this through an industrial tribunal.

The **Race Relations Acts** 1968 and 1976 make it unlawful for an employer to discriminate against a person on the grounds of race, nationality or ethnic origin. If a person suspects discrimination in areas such as recruitment, promotion or dismissal, he or she can approach the Commission for Racial Equality for assistance, with any further action also taking place at a tribunal.

### Health and safety

The control of health and safety at work goes back to the 19th century. Many rules and regulations extending back to this period were included in the 1961 **Factories Act**. This Act contains the following conditions:

1 There must be adequate toilet and washing facilities.
2 Lighting and ventilation must also be adequate.
3 Fire escapes must be provided and must be kept free from obstruction (as must stairs and passageways).
4 Moving machinery must be fenced for protection.

The **Offices, Shops and Railway Premises Act** of 1963 contains similar provisions. It ensures, for example, that offices are not overcrowded and that they are properly heated, lit and ventilated.

In 1974 the **Health and Safety at Work Act** (HASAWA) was passed. It states the duties of the employer and the employee regarding matters of health and safety.

*The employer's duties*

The following must be provided by an employer:

1 A safe working environment.
2 Safe machinery.
3 Safe working processes.
4 Safe entry and exit arrangements.

Employers have to take out employers' liability insurance (Unit 6) to compensate employees injured at work.

*The employee's duties*

Employees also have obligations under HASAWA, as follows:

1 To take reasonable care of themselves and others whilst at work.
2 Not to interfere with anything provided for their own safety or the safety of others.
3 To report defects in equipment, working areas, etc.
4 To cooperate with the employer to maintain safety regulations and procedures.

## 18.6 Controlling the Relationship Between Firms

### The law of contract

This forms the legal basis of transactions between two firms, as well as between firms and employees, and between firms and consumers. A contract is an **agreement** between two people (limited companies are separate legal 'people' in the eyes of the law: Unit 4) which can be enforced by law.

For a contract to be created, there must be an **offer** made by one person, which is **accepted** by the other. **Consideration** must be given by the parties: the product is given on the one hand and payment for it is given on the other. Both parties must have the **capacity** to enter into a contract – they cannot be under-age, drunk or insane, for example – and must have the **intention** that the contract will be legally binding on them.

Most contracts are entered into by firms very easily: they can be created over the telephone, by letter, or through a face-to-face meeting. Other contracts, such as those involving the purchase of property, are subject to more complex procedures. Should a business fail to meet its obligations under a typical trading contract, it will probably have to pay **damages** – financial compensation – to the other party.

### Competition law

Firms, through government policy, natural growth, or merger or takeover (Unit 4), can become **monopolies**, sole suppliers of a product or service. Some public corporations, such as British Coal, are monopolies or near-monopolies in their fields: they can be of benefit to the public even though they are monopolies, and – because they are in the public sector – they are controlled by the Government in various ways (see next page).

Monopolies are discouraged in the private sector. Business in this sector operates through the profit motive and competition between firms should provide customers with low prices and a variety of goods. If one firm becomes a virtual monopoly, however, it can use its power in the

**Fig. 18.2** Protecting the public Courtesy: *The Guardian*

market to make its products more expensive than they would be if competition existed. It may also become inefficient through a lack of competition.

The **Fair Trading Act** of 1973 set up the Office of Fair Trading, under a Director-General of Fair Trading. Trading matters are examined and any 'restrictive practices' are controlled. A restrictive practice may occur when, for example, two or more firms agree to fix prices and not to compete with one another.

There is also a **Monopolies and Mergers Commission**, which works closely with the Office of Fair Trading. It checks whether any proposed merger between two large companies would lead to a situation that is not in the interests of consumers. The Commission also investigates industries where possible monopolies exist and makes recommendations for improvements in trading practices.

The European Community operates a 'Competition Policy', which also seeks to control the number and level of monopolies in its member countries. It is designed to ensure that trade in the Community takes place on the basis of free and fair competition.

### Company law

UK governments have passed a number of **Companies Acts**, which control the operation of limited companies. Other Acts, such as the **Partnership Act** of 1890 (Unit 4), control the workings of other forms of business organization.

There are also a number of European Community directives in company law: they include the Second Directive, which states minimum levels of capital for PLCs, and the Fourth Directive, which explains rules regarding company annual accounts.

## 18.7 Controlling the Relationship Between Firms and Consumers

Consumers enter into contracts when buying goods. Under the law of contract, a consumer can take legal action against a firm if it fails to meet its part of the agreement. To support the law of contract and to give consumers much greater protection, governments – particularly in the last 25 years – have brought out a range of **consumer protection laws**. There are also a number of **Government and non-government agencies** (see page 123) which help to develop and enforce consumer protection.

### CONSUMER PROTECTION LEGISLATION

There are several important UK Acts and EC Directives which firms must obey when selling goods or providing services.

### UK Acts

**Unsolicited Goods and Services Act** 1971. This prevents firms delivering unordered items to people or other firms and then demanding payment for them. If unsolicited goods are received, they can be kept if the sender – following notice from the person receiving them – fails to collect them.

**Sale of Goods Act** 1979. This Act brought together various other Acts relating to the sale of goods. Its provisions only refer to goods (not services) bought from traders who normally deal in those goods. Under this Act, goods must be of **merchantable quality**, i.e. they must be fit to be sold. They must also be **fit for the purpose for which they were bought** and – if sold by description – they must **match their description**.

**Supply of Goods and Services Act** 1982. This Act extended the protection given under sale of goods legislation to **services**, such as hairdressing and package holidays.

**Foods and Drugs Act** 1955. This Act protects the consumer by making the sale of unfit food a criminal offence: it sets food labelling regulations and establishes rules on hygiene in premises dealing with food.

**Weights and Measures Acts** 1963 and 1979. These Acts force manufacturers to state quantities of packaged goods on the package and make it an offence to sell goods which are underweight or short in quantity. Certain goods must be sold in fixed weights or measures, such as milk, and other standard sizes are encouraged so prices can be compared.

**Trade Descriptions Acts** 1968 and 1972. Under these Acts, any false description – verbal or written – given to a good or service is a criminal offence. Trading standards officers enforce the Acts' provisions.

**Consumer Credit Act** 1974 and **Financial Services Act** 1986. People or businesses lending money or offering financial services are controlled by these Acts, for example by making them become registered. Companies lending money on credit must state clearly the **APR** – the 'Annual Percentage Rate' – which is the true cost of borrowing the money: and advertisements offering credit must not mislead people.

**Consumer Protection Act** 1987. Under this Act, it is an offence to supply customers with goods which do not meet general safety requirements.

### EC directives

The European Community's directives provide a range of protection for consumers. One example is in the area of **food law**, with directives to control food additives (permitted colours, preservatives, etc), the type of materials that can come into contact with food (e.g. for packaging), and food labelling and advertising, which must not be misleading. Certain foodstuffs – such as coffee, chocolate, jams and honey – are subject to special requirements concerning their composition or labelling.

There are many other EC measures on consumer protection. These are being 'harmonized' between the Member States for the 'Single Market' of 1992. Examples include:

1 The **Misleading Advertising Directive**, which protects people against unfair advertising practices.
2 The **Doorstep Selling Directive**, which provides for a week's 'cooling-off' period if certain goods are bought by people at their homes.
3 The **Consumer Credit Directive**, which gives the same sort of protection as the 1974 Consumer Credit Act above.
4 The **Toy Safety Directive**, which should lead to toy safety standards being harmonized.
5 The **Price Indication Directives**, which will harmonize the display of product selling prices in Member States.

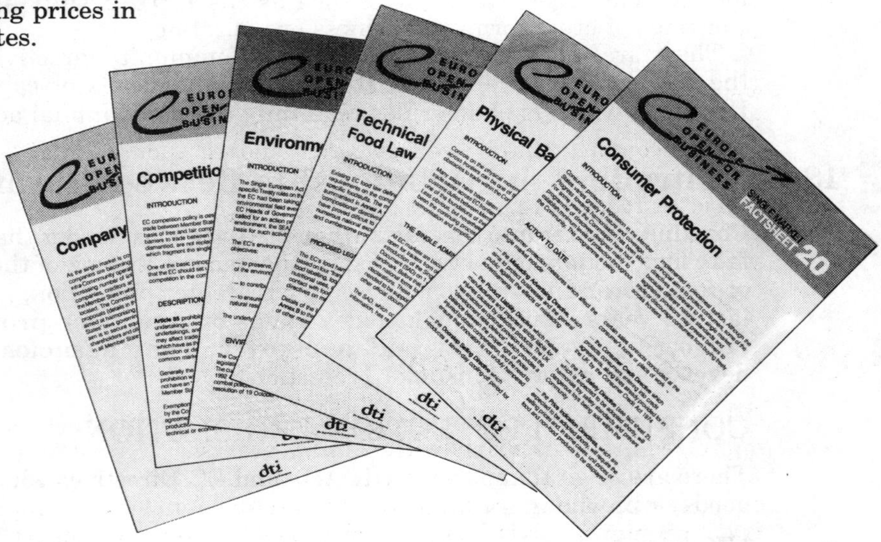

Fig. 18.3 Influence of the European Community

## 18.8 Controlling Firms Through Taxation and Financial Policies

Companies, like individuals, are liable to pay taxes on their income: the levels of these taxes are set by the Government. It can use the rates of such items as **Corporation Tax** (on company profits), **Value Added Tax** – charged on company purchases and sales – and **Employers' National Insurance contributions** to control its own level of income and the performance of the economy in general.

By altering other factors such as income tax levels, interest rates and credit restrictions, the Government can again directly and indirectly affect firms: a rise in income tax, for example, will reduce general levels of demand in the economy and firms may find it harder to sell their goods. Increased interest rates or 'tighter credit' means higher borrowing costs for firms and greater difficulty in selling their goods on credit.

The Government is also a major buyer of goods and services. It will exert, through levels of public expenditure and other financial policies, a lot of influence in the economy, by providing contracts for new roads and hospitals, for defence matters, for educational supplies and so on.

## 18.9 Controlling Trade Unions

Trade union power has come under attack by the Conservative Governments of the 1980s. The **Employment Acts** of 1980 and 1982, and the 1984 **Trade Union Act**, are examples of laws which control the operations of unions. Under these Acts, principal union officers must be elected by secret ballot every five years and strike action must be authorized by secret ballots. Trade unions can apply to the Government for refunds of money towards the cost of these ballots.

## 18.10 Controlling International Trade

Governments have a range of controls available (Unit 3) which may allow them to stop 'free' trade. These controls include tariffs, quotas, subsidies and embargoes. Membership of the European Community means that the United Kingdom follows Community policy in encouraging free trade between Member States.

## 18.11 Local Government

The actions of local authorities may both assist and control firms which operate in their areas. Recent changes in the rate system, leading to a more standardized system of business rates in England and Wales and in Scotland, mean that local government has lost much of its control here. It still exercises control on firms through **planning** policies: it will handle the planning applications from firms and so affect any expansion plans. The authorities will also control levels of **pollution** created by industrial activity. Local authorities also provide aid to business in their area (Unit 19).

## 18.12 Government Agencies Supporting Consumer Protection

There are both Government and non-government agencies contributing to the consumer protection field. The **Office of Fair Trading** is the Government's main agency in this area. As well as working with the **Monopolies and Mergers Commission** in controlling various restrictive practices, it is involved in publicising and encouraging fair trading practices and codes of conduct. It also licenses firms' lending under the 1974 Consumer Credit Act. There is further involvement at central government level through, for example, the **Ministry of Agriculture, Fisheries and Food**.

The involvement of **local authorities** includes employing people involved in trading standards and weights and measures (environmental health), and offering advice on consumer problems.

## 18.13 Pressure Groups and Other Agencies

Other important agencies exist, often operating as **pressure groups**. A 'pressure group' is an organized group of people with similar interests, who attempt to influence others.

A pressure group may try to gain further public support, to influence a government to change policy along the lines that the group wants. For example, the **Campaign for Nuclear Disarmament** (CND) seeks to persuade people to support a defence policy involving no nuclear weapons. The work of the pressure group may more directly involve the business world. A **trade union** (Unit 15), such as the Union of Communication Workers, is an example of a pressure group which acts to improve the pay and working conditions of its members. It will still attempt to exert political influence on the Government (e.g. through the TUC), for the benefit of its members.

Some well-known further examples are as follows:

The **British Standards Institute** is an independent organization which sets minimum standards for many consumer products. Its 'Kitemark' (fig. 18.4) is well known as a symbol guaranteeing that the product to which it refers has been tested by the BSI and found to be satisfactory.

**Fig. 18.4** The BSI 'Kitemark'

The **Advertising Standards Authority** (ASA) is another independent body, which sets out to control the advertising standards of firms. The advertising industry has established a voluntary code of practice, enforced by the ASA, which receives complaints from members of the public.

The **Automobile Association** and the **Royal Automobile Club** (AA and RAC) are motoring organizations which campaign on behalf of the motorist.

**The TUC, the CBI** and the various **trade associations** (Unit 15) are important pressure groups.

**Local residents' associations** may try to pressurize their local council to improve some aspect of local life.

**Citizens Advice Bureaux** give independent advice to consumers.

**Consultative Committees** of the nationalized industries (Unit 4) act as pressure groups in these industries.

The **Consumers Association** is an independent body which examines and reports on goods and services provided by firms, in its own publication, 'Which?' magazine.

The **Association of British Travel Agents** (ABTA) helps safeguard the holidays of customers who book with one of its member firms. ABTA keeps a central fund to provide compensation.

**Shopping by post?**
**Play it safe.**
*Look for the initials*
**MOPS**
**For full details send a 9" x 6"**
**stamped addressed envelope to:**
**The National Newspaper**
**Mail Order Protection**
**Scheme, 16 Tooks Court,**
**London EC4 1LB.**

THE NATIONAL NEWSPAPER
MOPS
MAIL ORDER PROTECTION SCHEME

**Fig. 18.5** MOPS: Consumer protection when shopping by post

The 1980s have produced a growing interest in our environment. People are becoming increasingly concerned over matters and acts which harm the environment: groups such as **Friends of the Earth, Greenpeace** and **ASH** (Action on Smoking and Health) cater for this increased interest. They will also influence firms both directly and indirectly, through such action as campaigning for new laws on the safe disposal of toxic waste, pressing the Government to publicize further the harmful effects of smoking and directly confronting companies which they believe are harming the environment through their policies.

**The media**

In the United Kingdom there is a great deal of **investigative TV and journalism**. Newspapers, television and radio stations investigate the complaints of their readers, viewers or listeners. Personalities such as Esther Rantzen have, through their television or newspaper work, publicized the activities of firms and individuals who exploit consumers; and they have helped to establish better controls over these 'sharp practices'.

## 18.14 Summary

Anyone who decides to set up in business will immediately find that there is a seemingly never-ending list of laws, rules, regulations and organizations which influence and control the operation of the new business. On a local basis, there is the local authority; the Government and various non-government pressure groups exert control on a regional or national basis; and the European Community is a major international influence on a firm. Most of these institutions also provide assistance to both new and existing businesses, as explained in the next unit.

# 19 AIDING BUSINESS ACTIVITY

## 19.1 Introduction

Many of those organizations which exercise **control** over the business environment (Unit 18) will also provide **aid** to firms. This assistance may come from local or central government, the European Community, or non-government sources such as trade associations and local Chambers of Commerce. Fig. 19.1 summarizes the sources of aid mentioned in the unit.

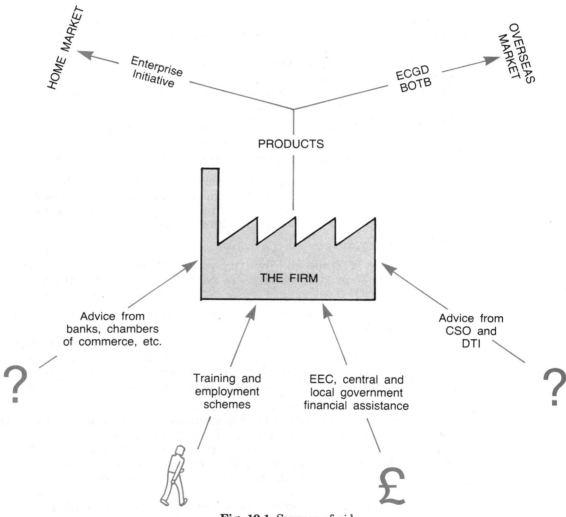

**Fig. 19.1** Sources of aid

## 19.2 Local Government

Unit 18 explained the controls that local authorities have over firms in their areas. Local government also provides aid to business.

Local authorities will have **planning and development** policies. They can grant planning applications to allow firms to expand; they also build industrial parks and allow grants to local business. They are responsible for certain **roads** in their area and their policies here can help firms by reducing road congestion. Local government influences the areas of education and housing. Through **education** and training policies, an awareness of the work of commerce and industry can be encouraged, and local authority **housing** can be used to attract workers to the area. Finally, a local authority, through its own **buying** decisions, can act as a customer for local firms, which may lead to lower unemployment in the area.

## 19.3 Aid from Central Government

The UK Government provides assistance to firms, particularly in these areas:

1 The provision of **information services**.
2 Help to **exporters**.
3 Various kinds of **financial assistance**.
4 **Training and employment schemes.**

In providing this assistance, it is supported by various EC initiatives.

### Information services

The Government provides a range of general and specific publications and information services, which are designed to assist firms trading in both home and overseas markets. The **Central Statistical Office** (CSO) is the Government's main provider of general statistical information. Its publications, which can be used by business in analysing statistics and forecasting trends, include the following:

1 'Annual Abstract of Statistics': this contains details on many aspects of economic and industrial life.
2 'Social Trends': this includes statistical information on population, employment, income and wealth.
3 'Regional Trends' also contains employment statistics, as well as information on regional and national population movements and income levels.
4 The 'CSO Blue Book' shows how the nation spends and earns its money; the 'CSO Pink Book' contains balance of payments details.

The above are annual publications: there are also a number of monthly publications, such as the 'Monthly Digest of Statistics' and 'Economic Trends'.

### *The Department of Trade and Industry (DTI)*

The DTI plays an important role in providing UK business with advice and assistance. In 1988 it launched the **Enterprise Initiative**: this contained business consultancy services such as the 'Marketing Initiative', the 'Design Initiative' and the 'Manufacturing Initiative', which provide certain firms with free or subsidized advice.

### Assistance to exporters

The Department of Trade and Industry provides specific help and advice to exporters. The following information and assistance is available from the Department's **British Overseas Trade Board** (BOTB):

1 Use of its Statistics and Market Intelligence Library, which contains up-to-date information on exporting.
2 An Export Intelligence Service, which issues information on export opportunities.
3 A Trade Fairs Overseas Scheme, which helps exporters attend overseas trade fairs.
4 A Market Prospects Service, which gives advice about the possibility of selling overseas.
5 An Export Market Research Scheme, to assist potential exporters with overseas market research.

The **Export Credits Guarantee Department** (ECGD) is part of the Department of Trade. It provides UK exporters with a form of credit insurance. An exporter, selling overseas on credit, takes the risk of the importing firms not paying for the goods. The exporter can pay a premium to the ECGD: in return, the ECGD checks the status of importers (and the importing country's payments record is also taken into account) and normally agrees to meet most of the cost of any bad debts.

The DTI has operated a number of other initiatives to assist companies in exporting. To help companies prepare for the Single European Market in 1992, for example, it has set up 'Spearhead', a database which is available to firms and which contains information about current and likely future EC measures.

UK businesses can obtain further advice and assistance from UK consular and embassy officials based in the importing country.

### Financial assistance

Firms are encouraged to locate in certain parts of the country (Unit 2). The Government's **regional policy** has included giving financial help through rent subsidies and capital grants, and setting up Enterprise Zones that are free from many government regulations. One illustration is the DTI's **Regional Enterprise Grant**. In 1988, a small firm employing fewer than 25 in one of the Development Areas could receive financial help for certain projects as follows:

1 Grants of 15 per cent of the cost of fixed assets up to £15 000.
2 'Innovation' grants for the project, up to 50 per cent of its cost (up to £25 000).

**Subsidies** are available from the Government, sometimes made to struggling firms to help them stay in business (so that employment levels are kept up and to ensure that the industry remains part of the UK economy). Industries such as agriculture may also receive government subsidies. The European Community closely monitors any subsidies awarded, to ensure that free competition exists.

The Government also provides financial incentives to encourage individuals to **set up in business** on their own. 'Enterprise allowances' have been made available to unemployed people who set up their own businesses. In addition, banks and other companies—who may otherwise be unwilling to lend money to new or newly expanding firms, because of the higher risks involved—can have most of these loans guaranteed by the Government.

### Training and employment schemes

The Government operates various national training schemes such as ET and the YTS (Unit 13). Other training, education and employment initiatives to help business have been taken: they include the **Restart** scheme, devoted to the long-term unemployed and the **Technical and Vocational Education Initiative** (TVEI) scheme, which encourages schools to take greater account of the business world when educating children.

## 19.4 The European Community

The European Community may provide direct **financial assistance** to UK firms, for example through awarding agricultural or other subsidies. Other examples of EC financial support include loans issued to businesses by its European Investment Bank and grants for retraining which have been awarded through the European Social Fund.

The Community also provides **information** about dealing with other EC countries and firms. One way in which this is done is through the 'Centres for European Business Information', found in Birmingham, Glasgow, London and Newcastle. Specific advice can be obtained on research and development, market intelligence, technical standards and rules, and sources of finance.

## 19.5 Non-Government Organizations

Many independent organizations contribute both advice and financial assistance to UK industry. Commercial banks (Unit 5) are an important source of finance and advice for home and exporting companies. Other organizations include trade and professional associations, Chambers of Commerce, and the Confederation of British Industry (Unit 15).

## 19.6 Summary

The United Kingdom Government acts as the major body in helping our industry and commerce. Its assistance—and its control (Unit 18)—is carried out for the benefit of individual firms and for the economy in general. The range of help includes assistance to exporters, giving grants to business, establishing and encouraging schemes to improve training and levels of employment, and providing a wealth of statistical information about the economy. In doing all this, it is supported internally by local government and other organizations and externally by the European Community.

# 20 THE IMPACT OF CHANGE

## 20.1 Introduction

The United Kingdom's economy is 'dynamic', i.e. it is ever-changing. All firms will be affected by changes that are taking place. Changes occur in the following areas:

1 The firm's **markets** and the **tastes** of its consumers.
2 **Production methods** used by the firm.
3 **Communication systems and office technology** available to it.
4 The **social attitudes** of its workforce and customers.

The managers of some firms will wait for changes to take place and then – by being flexible – will react to these changes. Other managements may have a more positive approach, where they set about influencing the way that change takes place, for example through their market research and other marketing policies.

## 20.2 Changes in Markets and Consumer Tastes

The market for a firm's products will be affected by changes in the **population size and structure** (Unit 1). The level and effects of these changes can be forecast by firms, using government-produced statistics. The level of **prices** (inflation levels) and **consumer incomes** are other factors influencing future demand for products, leading to market changes.

Consumer **tastes and fashions** are also subject to change. These changes are far less predictable and therefore much harder to forecast. Many firms diversify into other markets as an insurance against the demand for their original product falling due to changes in taste or fashion.

## 20.3 Changes in Production Methods

**Fig. 20.1** Monitoring and controlling an automatic spot welder Courtesy: *RTZ Ltd*

**Automation** is widely found in companies. Automatic equipment – usually controlled by computers which have been specially programmed for the task – has largely replaced labour both on mass-production lines and in the operation of single machines. The benefits to the company from automation are as follows:

1 Production levels increase, which can lead to lower prices for the consumer.
2 Quality control becomes easier when machines such as robots are involved (the robot does the same task to the same standard of performance every time).

Automation can, however, bring problems to a company:

1 If the product is unsuccessful, the company has invested large sums of money in expensive machinery.
2 Workers may have to be made redundant, although early retirement schemes and 'natural wastage' – where people who leave for other jobs are not replaced – may help to avoid this.

There are many examples of automation and the use of modern technology in the production process. Important examples include computer-aided design and manufacture, and materials development and handling.

### Computer-aided design (CAD)

Production design staff can use a computer-aided design package to program a computer to copy the product design onto its screen. The computer can show the design from all angles and **rotate this design on screen**. It also allows the designer to **make alterations** to the design and to see immediately the effects of these alterations.

**Fig. 20.2** CAD being used at THORN security  Courtesy: *THORN security*

### Computer-aided manufacture (CAM)

Computer-aided manufacture uses the computer in the manufacturing process itself. The computer can assist with production planning, production control and quality control (Unit 8).

A development out of CAM is **Computer Integrated Manufacture** (CIM). This is where different manufacturing systems are brought together through a computer communications link: engineering and design, planning and administration, and factory floor automation can all be linked in a CIM network. Suppliers can also be brought into the information network to speed up design, development and planning of the production processes still further. Fig. 20.3 illustrates a CIM network.

### *Robots*

One aspect of CAM is the use of robots in production. Robots have the advantage of being able to do repetitive, boring tasks throughout the working day, without getting tired; and they can

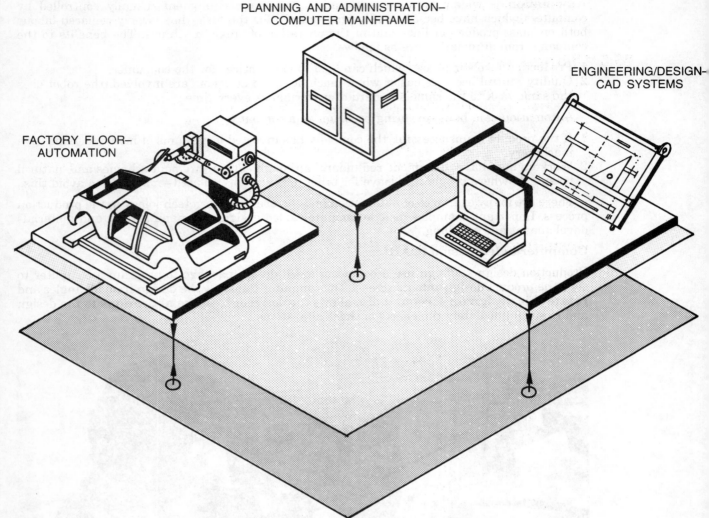

PLANNING AND ADMINISTRATION–
COMPUTER MAINFRAME

ENGINEERING/DESIGN–
CAD SYSTEMS

FACTORY FLOOR–
AUTOMATION

**Fig. 20.3** Computer Integrated Manufacture  Courtesy: *STC plc*

also sometimes be used where the production tasks could be dangerous to humans (e.g. in the atomic energy industry). Robots can be **reprogrammed**, if necessary, if the tasks change or if new products are to be made.

### Materials development and handling

Improved scientific and technological knowledge has led to improvements in the strength and durability of many materials used in production; and new, 'man-made', materials are continually being introduced. These developments can help production staff to manufacture improved products; but heavy costs can be involved, for example, in re-tooling machines to deal with the new materials.

**Automatic handling** systems are widely found, leading to improved materials handling procedures. Automation in warehouses – for example, through the widespread use of conveyor belts to move the materials, and the use of computer databases to record their movement – has led to increased efficiency.

## 20.4  Changes in Office Technology

An 'information revolution' has taken place in the business world, through the power, availability and use of computers and associated hardware and software. Word processors (Unit 17) are used to compose and store written communications, which can then be sent electronically using 'fax' machines (Unit 17) or communications software, rather than through the traditional postal channels.

Computer **databases** are used to store large amounts of employee, supplier, customer and other data, subject to the provisions of the Data Protection Act. Other computer software includes **spreadsheets**, which are used to handle numerical – usually financial – information. This information is entered into the spreadsheet, which is the electronic equivalent of a huge sheet of graph paper pland which can apply mathematical formulae to the numbers. Various calculations can be made – literally at the touch of a key – and the effects that come from changing any of the figures (such as the price) can be seen immediately.

Spreadsheets are often used to display and examine accounting information. Other, specialist, **accounting software** is available for firms to use on their computer systems.

## 20.5 Changes in Social Attitudes

Changes in the social attitudes of a society's members can affect the demand for a firm's goods or services. Attitudes to smoking, for example, have changed in the last 20 years, through increased publicity on tobacco's health risks and through the actions of pressure groups such as ASH (Unit 18).

Like tastes and fashions, social attitudes are difficult to predict for firms. Some firms may try to counter the actions of pressure groups through advertising and other promotional activities (e.g. trying to improve the image of tobacco by linking it with sporting activities through sponsorship): they are also likely to increase their range of products and their involvement in markets and market segments, as a form of protection against changing attitudes.

## 20.6 Resisting the Effects of Change

Changes which result from the factors described above may provide employees with greater job satisfaction and motivation (Unit 14). Employees may also **resist** change.

Fig. 20.4 is a summary of the reasons why a person may resist change.

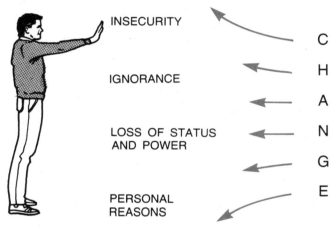

**Fig. 20.4** Resisting change

*Loss of power or status*

Change which leads to a person losing some power, prestige or status will be resisted by that person, because of the loss of self-esteem or the likely effects on wage or salary levels.

*Fear and insecurity*

It may be a part of human nature to reject new methods in preference for keeping the old, familiar working patterns and traditional ways of doing things. There is a natural fear for some employees that they cannot cope with new – often computerized or automated – processes and equipment.

*Personal factors*

Changes which are likely to lead to an individual being uprooted, having to move areas and leave friends and relatives, will be strongly resisted. Other changes, such as alterations in the licensing and the Sunday trading laws, which affect certain people's beliefs or living habits, will be strongly resisted by these groups.

**The effects of change**

People in employment, and those seeking work, will be affected by change in the following ways:

1 **New skills.** Modern working practices require employees to be more flexible than before. Much unskilled work, previously done by humans, is now done by robots and other automated procedures: workers need to possess higher levels of skills and education, to be able to cope with changing processes.
2 **Greater job mobility.** The pace of technological change leads to old jobs and industries dying, with new jobs and industries springing up to replace them. Most of us will change occupation at least once during our working lives, unlike our parents and grandparents who often stayed in the same occupation for the whole of their working lives.

**3 More leisure time.** One development, stimulated by the recent very high unemployment levels, is earlier retirement. Many firms encourage their employees to retire earlier than the statutory retiring age, by offering them financial incentives to do so. There has also been a general increase in leisure time available to employees, due to changing social attitudes to work and leisure.

## 20.7 Summary

The business world of the 1970s and 1980s has faced a pace of change that was previously unknown. New industries, often linked to technological developments, have grown, whilst at the same time traditional manufacturing and construction industries have declined in importance. These changes have produced trends, such as the increased numbers of women working and the growth of part-time jobs (page 16). Another trend in the UK economy has been the growth in the number of small businesses, encouraged by Government economic policies and developing out of the collapse of much of our industrial base.

Changes in a firm's markets, the tastes and social attitudes of its customers and the technology available to it, force its management to plan ahead. Changes in demand need to be anticipated; new management and production techniques must be used, so that the firm stays competitive; and initiatives must be taken if the firm is to remain in business.

# 21 SELF-TEST QUESTIONS AND ANSWERS

## Self-test Questions

### Unit 1 The economic framework of business

1 The four factors of production are _____, _____, _____ and _____.

2 Explain 'opportunity cost' and give one example of its relevance to business.

3 Distinguish between Direct and Indirect production.

4 All firms specialize to some extent. What benefits do they gain from this?

5 What is the main difference between a free market economic system and a planned system?

6 Give three advantages found in
   (a) the free market system;
   (b) the planned system.

7 Distinguish between Primary, Secondary and Tertiary forms of production.

8 Classify the following occupations as primary, secondary or tertiary:
   (a) shopkeeper          (e) forester
   (b) delivery van driver  (f) seaman
   (c) bricklayer          (g) banker
   (d) car body welder     (h) miner

9 A 'market' is a place where _____ and _____ are in contact with each other to determine a price.

### Unit 2 Regional and national factors

1 If an entrepreneur wishes to set up in business in the United Kingdom, what are the factors that influence where the new firm is located?

2 Name the three main influences on the overall size of the UK population.

3 Match the following descriptions with the unemployment terms they represent:
   (a) frictional      (i) lack of demand in the economy
   (b) structural      (ii) when people change jobs
   (c) seasonal        (iii) long-term change in demand or supply
   (d) cyclical        (iv) machines substituted for labour
   (e) technological   (v) changes in demand occur at certain points of the year

4 The two headings under which the mobility of labour can be analysed are _____ mobility and _____ mobility.

5 Give two factors which prevent or discourage workers from
   (a) changing occupation; and
   (b) getting work in another part of the country.

6 Outline briefly the ways in which central government tries to help regions suffering from high unemployment levels.

### Unit 3 International factors

1 Three reasons why a country takes part in international trade are to gain the benefits that come from greater _____, greater _____ and greater _____.

2 What factors have led to the United Kingdom becoming less important as a world power in manufacturing?

3 Give three reasons why the United Kingdom needs to trade with other countries.

4 Identify two major exports and two major imports of the United Kingdom.

5 Explain the difference between the Balance of Trade and the Balance of Payments on current account. How is each calculated?

6 Distinguish between tariffs and quotas.

7 Give two reasons why the UK Government may decide to restrict imports into the country. What problem may it face if it decides to do this?

133

8 Explain the role of the following in international trade:
(a) the EC and its CET;
(b) the IMF;
(c) GATT.

9 Explain the term 'multinational'.

10 Identify two problems that can arise for the UK through allowing multinationals to operate in its economy.

## Unit 4 Business organizations

1 Name three objectives that a private sector firm could have.

2 One difference between an unincorporated and an incorporated business is that the unincorporated business does not have a _____ _____ existence from its owner(s).

3 Explain 'limited liability' and state why the abbreviations 'PLC' or 'ltd' in a firm's name act as a warning to other firms.

4 Outline two advantages and two disadvantages associated with sole trader firms.

5 What benefits could a sole trader gain by taking on a partner?

6 What are the provisions of the 1890 Partnership Act, regarding
(a) interest on capital;
(b) share of profits and losses;
(c) other entitlements?
Under what circumstances does the 1890 Act come into force?

7 State the main difference between
(a) a public limited company and a private limited company;
(b) a public limited company and a public corporation; and
(c) the public sector and the private sector.

8 Give three reasons why UK governments have
(a) taken industries into public ownership;
(b) privatized certain firms.

9 Distinguish between worker cooperatives and retail cooperatives.

10 Explain the term 'franchising'.

## Unit 5 Business finance

1 Name two sources of finance for
(a) public corporations;
(b) local authority undertakings.

2 Distinguish between 'internal finance' and 'external finance' for a firm and give three examples of each type.

3 What is 'factoring'? How is it a source of finance for a firm?

4 Explain three differences between
(a) ordinary and preference shares;
(b) preference shares and debentures.

5 Name two types of institution through which a firm can obtain long-term capital.

6 Which factors determine the method of finance selected by a firm?

7 In addition to providing short-term and long-term finance for a company, in what other ways can a commercial bank help a company?

## Unit 6 Business risk and growth

1 Name one business risk that cannot be insured against. Why is this?

2 Explain the purpose of
(a) consequential loss insurance;
(b) fidelity guarantee insurance.

3 What is the difference between employers' liability insurance, public liability insurance and product liability insurance?

4 Give three reasons why the directors of a company may seek to expand that company.

5 State three popular methods of measuring the size of a firm.

6 How can a firm grow through
  (a) internal expansion;
  (b) integration?

7 Explain the difference between the three forms of integration.

8 Which of the following is an example of lateral integration?
  (a) a car manufacturer takes over a shoe company;
  (b) two car manufacturers merge;
  (c) a car manufacturer takes over a chain of car retailers.

9 What advantages are associated with vertical integration?

10 Explain the difference between 'internal' and 'external' economies of scale and name five internal economies of scale.

11 Give two problems typically faced by small firms.

12 How has specialization helped some small firms to survive?

## Unit 7 The structure of organizations

1 Name five departments found in most large manufacturing companies.

2 Describe two ways in which firms are organized internally.

3 Distinguish between
  (a) 'span of control' and 'chain of command';
  (b) line and staff organization.

4 From the following extract of an organization chart, identify
  (a) the span of control of the Chief Accountant;
  (b) the chain of command from the Managing Director to the Wages Clerks.

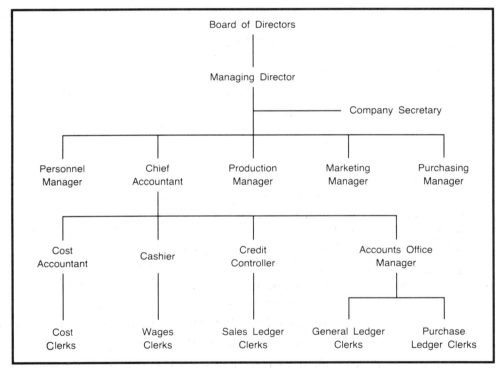

5 In the above chart, does the Company Secretary hold line or staff authority?

6 Explain the purpose of delegation.

## Unit 8 Production

1 Name four different costs of production faced by a car manufacturer.

2 What is the difference between
  (a) fixed and variable costs;
  (b) direct and indirect costs?

3 A firm produces 249 items at a total cost of £499.50: the total costs after making the 250th item are £500. What is
  (a) the firm's average cost of production;
  (b) the marginal cost of producing the last item?

4 Which of the following cost classifications is used in breakeven analysis?
average and marginal;
direct and indirect;
standard and budgeted;
fixed and variable.

5 Explain the importance to a firm of calculating its breakeven point.

6 From the chart below, state
   **(a)** the breakeven level of output;
   **(b)** the profit or loss made if 4000 units are made and sold.

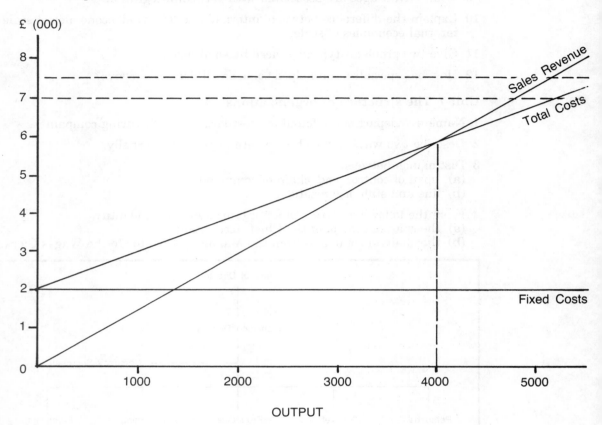

7 Calculate the breakeven level of output from the following:
   fixed costs £6000
   variable costs £1.50 per unit
   selling price £3.50 per unit

8 Distinguish between Job, Batch and Mass production.

9 Which of the following products would normally be produced using mass **production** techniques?

| bridges | televisions |
| double-glazed windows | cars |
| pavement slabs | curtains |

10 Explain the purpose of
   **(a)** production engineering;
   **(b)** production control;
   **(c)** quality control.

**Unit 9  Purchasing**

1 Name four items that a typical manufacturing company would have to purchase.

2 A purchasing department must provide the correct items in the correct _____, at the correct _____ and at the correct _____, and ensure they are delivered to the correct _____.

3 Describe the influences which must be taken into account by a purchasing department when establishing a purchasing policy.

4 State three stock levels that a stock control section will set.

## Unit 10 The accounting function

1 A firm's accountant will _____, _____, _____ and _____ financial information.

2 Which accounts are kept in
   (a) the Sales Ledger;
   (b) the Bought (or Purchases) Ledger?

3 Name the other two Ledgers which a company normally keeps.

4 Distinguish between 'profitability' and 'liquidity'.

5 Give one example of each of the following for a manufacturing company:
   (a) an expense;
   (b) a revenue;
   (c) an asset;
   (d) a liability.

6 Which two of the types of accounts in 5 above are used to calculate a firm's profit?

7 Give two examples of
   (a) fixed assets;
   (b) current assets;
   (c) current liabilities;
   (d) other liabilities.

8 What is the role of an auditor?

9 Explain why many firms set budgets.

10 Name, and state the method used to calculate, two ratios which check a firm's
   (a) profitability;
   (b) liquidity position;
   (c) use of its assets.

## Unit 11 Marketing

1 Name the 'four Ps' which make up the marketing mix.

2 In market research, what is the difference between 'desk' research and 'field' research?

3 Give three examples of
   (a) desk research;
   (b) field research.

4 Name and describe the four stages in the life-cycle of a product.

5 Which of the following pricing policies are 'high-price'?
   Capturing
   Maximizing
   Penetration
   Skimming

6 The three main forms of promotion are _____, _____ _____ and _____ _____.

7 Identify two reasons why firms advertise their products and give two benefits that can result from an advertising campaign.

8 Explain the difference between, and give an illustration of, 'persuasive' and 'informative' advertising.

9 State one suitable advertising medium for each of the following:
   (a) the launch of a new washing powder;
   (b) the launch of a new road running shoe;
   (c) a government health warning concerning the dangers of smoking;
   (d) a car boot sale;
   (e) a vacancy for a multinational's assistant managing director;
   (f) a special offer on Australian wines at a local Spar shop.

10 Which of the adverts in 9 is/are likely to be persuasive?

11 Give two advantages that newspaper advertising has over TV advertising.

12 Distinguish between personal selling and sales promotion.

13 Name five different methods used in sales promotion.

14 Branding products allows brand _____ to become established.

## Unit 12  Transport and distribution

1  Construct a diagram to show the four main channels of distribution used to get consumer goods from manufacturer to consumer.

2  Name four services provided by a wholesaler for
  (a)  the manufacturer;
  (b)  the retailer.

3  Give one example of
  (a)  a variety multiple;
  (b)  a department store.

4  Factors that determine the form of transport used include the _____ of the method of transport, the nature of the _____ and the _____ of delivery required.

5  State the form(s) of transport likely to be used for the following:
  (a)  the export of North Sea oil;
  (b)  importing Fiat cars into the UK;
  (c)  a machine part, at a company's London head office, urgently required at its Scotland office;
  (d)  a regional newspaper for the Midlands;
  (e)  moving radioactive materials from a nuclear power station.

## Unit 13  The personnel function

1  What is the difference between a job description and a job specification?

2  Give two advantages to a firm that come from promotion internally, rather than recruiting from outside.

3  If a firm wishes to advertise a post, name three external sources of recruitment that could be used.

4  Two Acts of Parliament which influence the content of the job advert are the _____ _____ Act and the _____ _____ Act.

5  What does an interview allow the interviewer to discover about the interviewee?

6  Name three different types of test that may take place at an interview.

7  Give five items of information that must be included in a contract of employment.

8  Why should a firm provide induction training for its new employees?

9  What is the difference between 'on-the-job' and 'off-the-job' training?

10  State three areas of work, other than recruitment, selection and training, for a typical personnel department.

## Unit 14  Work and its rewards

1  Give one reason why a manager should try to motivate his staff.

2  Name the five groups of needs suggested by Abraham Maslow.

3  What 'motivators' are there for employees, according to Herzberg?

4  State four of the elements that help provide job satisfaction.

5  Wage differentials result from factors such as the _____ of the work, the amount of natural _____ required to perform it, or the degree of _____ or level of _____ involved.

6  What is the difference between
  (a)  'time rate',
  (b)  'piece rate', and
  (c)  'flat rate' systems?

7  Name five different fringe benefits that a company may offer its workforce.

8  A person has a tax code of 375L. Her annual salary is £7800. State her
  (a)  tax-free pay;
  (b)  taxable pay.

9  Name one compulsory deduction, other than income tax, from a person's pay.

10  How is an employee's net pay calculated?

## Unit 15 Industrial relations

1 Name one example of
  (a) a craft union;
  (b) an industrial union;
  (c) a white-collar union.

2 Give three aims of trade unions.

3 What benefits do workers receive from union membership?

4 The central body of the trade union movement is the _____ _____ _____, and its equivalent for the employers is the _____ of _____ _____.

5 Name two other types of employers' associations.

6 Give two forms of non-strike action that a trade union can take, when in dispute with a firm.

7 ACAS stands for the _____, _____ and _____ _____.

8 How can ACAS help to resolve industrial disputes?

## Unit 16 Business documents

1 Which of the following business documents is/are sent by the buyer?
  Invoice        Advice Note
  Order          Statement
  Credit Note    Enquiry

2 What is a 'Pro-Forma' invoice?

3 Explain the different effects of a Debit Note and a Credit Note.

4 Give four items of information shown on an Invoice.

5 What purpose does 'E & O E' serve on a business document?

6 Describe two business documents used in foreign trade.

## Unit 17 Business communication

1 Give examples of internal and external business communication that take place.

2 Give one illustration where
  (a) a business letter; and
  (b) a business memorandum
  would be used by a firm's employees.

3 Besides letters and memos, what are the other major forms of written business communication?

4 State one advantage and one disadvantage to an employee of using a telephone rather than a business letter.

5 Name two formal meetings that will take place in a company.

6 What written details relating to a business meeting are sent out
  (a) before; and
  (b) after
  the meeting takes place?

7 Name three different forms of visual communication used in business.

8 Modern technology, such as computers, word processors and fax machines, is widely used to _____, _____ and _____ business communications.

9 Give four qualities of an efficient record-keeping system.

## Unit 18 Controlling business activity

1 Identify three important ways in which central government controls private sector firms.

2 Name three pressure groups. What objectives does each group have?

3 Name and state the purpose of three Acts of Parliament which control a firm's dealings with its employees.

4 Give three duties that an employee has under the 1974 HASAWA.

5 In a contract, one person or firm makes an _____ which is _____ by another. Both parties must have the _____ to enter the contract, and they must intend it to have _____ consequences. Both parties must also provide _____.

6 Name the Commission which checks whether proposed mergers between companies are in the public interest.

7 Explain the purpose of the following legislation:
   (a) the Trade Descriptions Act;
   (b) the Sale of Goods Act;
   (c) the Consumer Credit Act.

8 What role does the Advertising Standards Authority have in consumer protection?

### Unit 19 Aiding business activity

1 State two ways in which local government helps industry in its local area.

2 Name two central government statistical publications.

3 What is
   (a) the ECGD;
   (b) the BOTB?
   In what ways do they provide assistance to business?

4 Explain two ways in which central government provides financial assistance to business.

### Unit 20 The impact of change

1 Identify three types of change that can affect a company.

2 Name two advantages and two disadvantages that can result from a company automating its production processes.

3 What are 'CAD' and 'CAM'?

4 Give one example of how
   (a) a computer database; and
   (b) a computer spreadsheet
   are used in a company.

5 State two reasons why people resist change.

6 Give three ways that change affects people in, and seeking, employment.

## Answers to Self-test Questions

### Unit 1 The economic framework of business

1 Land, labour, capital, enterprise.

2 Having to forego one thing in order to have another: e.g. a company may have to forego bringing out a new product if it has just bought new machinery to improve production of existing products.

3 People producing what they need (Direct); people specializing (Indirect).

4 Greater efficiency; greater output and reduced unit costs.

5 Level of state control of the economy.

6 (a) High incentive; greater choice; greater competition.
   (b) Full use of resources; benefits of large-scale production; basic services will be provided.

7 Extractive; manufacturing/construction; commercial support services.

8 Items (e), (f) and (h) primary; (c) and (d) secondary; (a), (b) and (g) tertiary.

9 Buyers, sellers.

### Unit 2 Regional and national factors

1 Climate (agriculture); transport and communication systems; labour supply; situation of markets; external economies; government.

2 Birth rate; death rate; migration.

3 (a) matches with (ii); (b) and (iii); (c) and (v); (d) and (i); (e) and (iv).

4 Geographical, occupational.

5 (a) Inability to do work; pay levels.
   (b) Family ties; cost of housing.

6 Training and re-training schemes; regional grants/development areas and financial incentives.

## Unit 3 International factors

1 Choice, specialization, competition.

2 Increased competition from abroad; low-cost overseas manufacturers; weaknesses in UK management/labour/products.

3 Lack of natural resources; may reduce unemployment; need for foreign currency.

4 Exports: finished goods (e.g. industrial machinery) and semi-finished goods. Imports: finished goods, also fruit/vegetables and textiles.

5 Trade: 'visibles' (goods) only, calculated as visible exports less visible imports. Payments: visibles and invisibles, calculated as total exports less total imports.

6 Import duties (tariffs); physical restrictions (quotas).

7 To protect home industries; to protect 'infant' industries. Problem that other countries may reply 'in kind', leading to trade war.

8 **(a)** EC encourages free trade between member states: the CET fixes a common tariff level for other countries' imports;
  **(b)** IMF helps world trade, assists countries with trade problems, and seeks to keep exchange rates stable;
  **(c)** GATT tries to reduce trade barriers between countries.

9 A company producing in more than one country.

10 Multinationals may send their profits out of the UK; difficult to control their activities.

## Unit 4 Business organizations

1 Maximize profits; greater market share; survival.

2 Separate legal.

3 The liability of the company's owners (shareholders) is limited to the amount they have agreed to invest in the company. 'PLC' and 'ltd' warn traders that the company's owners do not have to meet its business debts out of their private wealth, and so traders may not recover trading debts from the owners.

4 Advantages: profits do not have to be shared; owner can make all the decisions. Disadvantages: long hours; problems if owner is ill.

5 More capital (expansion); partner shares responsibilities and burden of running the business.

6 **(a)** no entitlement;
  **(b)** shared equally;
  **(c)** interest on loans made by partners, at 5 per cent.
  The 1890 Act only operates if partners have made no other agreement.

7 **(a)** PLC can apply directly to the public to get share capital;
  **(b)** PLC in private sector and normally sets out to make profit; public corporation in public sector, normally providing public service;
  **(c)** Public sector state controlled and private sector in hands of individuals.

8 **(a)** Controls 'natural' monopolies such as water; ensures national security; ensures that unprofitable but vital services are provided.
  **(b)** Greater competition; wider share ownership in population; reduces the amount of government interference.

9 Worker cooperatives: a form of ownership/organization of private sector business, the employees running the firm. Retail cooperatives: a form of retail organization, supplied by the Cooperative Wholesale Society.

10 The franchisor company allows the franchisee to sell its products and supplies a range of marketing and other services.

## Unit 5 Business finance

1 **(a)** Treasury grants or loans; retained profits.
  **(b)** Local authority loans; retained profits.

2 Internal: generated from within the company, e.g. retained profits, trade credit, selling surplus assets. External: comes from other organizations, e.g. bank loan/mortgage, share capital, use of finance houses (leasing or HP).

3 Selling debts to a third party; it quickly releases (most of) the cash owed to the firm.

4 (a) Ordinary: voting rights, variable dividend, lowest priority for both dividend payment and repayment of capital. Preference: non-voting, fixed percentage dividend, ranked before Ordinary when it comes to dividend payment and repayment of capital.

  (b) (Preference points first): shares/long-term loans; normally not redeemable/normally redeemable; dividend paid out of profits/interest paid whether or not profits are made.

5 Commercial banks; Investors in Industry.

6 The type of project for which the capital is required; nature of the business; degree of risk involved; the cost of the method of finance.

7 Business accounts for handling receipts and payments of UK and foreign currency; savings/deposit accounts for surplus cash; bank giro (credit transfer) system for transfer of cash; advice on exporting, taxation, legal matters, etc.; night safes; provision of cash for wages.

## Unit 6 Business risk and growth

1 The company's products becoming unfashionable or obsolete; uninsurable because the risk cannot be accurately assessed.

2 Consequential loss: to cover a firm's loss of profits/income due to fire or other perils. Fidelity guarantee: to protect the firm against losses through dishonest employees.

3 Employers' liability: covers injury to employees. Public liability: covers injury to visitors on the employer's premises. Product liability: covers injury to buyers arising from employer's products.

4 For personal status and power; to obtain economies of scale; to improve the firm's chances of surviving.

5 Turnover (sales); capital employed; number of employees.

6 (a) By selling more products, or a new product, in existing markets; by selling its products in new markets.

  (b) Through merger with, or takeover of, other companies.

7 Horizontal: involves companies in the same industry and at the same stage of production. Lateral (conglomerate): the companies are in different industries/markets. Vertical: a company merges with or takes over another in the same industry, but at a different stage of production – either 'backwards' to the source of its raw materials, or 'forwards' to its customers.

8 (a) is lateral (b) is horizontal and (c) is vertical forwards.

9 The company gets a closer control over its suppliers and/or its markets; it now keeps the profits which were going to the other companies; economies of scale.

10 Internal: these relate to the firm itself, e.g. managerial, technical, financial, trading and risk-bearing economies. External: the firm gains through the industry as a whole growing.

11 Cost of borrowing is higher than for a large company; fewer products made and involvement in fewer markets, so higher risk.

12 Concentrating on a local market; providing a skilled, personal service; supplying expertise/components to large companies; providing items for which there is a limited, specialist demand.

## Unit 7 The structure of organizations

1 Production; Marketing or Sales; Accounts; Purchasing; Personnel.

2 By functions (departments); by products/markets.

3 (a) Span of control: the number of people directly controlled by someone. Chain of command: the formal line of communication from managing director through to the shop floor.

  (b) Line: the line of command within specialisms/departments. Staff: specialists outside the direct control of the department.

4 (a) Controlling the four staff directly under him.
  (b) Through Chief Accountant and Cashier.

5 Staff authority.

6 To pass on less important day-to-day decisions and work to subordinates, so that the manager can concentrate on the more important decision-making.

## Unit 8 Production

1 Cost of raw materials (e.g. sheet steel); wages of manufacturing staff; factory lighting and heating costs; costs of servicing and repairing factory machinery.

2 **(a)** Fixed costs do not vary with output; variable costs do.
   **(b)** Direct costs are directly associated with a particular product line; indirect costs apply to a range of products.

3 **(a)** Average costs £2.00 (£500 divided by 250).
   **(b)** Marginal cost of the 250th item is 50p (£500 less £499.50).

4 Fixed and variable costs.

5 It tells the firm how many products need to be made and sold before it starts to make a profit.

6 **(a)** 4000 units
   **(b)** Neither profit nor loss (the breakeven point).

7 Contribution is £3.50 less £1.50 = £2. The breakeven point is £6000 divided by £2 = 3000 units.

8 Job: production of a one-off item, made to customer's specialist requirements. Batch: production of a number of identical items. Mass: continuous or 'flow' production of a product.

9 Televisions and cars.

10 **(a)** To plan how a product is to be manufactured.
   **(b)** To ensure that production plans are being followed.
   **(c)** To check that waste from production is kept to a minimum.

## Unit 9 Purchasing

1 Raw materials; office stationery; manufacturing and office machinery; company cars.

2 Quantity, price, time, place.

3 Looking after the security of the stock (theft and deterioration); the need to guard against obsolesence; the need to help the company's cashflow.

4 Maximum; minimum; economic order quantity.

## Unit 10 The accounting function

1 Obtain, record, analyse, present.

2 **(a)** Customers (debtors)
   **(b)** Suppliers (creditors).

3 Cash Book; General Ledger.

4 Profitability: how much profit (or loss) the firm is making for the owner(s). Liquidity: whether it can repay the short-term debts it owes.

5 **(a)** Raw materials.
   **(b)** Sales.
   **(c)** Cash.
   **(d)** Bank overdraft.

6 Expenses and revenues.

7 **(a)** Machinery; vehicles.
   **(b)** Stocks; debtors.
   **(c)** Creditors; overdraft.
   **(d)** Capital: debentures.

8 To check that the firm's accounts give a true and fair view of its financial position.

9 So that financial plans can be drawn up for the future.

10 **(a)** Return on capital employed (net profit as a percentage of capital employed): net profit percentage (net profit over sales, multiplied by 100).
   **(b)** Working capital ratio (current assets to current liabilities): liquid assets ratio (current assets less stock, to current liabilities).
   **(c)** Rate of stock turnover (cost of sales divided by average stock): debtors' collection period (debtors over sales, multiplied by 365).

### Unit 11 Marketing

1 Price; promotion; product; place.

2 Desk research uses existing sources of information: field research involves obtaining new information.

3 (a) Government statistics; the firm's own statistical information; information from 'quality' newspapers.
  (b) Questionnaires (postal, telephone or face-to-face); test marketing; consumer testing panels.

4 Introduction: designing and launching the product. Growth: establishing brand loyalty amongst the population. Maturity: reaching peak sales and market saturation. Decline: market share falls.

5 Maximizing and skimming.

6 Advertising, personal selling, sales promotion.

7 To introduce new products onto the market; to boost sales. Improved company image; increased sales levels.

8 Persuasive tries to convince potential customers that they need the product or brand; e.g. TV advertising of different brands of jeans or of petrol. Informative gives non-persuasive details, e.g. newspaper advertising of jobs or college courses.

9 (a) TV (nationwide, mass product).
  (b) Specialist magazine (limited interest).
  (c) Posters/packaging.
  (d) Local newspaper.
  (e) National 'quality' newspaper.
  (f) Door-to-door leaflets.

10 Item (a), also elements of (b), (c) and (f) may be persuasive.

11 A more permanent message; can provide more information.

12 Personal selling uses sales staff to talk to customers, providing them with information and advice; sales promotion uses a variety of techniques to support the advertising campaign and 'push' the product.

13 Free samples; premium offers; competitions; price reductions; after-sales service.

14 Loyalties.

### Unit 12 Transport and distribution

1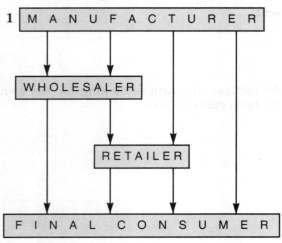

2 (a) Buying in bulk; storage; giving advice on sales performance; promoting the product.
  (b) Breaking bulk; giving product information; providing a choice of products; services such as giving credit, or delivering the goods.

3 (a) Marks and Spencer.
  (b) Debenhams.

4 Cost, product, speed.

5 (a) Tanker ships and lorries.
  (b) Ship, rail and car transporter lorries.

**(c)** Air or rail, then van or lorry.
**(d)** Delivery vans.
**(e)** Rail and road.

## Unit 13  The personnel function

1  Job description outlines the type of work; job specification describes the qualities needed by the worker to do the work.

2  Greater motivation for existing staff; less expensive/time-consuming.

3  Jobcentres, private recruitment agencies, newspapers.

4  Race Relations, Sex Discrimination.

5  Appearance; communication and social skills; general confidence; general suitability for the post.

6  Personality; aptitude; intelligence.

7  Names of both parties; job title; notice required; pay and intervals of payment; hours of work.

8  To motivate them and to enable them to settle down quickly.

9  On-the-job: instruction at work, often by an employee skilled in the work being taught. Off-the-job: external training, e.g. taking qualification at local college.

10  Looking after staff welfare; keeping staff records; handling industrial relations.

## Unit 14  Work and its rewards

1  Improves efficiency and helps avoid industrial disputes.

2  Basic; safety; social; ego; self-fulfilment.

3  Having work recognized; feeling of achievement; promotion or advancement available; being given greater responsibility.

4  Pay; hours; environment; security.

5  Location, ability, danger, qualifications.

6  **(a)** Payment per hour worked.
   **(b)** Payment for each item ('piece') made.
   **(c)** Fixed payment per week/month.

7  Company cars; subsidized travel; company products at a discount; cheap loans/mortgages; membership of private health schemes.

8  **(a)** £3750.
   **(b)** £4050 (£7800 − £3750).

9  National Insurance contributions.

10  Gross pay calculated (e.g. hours worked times rate per hour); compulsory deductions, e.g. tax, and voluntary deductions, e.g. trade union subscription, are taken off gross pay to leave the net pay.

## Unit 15  Industrial relations

1  **(a)** National Graphical Association.
   **(b)** National Union of Mineworkers.
   **(c)** National Union of Teachers.

2  To protect their members (e.g. against unfair dismissal); to negotiate with employers on behalf of their members; to influence employers and the Government for the benefit of their members.

3  Support in individual or group disputes; the chance of improved pay and conditions; opportunity to join training, social and other schemes run by the union.

4  Trades Union Congress, Confederation (of) British Industry.

5  Local Chamber of Commerce; trade association, e.g. Road Haulage Association.

6  Overtime ban; work-to-rule.

7  Advisory, Conciliation (and) Arbitration Service.

8  Through its conciliation service finding common ground for further negotiations; through its arbitration service, where an independent third party makes the settlement.

## Unit 16 Business documents

1 Order, Enquiry.

2 An invoice requesting payment for the goods before despatch; also used where goods sent on 'sale or return' basis.

3 The effect of a Debit Note is to increase the Invoice total: a Credit Note reduces the amount owed by the buyer (e.g. due to return of faulty goods).

4 Addresses of seller and buyer (including delivery address); details of the goods to be sold; unit prices and total price; VAT and discount adjustments.

5 'Errors and Omissions Excepted', so that any errors on the Invoice, such as undercharging for the goods, can be corrected later by the seller.

6 Bill of Lading; gives details and destination of the goods. Certificate of Origin; states the original country of origin of the goods.

## Unit 17 Business communication

1 Internal: memos, telephone, notices, meetings. External: letters, telephone, fax, telex, publication of annual accounts.

2 (a) From the Purchasing Department to a possible new supplier, requesting prices, etc.
(b) From Stores to other departments, informing them that new stationery has been received.

3 Minutes of meetings; reports; notices; company magazines.

4 Advantage: speed. Disadvantage: no written record of the conversation.

5 Safety Committee meeting; meeting of Board of Directors.

6 (a) Agenda.
(b) Minutes.

7 Charts/graphs; maps; pictures/photographs.

8 Prepare, transmit, store.

9 It can be expanded; the information is secure/protected; the system is easily understandable; easy access for authorized users.

## Unit 18 Controlling business activity

1 Through its health and safety laws; by controlling monopolies and mergers; through consumer legislation, e.g. on the sale of goods.

2 Action on Smoking and Health: to persuade people to give up smoking tobacco. Greenpeace: to protect and improve the world's environment. National Union of Mineworkers: to protect miners' pay, improve working conditions and help mining communities to survive.

3 Health and Safety at Work Act: to make sure that employers follow certain health and safety practices. Race Relations Act: to help prevent racial prejudice in employment. Equal Pay Act: to ensure equal pay for men and women doing similar work.

4 To take care of themselves and others at work; not to interfere with safety or other equipment; to work with the employer on health and safety matters.

5 Offer, accepted, capacity, legal, consideration.

6 Monopolies and Mergers Commission.

7 (a) To stop false descriptions being made about goods.
(b) To ensure that goods for sale in shops are of suitable quality and fit for their intended use.
(c) To register and control firms which give credit.

8 It controls the advertising industry, e.g. by considering complaints about specific adverts made to it by members of the public.

## Unit 19 Aiding business activity

1 By allowing factory/office extensions to be built; by helping in the disposal of the firms' waste materials.

2 Social Trends; Regional Trends.

3 (a) Export Credit Guarantee Department, providing 'bad debts' insurance for exporters.
(b) British Overseas Trade Board, providing a wide range of services to exporters, such as the Export Market Research Scheme which helps with overseas market research.

4 Subsidies for struggling firms, to help them stay in business and provide employment; regional policy/enterprise zone grants, to encourage firms to set up in business there.

## Unit 20 The impact of change

1 Changes in consumer tastes, changes in production methods, changes in technology available to it (e.g. communications technology).

2 Advantages: increased production levels, easier quality control. Disadvantages: possible redundancies, the investment in expensive equipment may not pay off.

3 Computer-Aided Design; Computer-Aided Manufacture.

4 **(a)** Records of suppliers, customers or employees.
   **(b)** Calculating profit or loss, or breakeven points.

5 The change may lead to loss of status or personal power; fear of the new methods and systems.

6 The need to gain new skills and expertise; the need to change occupations more frequently than in the past; more time for leisure activities.

# 22 TYPES OF GCSE EXAMINATION QUESTIONS

## 22.1 Introduction

In addition to your teacher, there are three further sources of information about the types of questions used in examination papers in Business Studies. Details of the exam can be checked in the course syllabus; specimen examination questions are available; and past examination papers can be studied.

The **syllabus** provides information about the form that the examination will take. For example:

**Scheme of Assessment**
The examination will consist of two written papers and an internal assessment of coursework.

**Examination Papers**
Allocation of marks 70 per cent.
All questions will be compulsory and will be drawn from any part of the syllabus. All of the assessment objectives will be tested. The use of a calculator is permitted.

**Paper 1**
Allocation of marks 35 per cent. Working time 1½ hours. Three structured questions based on case studies or other stimulus material.

**Paper 2**
Allocation of marks 35 per cent. Working time 1½ hours. One extended case study.

*(Part of the NEA Business Studies syllabus)*

Summaries of the various Examining Groups' examination requirements are given in the 'Assessment patterns and weightings' section on page x. There is also a brief syllabus analysis on page viii of this book. You can obtain your own syllabus for the examination you are taking: addresses of the Examining Groups are given on page xiii. It is likely that your school or college library will have a copy of the syllabus, in the Reference section, for you to study. Your teacher or librarian can advise you.

**Specimen examination questions** provide a guide to the standard and the structure of the questions you will face in your examination. These specimen questions are sometimes included in the syllabus booklet, or they may be published separately by the Examining Group.

**Past examination papers** for GCSE Business Studies are available (normally at a small charge) from the various Examining Groups: they may also be available for study in your school or college library. These papers obviously provide the best illustration of the type of questions and the structure of the exam paper. A word of caution, however. The GCSE is a new examination and the Examining Groups are still heavily involved in revising syllabuses and examination procedures. You therefore need to check – with your teacher, or in the syllabus – that the examination you will be sitting will have the same structure and type of questions as these past examination papers.

## 22.2 Short-answer Questions

To answer these questions, you are required to provide a word, phrase or sentence as the answer. They are not very popular methods of testing your understanding of business, since they are rather limited in scope; other forms of question are more appropriate for testing higher levels of understanding.

The main features of these questions are as follows:

1 A limited answer only is required. This answer is normally descriptive, although sometimes you may be asked to do a calculation.

2 Typical questions (see next page) require you to either define a set of initials, provide an example of a business activity or organization, or give a brief description of this activity/organization.

3 The exam paper often doubles as your answer book: the short-answer question is given as a statement, or as the first part of a sentence, and you have to complete the line or lines provided for your answer.

**4** Marks for each short-answer question are normally given in brackets at the end of each question.

Examples of short-answer questions are as follows:

**Q.2** CBI stands for the _____

_____ **(1)**

**Q.6** **(a)** ONE example of a pressure group is _____

_____

**(b)** State briefly what this group is trying to achieve _____

_____

_____ **(2)**

(*LEAG GCSE Business Studies Paper 2B, 1988*)

In answering question 2, you should simply have to write 'Confederation of British Industry'. In question 6, a pressure group would have to be named in part (a) (e.g. 'Friends of the Earth'); part (b)'s answer would describe its work (in this example, by a phrase explaining its interest in environmental matters and perhaps mentioning its interest in controlling 'toxic waste' business pollution).

## 22.3 Data-response Questions

These are currently the most popular form of exam question in GCSE Business Studies. They have a number of features:

**1** An 'information component' – the **data** – sets the scene and is used in answering the questions – the **response** – that follow.

**2** The information component may be wholly descriptive; it may consist partly (or mainly) of numerical data, e.g. final accounts; and some of it may be organized diagrammatically, such as the use of a bar chart or graph to show a company's progress.

**3** The length of the information will also vary: there may be a little or a substantial amount, which has to be studied at the time of the examination; or it may be in the form of a 'seen case study', sent out to candidates about a month before the examination. Some structured questions may also introduce additional elements of information as you work through them.

**4** The question is a **structured** one: the various questions are organized on an 'incline of difficulty', easier ones being provided at the start, with the more difficult ones following.

**5** Marks are again normally shown in brackets at the end of each question.

**6** The exam paper may once again act as the answer book. Guidance is given as to the length of answer required, by the number of blank lines which follow each question.

### DESCRIPTIVE QUESTIONS

The information provided in a data-response question will be at least partly descriptive. This tests your ability to:

**1** Read the information carefully (more than once).

**2** Read and study the requirements of the various questions.

**3** Identify the relevant items of data or information to use in answering each question.

You will also have to use your knowledge of different syllabus areas in answering these questions and also – if possible – draw on any work experience you have. The information on the GCSE contains a section on grade criteria (page xv), which explain the type of skills that candidates have to demonstrate to achieve grades C and F. These criteria give an indication of the skills you need to answer these data-response questions.

The style of your answer is important. A valuable approach is to **plan** briefly your answer, identifying key words and points that need to be made, and the order in which they are to appear. Only **relevant** information should be included: do not write down information simply because you can recall it. A final tip is to include as many up-to-date **examples** as you can, to support any general points that you have to make to answer the question.

An example of a descriptive data-response question is given overleaf.

QUESTION A (Units 13 and 18)

Read the advertisement below which is to appear in a local newspaper.

---

## Wanted for small office in the town centre

### TRAINEE CLERK
### TO UNDERTAKE GENERAL OFFICE DUTIES

She must be aged 16–18
have good English and Maths GCSE grades
and RSA Typewriting Skills Stage 1 or Joint RSA/GCSE grade C

### SALARY £6000 per annum

Hours–35 per week on flexitime–no Saturday working
Luncheon Vouchers

---

(a) What is the meaning of the terms:
   (i) 'luncheon vouchers'
   (ii) 'flexitime' **(4)**

(b) How does the above advertisement break current laws on discrimination? **(2)**

**Julie lives on the outskirts of town. She is qualified for the job advertised above. She is also interested in a job in her local hypermarket as a checkout operator. It pays £100 per week for 39 hours on shifts Monday–Saturday.**

(c)  (i) What are the advantages for Julie of the hypermarket job?
    (ii) What are the disadvantages for Julie of the job in town? **(12)**

(d) Julie is offered both jobs. She decides to take the job in town. She makes her decision because of what she learned about the firms at the interviews. What kind of things may have persuaded her to take the town job? **(12)**

(e) What qualities other than those mentioned in the advertisement will interviewers be looking for in the applicants? **(10)**

           **(40 marks out of 200)**
           (*SEG GCSE Business Studies Paper 1, 1988*)

For an outline suggested answer, see Unit 23.

## NUMERICAL AND DIAGRAMMATIC QUESTIONS

The GCSE syllabuses contain topics–accounts, production, marketing, etc–which are often assessed using diagrams and/or numbers. Diagrams popularly used include breakeven charts (see below) and histograms. Final accounts questions are good illustrations of those data-response questions containing numerical information.

In answering these questions, you have to study and interpret the information provided and will probably have to calculate and/or display figures. Any calculations made should be supported by your **workings**, so that the examiner can see how an answer has been obtained. All diagrams must be **plotted** accurately, **labelled** clearly, and be given a suitable **title**.

An example of such a question is shown below.

QUESTION B (Unit 8)

Top Sports Ltd is a small family owned manufacturing business which sells vests to a number of athletics clubs. Past and present sales figures suggest that next year the firm will be able to sell 10 000 vests at £2.50 each, or 8000 vests at £2.60 each.

Top Sports decides to fix the price of its vests next year at £2.50 each.
(a) Explain why Top Sports chose the price of £2.50 instead of £2.60 each. **(3)**

Fixed costs of production next year are estimated at £10 000 and variable (direct) costs at £1 per vest.
(b) Construct a breakeven chart to show next year's
   (i) breakeven level of output **(4)**
   (ii) expected profit at 10 000 sales. **(2)**

(c) If the Government decided to increase the rate of VAT, so that the price of Top Sports vests would have to rise by 4 per cent, explain the effect of this on next year's
   (i) breakeven level of output
   (ii) expected profit. **(6)**

           **(15 marks out of 40)**
           (*LEAG GCSE Business Studies Paper 2A, 1988*)

For an outline suggested answer, see Unit 23.

## 'SEEN' AND 'UNSEEN' CASE STUDIES

The term 'case study' is widely used to describe a type of data-response question. In a case study, the information in the question usually gives a situation (often describing the background of a company or of its owner), upon which a business problem is built. The structured questions in some way relate to this business problem.

'Unseen' case studies – where candidates are given the case study at the start of the examination – are tackled in the same way as other data-response questions.

Some Groups operate examination papers which are based on 'seen' case studies. Here, the case study is sent out in advance of the examination: candidates study this detail and then answer unseen questions given to them at the start of the exam. With seen case studies, there is an opportunity to examine in depth the information provided and to plan for certain expected questions. If, for example, the case study contains a range of financial costs and revenues associated with a company, candidates can anticipate being asked to calculate ratios related to the company's profitability or liquidity, or perhaps to prepare a breakeven chart. In these situations it is important to try to anticipate likely questions: but it is still necessary to revise thoroughly all aspects of the syllabus, and not to rely wholly on 'hunches' about possible areas of questioning.

# 23 GCSE QUESTIONS AND ANSWERS

## Short-answer Questions

**1** (Unit 4)
Describe one important economy of scale. **(1)**

*(LEAG GCSE Business Studies Paper 2B, 1988)*

**2** (Units 10 and 16)
 **(a)** **(i)** Name one business document used to keep records.
   **(ii)** What sort of information is contained in this document?
 **(b)** What is the main purpose of a budget? **(2)**

*(LEAG GCSE Business Studies Paper 2A, 1988)*

**3** (Unit 17)
 **(a)** **(i)** Name one method of communication.
   **(ii)** Suggest one situation in which this method of communication would be most useful.
 **(b)** Give one reason why communication is important in the business world. **(2)**

*(LEAG GCSE Business Studies Paper 2A, 1988)*

## Data-response Questions

QUESTION A (Units 13 and 18): see page 150.

QUESTION B (Unit 8): see page 150.

QUESTION C (Units 1, 2 and 12)
London Newspapers plc is aiming to launch a new London and surrounding counties evening newspaper. This will involve setting up a modern production and distribution plant at one of four sites (A, B, C or D) shown on the map below.
 **(a)** Explain the main characteristics of the consumer market for a London evening newspaper. **(3)**
 **(b)** What channel of distribution and form of transport would you suggest as the most appropriate to deliver newspapers from the production site to the retailer? **(4)**
 **(c)** Explain at which site (A, B, C or D) you would locate the new production and distribution plant. Give reasons for your answer. **(8)**

**(15 marks out of 40)**

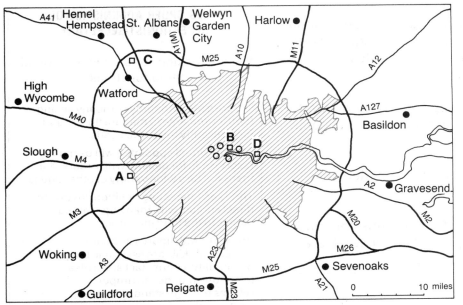

KEY
■ Greater London
○ British Rail main line stations
M25 Motorways

□ POSSIBLE LOCATION SITES
A Existing warehousing at Heathrow Airport
B Existing newspaper offices in Fleet Street (Central London)
C A site close to the M1/M25
D A site in London's Dockland (a redeveloped industrial zone)

*(LEAG GCSE Business Studies Paper 2A, 1988)*

QUESTION D (Units 2 and 5)

Anglia Fashions is a private company designing and manufacturing clothes mainly for 15 to 19 year olds. The managing director of the company has suggested that the company expand its output by building a new factory.

**(a)** **(i)** Suggest one internal source of finance, and                                                                 **(1)**
   **(ii)** one external source of finance which might be available to Anglia Fashions to pay for the building of a new factory.                                                                **(1)**
  **(iii)** Suggest which one of these sources of finance would be best for Anglia Fashions to use in this situation. Give one reason for your answer.                                        **(3)**

**(b)** The structure of the UK population in 1981 is shown in the diagram below.
   **(i)** Explain two effects the changes in population structure are likely to have on the demand for Anglia Fashion's products over the next 10 years.                                  **(4)**
  **(ii)** Suggest three ways in which Anglia Fashions would overcome these effects.              **(6)**

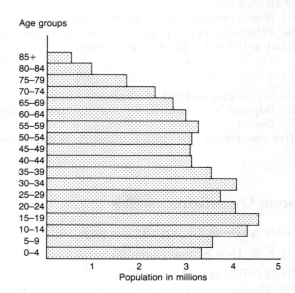

(*LEAG GCSE Business Studies Paper 2B, 1988*)

QUESTION E (Units 2, 13 and 14)

**(a)** Read the information given in the two advertisements and answer the questions which follow.

**Advertisement A**                                  **Advertisement B**

**ALTAMY LTD**

require a hard working, energetic young person to work in the challenging world of double glazing sales.

The successful applicant will be smart, lively and able to get on well with people.

Training will be provided.

The pay is based on commission, and earnings of up to £300 per week are possible.

**Weltex Limited**

**SALES ORDER ADMINISTRATOR/ RECEPTIONIST/SECRETARY**

We are looking for someone to do all three functions!

We are a busy, friendly company selling food ingredients to manufacturers and have recently moved to Leeds.

The individual appointed will be mainly responsible for dealing with orders, but there will be a wide variety of other duties.

This is an interesting position, involving direct contact with many household names in the food industry.

An ability with figures and some secretarial skills are essential, but good personality, charm, tact and a pleasant telephone manner are important. The pay reflects the high standard and experience we are looking for.

(i) In **advertisement A**, state with reasons what kind of training might be given to the successful candidate. **(10)**

(ii) In **advertisement B**, what is meant by 'dealing with orders'? Use examples to illustrate your answer. **(10)**

(iii) Explain what a firm should consider about a job before employing new people. Use examples from the advertisements to illustrate your answer. **(15)**

(iv) Apart from good pay, say what there is about these two jobs that might motivate the successful applicants, and explain why you think so. **(15)**

(b) The following is an internal memo from the Personnel Officer in Altamy Ltd (see advertisement A).

---

MEMO                                                            Date: 05.05.88

From: Personnel Officer                                     To: Head of Sales

Below is a summary of the number of staff who left and were replaced last year. It is fairly obvious that a problem exists in your department. I should like to discuss your views on this at our next meeting. Please come prepared with a short report, saying why your department has this problem, and outlining any action you feel we might take to improve matters.

**Staff turnover**

| Department | Total number employed | Left and replaced |
|---|---|---|
| Assembly | 150 | 10 |
| Maintenance | 10 | 1 |
| Office | 12 | 2 |
| Sales | 5 | 4 |

---

Answer the memo with the kind of report you would expect the Head of Sales to write, including the following points.
1 The nature of the main problem;
2 why it is a problem to the firm;
3 what might be done about it. **(15)**

(c) In recent years there has been a change in the proportion of men and women in the Weltex labour force. The graph below shows this change. (See advertisement B).

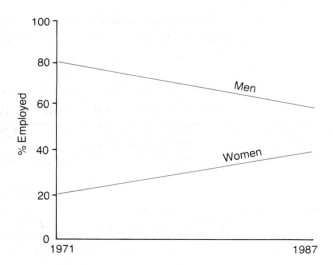

What has happened to the proportion of men and women employed in Weltex Limited? Give reasons why you think this might have happened. **(15)**

(*NEA Syllabus A Business Studies Paper 1, 1988*)

QUESTION F (Units 3 and 17)

Study the information below carefully, and answer the questions.

Oldport Docks

| *Imports* | '000 Tonnes | *Exports* | '000 Tonnes |
|---|---|---|---|
| Iron ore and other metals | 1 900 000 | Coal and coke | 500 000 |
| Timber | 200 000 | Iron and steel | 150 000 |
| Fruit | 104 000 | Chemicals | 100 000 |
| Others | 55 000 | Others | 50 000 |

(a) Why does the United Kingdom import metals, timber and fruit? **(5)**

(b) Why do we buy cars from other countries when we can produce our own? **(4)**

(c) Draw a bar chart in your answer book to show clearly the different amounts of exports from Oldport docks. **(4)**

(**13** marks out of **80**)

(*WJEC Business Studies Paper 2, 1988*)

QUESTION G (Units 4, 5, 10 and 11)

F Brown is the sole owner of a small market garden business. It is on the edge of a medium sized town. The firm has a small shop on the site, selling its produce. Brown has decided to expand the shop and buy in flowers, vegetables and garden equipment from wholesalers. Brown is a good gardener but has few business skills.

(a) What extra costs might be involved in expanding the business? **(8)**

(b) Brown needs advice on how to finance this expansion. Where could he get this advice? **(4)**

(c) Brown considers two alternatives:
  (i) Borrowing the money from a bank
  (ii) Taking on a partner
  What are the advantages and disadvantages of each? **(12)**

(d) To increase his sales Brown decides he will need to advertise.
  (i) How could he find out the type of consumer he should be trying to reach? **(8)**
  (ii) What methods of advertising is Brown likely to use?
    Give reasons to support your ideas. **(8)**

> **BROWN'S GARDEN SHOP**
> Now Open
>
> The Cheapest Garden Produce in Town
> Our Carrots improve your Eyesight
>
> **ALL HOME GROWN PRODUCE**
>
> On the A599 2m south of the Town Centre
> 'You know what you are getting at Browns'

(e) He produces the above advertisement. In what ways would you change it to make sure that it did not break the Advertising Standards Authority's Code of Practice. **(6)**

(**46** marks out of **200**)

(*SEG GCSE Business Studies Paper 1, 1988*)

QUESTION H (Units 7, 8 and 14)

Look at the organization chart on the next page and answer the following questions.

(a) How many levels of authority exist above the shop floor? **(1)**

(b) All the departments are divided into sections. What do you think the other three sections of the Marketing Department might be? **(3)**

(c) The Managing Director needs to tell the workforce about a new payment system.
  (i) List three ways in which he could do this. **(3)**
  (ii) Choose one way from your list and explain why it would be an appropriate method in this situation. **(2)**

(d) Gary Jones is one of the biscuit makers. Under the new payment system he will be paid on a piece rate, while the office staff are paid a salary.
  Explain the two payment systems mentioned.
  (i) piece rate **(2)**
  (ii) salary **(2)**

(e) Explain why Gary might not like being paid piece rate. **(2)**

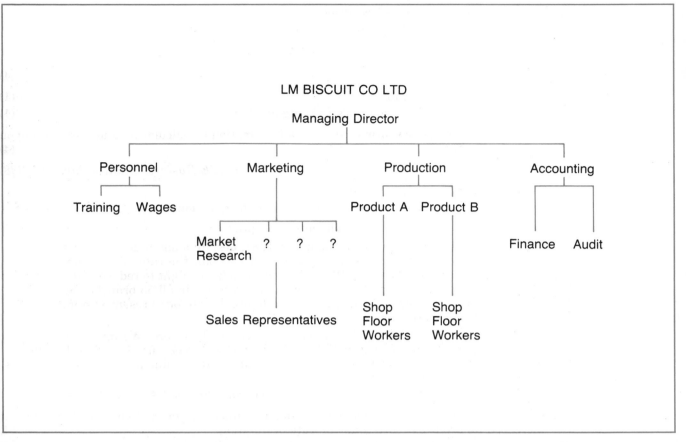

LM BISCUIT CO LTD

Managing Director

Personnel — Marketing — Production — Accounting

Personnel: Training, Wages

Marketing: Market Research, ?, ?, ? — Sales Representatives

Production: Product A, Product B — Shop Floor Workers, Shop Floor Workers

Accounting: Finance, Audit

**(f)** LM Biscuits could make their biscuits using a job, batch or flow system of production. Say, giving a reason, which of these three methods is likely to be used by the company. **(3)**

**(18** marks out of **100)**

(*MEG GCSE Business Studies Paper 1, 1988*)

QUESTION I (Unit 10)

Data Information is a public limited company with a large number of individual shareholders. The balance sheet shown below was presented to shareholders at their annual general meeting.

Data Information plc. Balance sheet as at 31.12.87

|  | £m | £m | £m |
|---|---|---|---|
| Fixed assets |  |  |  |
| Land and building |  | 80 |  |
| Machinery |  | 70 |  |
|  |  |  | 150 |
| Current assets |  |  |  |
| Stock | 110 |  |  |
| Debtors | 5 |  |  |
| Cash | 5 |  |  |
|  |  | 120 |  |
| Current liabilities |  |  |  |
| Creditors | 10 |  |  |
| Overdraft | 10 |  |  |
|  |  | 20 |  |
|  |  |  | 100 |
| Net assets employed |  |  | 250 |
| Financed by |  |  |  |
| Ordinary shares |  | 100 |  |
| Long term bank loan |  | 100 |  |
| Reserves |  | 50 |  |
|  |  |  | 250 |

(a) Explain what is meant by the terms
    (i) fixed asset
    (ii) debtor
    (iii) creditors
    (iv) reserves.    **(4)**

(b)   (i) What is working capital?    **(1)**
    (ii) Calculate Data Information's working capital.    **(1)**

(c) Analyse the business performance of Data Information by calculating and commenting on two relevant ratios.    **(4)**

*(LEAG GCSE Business Studies Paper 1, 1988)*

## QUESTION J (Units 11, 13, 19 and 20)
Study the information below carefully, and answer the questions.

### Directors Report

The company continued to expand in 1987, despite a small decline in its market share. It increased its profit by more than the rate of inflation, despite fierce competition. We have continued in our fight to reduce costs. Our new computer booking system will be installed in all 56 branches by the end of September 1988. It is very different from our present system and much more efficient.

Competition in the tourist industry is increasingly severe. We intend to try and regain our market share by introducing special offers for all customers who book a holiday of more than £200 in value at any of our branches.

*(Extract from the 1987 Annual Report)*

(a) Suggest reasons why the firm suffered a small decline in its market share in 1987 and yet increased its profit by more than the rate of inflation.    **(4)**
(b) Comment on whether you think the special offers will, in fact, increase profits.    **(3)**
(c) What problems might the new computer system cause?    **(5)**
(d) The firm agrees to employ one YTS employee in each of their branches.
    (i) What is the YTS scheme?    **(5)**
    (ii) What problems might the trainee cause the firm in the first few weeks of employment?    **(5)**

**(22 marks out of 80)**

*(WJEC Business Studies Paper 3, 1988)*

## QUESTION K Case Study: (Units 4, 8, 10, 11 and 14)

### Parry Games Ltd

Parry Games Ltd is a family business based in the East Midlands which makes card games for a large retail chain. The business has been profitable for a number of years but has not expanded very much because the Parry family are unwilling to involve outsiders in the ownership of the business. Over 90 per cent of their sales go to one buyer whom they have dealt with for 25 years and their other sales go to a number of small toy shops who are also regular customers.

Parry's produce a variety of card games and sales of their products have been growing slowly over the last five years. They do not employ a sales force as the Managing Director takes responsibility for dealing with their customers and for all marketing of the products.

Over the last five years Parry's have experienced a steady increase in their raw material costs as the price of imported paper has risen. Wage costs have also gone up in line with other businesses. Parry's have found it difficult to pass these increased costs on to their customers by increasing the price of the card games. Information from the Accountant, shown in figure A, shows the effect of these developments on the profits of the business.

Parry's have recently encouraged their workers to produce new ideas for games in a suggestion scheme. One idea, from Paula Long, a designer, has interested the Managing Director. Paula suggested that Parry's should produce a board game called 'Enterprise' based on running a small business. With their sales of card games only increasing slowly, the

Managing Director likes the idea of a new product and decides that a consumer survey is needed to find out if there is a market for 'Enterprise'.

As a result of this market research, the Managing Director is able to forecast sales of about 16 000 board games per annum. This then allows the Accountants to produce a budget for 'Enterprise', which is shown in figure B. The market research has also shown that consumer attitudes towards 'Enterprise' are quite favourable. However, the Managing Director is worried about the changes in sales force that will be needed to compete in the large board game market. A final decision about 'Enterprise' now has to be taken.

**1 (a)** Suggest two objectives that a family business like Parry's might follow. **(2)**

**(b)** Why are many family businesses organized as private limited companies? **(3)**

**(c)** Why might working for a family business be better than working for a large business? **(3)**

**Figure A**

PARRY'S RESULTS 1983/1987

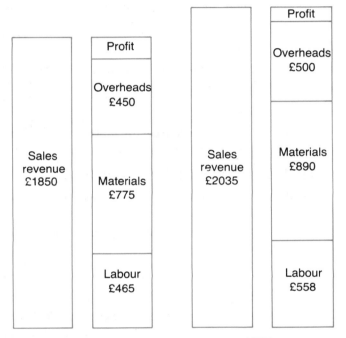

1983
FIGURES IN THOUSANDS

1987
FIGURES IN THOUSANDS

**Figure B**

BUDGET FOR 'ENTERPRISE'

| Revenue | |
| --- | --- |
| Sales volume (forecast) | 16 000 units |
| Selling price | £20.00 Per unit |

| Costs | |
| --- | --- |
| Labour | £5.00 Per unit |
| Materials | £8.50 Per unit |
| Increase in overheads | £50 000 |

**2** The Accountant can calculate the business's profitability by using the ratio

$$\frac{\text{profit}}{\text{sales revenue}} \times 100$$

(a) What is Parry's profit for 1983 and 1987? **(2)**

(b) Using the ratio the Accountant calculated that profitablity for 1983 is 8.65 per cent. What is it for 1987? **(3)**

(c) (i) What changes have taken place which might have influenced profitability? **(4)**
    (ii) Suggest reasons why these changes may have occurred. **(4)**

3 (a) Parry's carry out a survey to find out customer opinions about 'Enterprise'. Write a report for the Managing Director that outlines the stages that the business would need to go through both in planning and carrying out the survey. **(12)**

   (b) What information would the Managing Director expect to find out from market research about 'Enterprise'? **(6)**

4 The idea for 'Enterprise' came from a suggestion scheme.

   (a) Explain two other ways in which the workforce could give management ideas about the business. **(6)**

   (b) Why would the business want to involve the workforce in making decisions? **(5)**

5 Making use of information in the case study, and in figure B, plus any ideas that you would like to add, what would you recommend the company do about 'Enterprise'? Give reasons for your decision. **(2)**

**(52 marks out of 62)**

*(MEG GCSE Business Studies Paper 3, 1988)*

## Answers

These answers are entirely those of the author, and the various Examination Groups accept no responsibility for the accuracy or method of working.

### SHORT-ANSWER QUESTIONS

1 Financial: larger companies can borrow at cheaper rates than smaller companies.

2 (a) (i) Invoice.
      (ii) Description of goods; financial information (unit and total prices, VAT, discounts); details of buyer and seller.

   (b) To forecast future income and expenditure.

3 (a) (i) Oral.
      (ii) Goods required urgently; could be ordered over the 'phone.

   (b) Transfer of information quickly and efficiently keeps costs down.

### DATA-RESPONSE ANSWERS

**Question A (page 150)**

(a) (i) 'Perk' of voucher having a cash value; redeemed against food bought, typically in lunch hour.
    (ii) Staff allowed to start any time between (say) 8 and 10 a.m., and finish between (say) 4 and 6 p.m.; total hours (35 in this example) must be worked.

(b) Assumes females only ('She . . .'): sex discrimination.

(c) (i) Easier to get to (save time and lower travel costs); probable staff discount on goods sold; shift-work may allow her more free time during the day; work may be less demanding; more likely to be chance of promotion in a large organization.
    (ii) Travel (cost and time); may dislike working in a small office; may be fewer promotion chances.

(d) Pay is higher; 'perks' (luncheon vouchers) offered; lower hours; hours may be more sociable; no Saturday work; greater range of duties (more interesting work); may have liked the atmosphere of the office at interview.

(e) Reliability (attendance); personality; acceptable 'business' appearance; personal motivation to do well; ability to work with others.

**Question B (page 150)**

(a) Obtain greater market share and higher revenue (and profit):
    revenue at £2.50 = £2.50 × 10 000 = £25 000
    revenue at £2.60 = £2.60 ×   8000 = £20 800: £4200 lower.

**(b)**

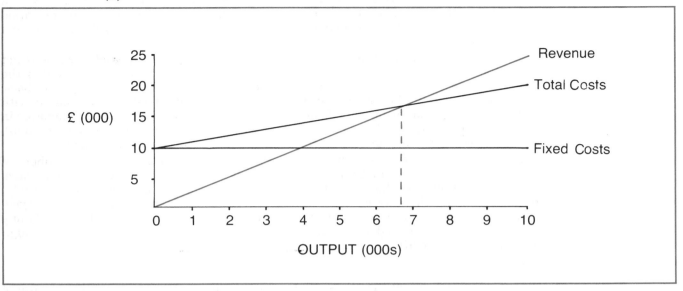

(i) Breakeven output 6667.

(ii) Expected profit: total revenue £25 000 (from (a)), total costs £10 000 fixed and £10 000 variable (10 000 × £1) = £20 000. Profit of £5000.

(c) (i) New price of £2.60 (£2.50 plus 4 per cent i.e. 10p). Contribution is £1.60 (£2.60 − £1); divided into fixed costs of £10 000 gives break-even point of 6250.

(ii) Information in question states a price of £2.60 should result in 8000 sold (total revenue £20 800, from (a)). Total costs £10 000 + £8000 (8000 × £1) = £18 000; profit £2800.

## Question C

(a) Many commuters – likely to be more men, often medium to high income; people interested in events (entertainment); people interested in buying/selling (cars, property etc); people looking for work or new jobs.

(b) Use of company's own (road) transport: direct to newsagents' shops and paper stands.

(c) Site A: existing buildings, so no need to build (cheaper?); near motorway, so delivery could be quick.

Site B: no need to build; expensive rents? Central site, suitable for distribution to commuters.

Site C: cost of building; near motorway, for good distribution.

Site D: possible building grants (development area); close to central London for commuter market.

Any of the sites could be selected, with reasons given such as those above.

## Question D

(a) (i) Retained profits.

(ii) Bank loan.

(iii) Retained profits: avoids the expense of interest payments on bank loan.

(b) (i) Forecast fall in the number of the 15 to 19 age group will reduce total demand for Anglia's goods; growth in number (and importance) of young middle-aged, many of whom will have bought Anglia's products.

(ii) Move into clothes market for other age-groups (as age-range numbers are changing); attempt to increase market share for 15 to 19 group, e.g. through more advertising; diversifying into other related products, e.g. clothing accessories.

## Question E

(a) (i) Induction training to introduce the company and its products, to provide motivation; training in technical specifications, etc, of products to assist in selling the products; training in selling techniques, to improve sales performance.

(ii) Handling the paperwork from customers; ensuring customer orders are dealt with and sent as quickly as possible; liaising with customers if any problems over orders.

(iii) Need to analyse the elements of the job (what it entails), so that the skills, knowledge, attributes and abilities of applicants can be assessed for their suitability. Advert B contains 'ability with figures' and 'some secretarial skills', which relate to job content; also 'a pleasant telephone manner' indicates what is involved in the job.

(iv) Job A's main motivation seems to be pay (commission-based: sales must be made for income to be earned); dealing with customers may provide motivation since it is a challenge to sell to them. Job B's range of work should motivate, because of the varied tasks done daily; also dealing directly with customers can provide interest and stimulation.

(b) The report could point out that the commission system of payment used in Sales is not used in the other departments, and is the main reason for the turnover; linked to this, the company's expectations of its sales staff may be too high, and rewards (e.g. lack of basic pay, no company car, low rate of commission) may be uncompetitive compared with similar firms. It is a problem to the firm because training new staff is expensive; morale in the department – and therefore performance – will be low. Improvements in pay (system), 'perks' (e.g. company car) and conditions of work could reduce sales staff turnover.

(c) Previous ratio 4:1 in favour of male staff. Present ratio is 3:2. Increased numbers of women workers available in 1987, with more women returning to work after marriage/family; automation may have resulted in changes in working practices, and (possibly) unskilled women, who may be more willing to tolerate lower pay, have been employed. Likely to be more part-time jobs, which often suit women from traditional domestic/family backgrounds, Possible reduction in full-time (male-dominated) posts, e.g. through redundancy or automation.

## Question F

(a) Because of specialization: the UK specializes in certain goods/services, at the expense of others, because it is cost-effective to do so. Land may be devoted to growing cereals or livestock, rather than timber or fruit; certain timber and fruits (e.g. tropical fruit) cannot be grown, or are comparatively expensive to grow, because of the climate here. Some ores and metals are not naturally found in the UK, or are too expensive to extract, and so are imported.

(b) Specialization is again one reason. Factors of production are devoted to making that which we are best at producing: the surpluses produced are traded (exported), and goods imported in return. Also, consumer choice and a relatively free market (some quotas) encourages competition from overseas (which can result in more efficient home production).

(c) Bar chart showing tonnes (000s) exported from Oldport docks.

| Others | 50 |
|---|---|
| Chemicals | 100 |
| Iron and steel | 150 |
| Coal and coke | 500 |

## Question G

(a) Building costs (only a 'small shop'); stockholding costs increase; delivery costs increase; interest costs of borrowing any money required for expansion; insurance costs likely to rise; more wages for any new assistants.

(b) Likely sources include his accountant; his bank; possibly the DTI through Enterprise Initiative or similar.

(c) (i) He remains in complete control of the business; the borrowing total can be fixed; the bank's advice and resources can be used; BUT interest rates may rise; the bank may call in the loan; he has to pay the interest on the loan, and the loan itself must be paid back in the future.

    **(ii)** Workload shared; partner can bring in business expertise; interest does not have to be paid on new capital: BUT he is no longer in full control; he has to share profits.

**(d) (i)** Market research: e.g. surveys of customers presently using his shop via questionnaires; examine sales records, to check main product lines sold; check product ranges sold by competitors; check competitor advertising (type and frequency).

    **(ii)** Any methods largely limited to the local town – e.g. local paper; direct mailshot (leaflet through doors); freesheets; local cinema; local radio. Cost is the major factor: where possible, targeted to likely interest groups (e.g. leaflet to local gardening societies). National or regional forms (TV, gardening journals) unrealistic due to cost and size of this market.

**(e)** Unlikely to be the 'cheapest garden produce in town' (change to 'competitive prices' or similar); not a statement of fact that his 'carrots improve your eyesight'; not all produce is 'home grown' (rephrase to 'home-grown market garden produce sold'); perhaps change last sentence to offer a refund if customers not fully satisfied with freshness or quality.

## Question H

**(a)** Three – MD, Production Manager, Product A and B managers/supervisors.

**(b)** Advertising; Public Relations; Customer Records (or Credit Control).

**(c) (i)** Company magazine or staff noticeboard; notice in pay packets; mass meeting or meeting of worker representatives.

    **(ii)** Meeting: gives the employees the chance to ask questions and management the opportunity to clear up any misunderstandings.

**(d)** Piece rate: payment for each item produced (to acceptable quality), paid weekly, often in cash. Salary: fixed amount, paid monthly, often direct into bank account.

**(e)** Depends on his ability to produce high number of items, putting him under pressure. He may not be as quick a worker as others and thus earns less.

**(f)** Job production unlikely. Batch is the most likely; batches of different types of biscuits (Product A and Product B?) made. Flow system also possible, if only two varieties being made: continuous production of these two types.

## Question I

**(a) (i)** Item owned by the PLC, used by the PLC to make its profit: e.g. machinery.
    **(ii)** Customer who buys on credit and who owes the PLC the cost of the goods bought.
    **(iii)** Suppliers of goods bought by the PLC on credit.
    **(iv)** Retained profits, kept for future expansion or in case of emergency.

**(b) (i)** Excess of current assets over current liabilities: used in meeting short-term debts (e.g. paying trade creditors).
    **(ii)** Current assets £120 million; current liabilities £20 million; working capital £100 million.

**(c)** Working capital ratio = £120:£20, or 6:1. Very high – money tied up in excessive stock. 'Acid Test' ratio = £10:£20, or 1:2. Insufficient liquid funds (ignoring stock) to meet demands of creditors.

## Question J

**(a)** Less advertising than its rivals due to cost control, leading to lower costs but a loss of some of its market: and/or increased prices, making it slightly less competitive (lower market share), but larger profit margins leading to higher overall profit.

**(b)** May encourage customers to book holidays with them: but depends on the proportion of holidays costing over £200 sold by them, and will eat into profits even if market share increases.

**(c)** System breakdown/failure – is there a back-up system if the new one does not work at the outset? Difficulties for staff – has training been adequate? Suspicion, fear or fall in morale – staff may dislike new working practices.

**(d) (i)** Two-year Government scheme for young adults (16+) which gives the chance of on-the-job training and off-the-job study for qualifications, but with no automatic guarantee of a job at the end.
    **(ii)** Settling-in problems: getting to know staff and working practices. Errors may be made, e.g. in booking holidays, which could prove costly to the firm.

## Question K Case Study

**1 (a)** Survival: customer satisfaction.
  **(b)** Benefit of limited liability; affairs can be kept private.
  **(c)** Less impersonal, more friendly: more relaxed.

**2 (a)** 1983: £1850 − (£465 + £775 + £450) = £160 (thousand).

1987: £2035 − £1948 = £87 (thousand).

**(b)** 1987 = 4.28 per cent.

**(c)** Increased raw material and wages costs, with prices not being passed on. Sales revenue has increased by 10 per cent: but labour costs are up by 20 per cent, materials by 15 per cent and overheads by 11 per cent. Sales price has absorbed these increases, resulting in reduced profit margins.

**3 (a)** The report could mention typical stages involved with market research – problem definition; formulation of the survey; data collection (field and desk research); analysis and tabulation of the data; interpretation of results; recommendations and conclusions.

**(b)** Consumer attitudes; existing competition; estimated sales and costs.

**4 (a)** Through consultative or other committees, where managers and workforce meet on a regular basis; through direct worker participation in decision-making, e.g. at Board level with worker directors.

**(b)** Improves morale, motivation and efficiency; improves communication and knowledge about business decisions.

**5** A decision to go ahead with 'Enterprise' could be argued on the figures – sales revenue £320 000, total costs £266 000 (£13.50 × 16 000, plus £50 000): profit £54 000. The break-even point is under 8000 sales: contribution £6.50 per unit, divided into £50 000 fixed costs. It also brings the firm into a new market segment (board games), and it will strengthen the sales force (which could benefit other games' sales, which are only increasing slowly). A decison not to go ahead may be argued on the basis of the MD's fears over the competitive board-game segment, and possible problems with the sales force.

# 24 GCSE COURSEWORK

## 24.1 Introduction

All students taking full-time two-year courses in GCSE Business Studies will have to carry out coursework. There are some exceptions to this: older students, taking a one-year GCSE at a local college for example, may face some different tasks. You will need to check the exact position with your teacher, or with the Examining Group, because the syllabuses vary in their individual coursework requirements (summarized on pages xi-xii). Some, or all, of your coursework grades or marks will count towards your overall GCSE assessment.

You will need to consult regularly with your teacher concerning your coursework. Although your teacher cannot do the work for you, he or she can provide you with advice, for example, on how to get information. You should also learn how to analyse this information and how to present and summarize your findings.

## 24.2 Coursework Skills

Although the demands made by different items of coursework will vary, the following skills are often used.

### Research

Your main task here is to **gather information** about a business problem, a theme, a company, or whatever else acts as the focus of your coursework assignment.

Remember that you will not score high marks simply by including the information gathered in the assignment (e.g. enclosing all the leaflets that you have collected from a bank or building society). The information therefore needs to be **relevant** to the task or problem you are researching into.

The information may be **original**, e.g. the results of a survey you have conducted: or it may already be **published**. Popular sources of general business information include banks, articles in business magazines and newspapers, visits to firms or listening to a visiting speaker from a business organization, and electronic sources (e.g. Prestel).

### Analysis

Once you have collected the information, you have to analyse it. The first step is to **understand** the information (your teacher may have to guide you here): not only understanding its **content** but also its **relevance** to your coursework and its **limitations** (what the information misses out can be as important as what it includes). The information must therefore be studied carefully: you may have to rearrange it, so that it ties in more closely with your assignment.

### Presentation

Your coursework assignments will be assessed by other people: they must, therefore, be capable of being **understood by others**. Where there is a lot of information, you will need to **summarize** it for the assignment. Another decision that you must take concerns the use of **diagrams** or other forms of pictorial communication: be prepared to use charts, graphs or other visual forms to highlight your research and findings.

Coursework findings are often presented in the form of a **report**. Your teacher will advise you on an acceptable business report layout, this often consists of the following:

1 The Title and list of Contents.

2 An Introduction, which explains the purpose of your coursework.

3 The Investigation section, outlining what you have done to investigate the problem or activity.

4 The Analysis section, which gives details of your work in assessing what you have discovered.

5 The Results and Conclusions section, which contains your detailed comments on conclusions reached, and why they have been reached.

6 A Bibliography and an Appendix, containing details of the sources you have used, copies of questionnaires used, etc.

## 24.3  Skills Often Assessed through Coursework

Undertaking coursework usually requires you to demonstrate skills that are not normally assessed in the traditional type of examination. The more important of these skills are listed below and should be remembered if and when you have to select your own areas of coursework.

1  Search skills: testing your ability to decide what information you require, where to find that information, and how best to collect and record the information.

2  Cooperative skills: the ability and willingness to work with other people in carrying out the various elements of the coursework.

3  Problem-solving skills: the ability to identify a particular (business) problem, set objectives which allow you to tackle the problem and establish possible solutions (including the 'best' solution) to the problem.

4  'Awareness' skills: your ability to adapt as the coursework leads you into previously-unconsidered areas of research and study.

5  Integrative skills: your ability to draw upon the whole range of Business Studies content and ideas (e.g. bringing in aspects of health and safety, other legal aspects, ideas from accountancy, cost-benefit analysis, etc) in carrying out the assignment.

6  Perseverance skills: your willingness to carry out the task from start to finish, with appropriate assistance and advice.

## 24.4  How to Approach Coursework

Your coursework topic may be set by the Examining Group (e.g. LEAG). A more popular approach at the moment is to allow you to select your own area of research, following discussions with your teacher. There are a number of points that you must bear in mind when selecting an area for coursework:

1  The topic chosen must be one that is on the syllabus: ideally, it should give you the chance to integrate different areas of your syllabus.

2  It must be 'suitable' in that
(a)  it allows you to research into some business aspect, activity or problem;
(b)  it can be completed in the time available;
(c)  it gives you the opportunity to demonstrate your knowledge and understanding of some aspects of the business world.

3  The topic must relate to the skills in Section 24.2: it must be capable of being researched, analysed, evaluated and presented by you.

4  The topic must lead you to produce your own work and not the work of others (e.g. by simply copying out information from published materials).

## 24.5  Examples of Coursework

The following examples are taken from the assignments set by London East Anglian Group (LEAG). The candidates are encouraged to make use of all relevant syllabus areas and also to use appropriate techniques of investigation. The results of their research are to be presented in report form, with diagrams being used where appropriate. Finally, LEAG states that materials from the 'background work' and any pamphlets, leaflets or other materials collected, are not to be included in the report.

**Coursework assignment no. 3, 1989**

LEAG: GCSE BUSINESS STUDIES COURSEWORK ASSIGNMENT NO. 3
INFLUENCE OF A PRESSURE GROUP ON BUSINESS ACTIVITY

**Background Work**
You are required to investigate the work of a pressure group on business in general or on businesses in your local area.

Select an example of a pressure group which seeks to influence business activity. You can use a wide definition of the term 'pressure group'.

Identify clearly what this group is trying to achieve.

For example:

protection of the consumer/employee/local trader;
promotion of local business activity or a type of business activity;
an environmental issue.

**Activity One**
Investigate the influence on business activity of the pressure group you have selected.

**Activity Two**
Investigate how this business activity is additionally influenced by local and/or national government.

*Possible approaches*

There are many pressure groups from which you could make your choice. The group chosen should of course be one which has an influence on business activity: trade unions or environmental pressure groups are likely selections here. Your choice of pressure group will also be influenced by the number and nature of local businesses, if you planned to survey your local business community.

The research you would undertake would probably start with a study of the pressure group's organization: where it is based, names of key personnel, how it publicizes itself, etc. From this research, you could collect its various leaflets and publications and assess how much business-relevant information they contained. Hopefully, the objectives of the pressure group would be stated in its literature. If it has a local office, you could – after consultations with appropriate people, such as a parent/guardian, or teacher – arrange to visit the office and discuss your ideas and plans with an official. It would also be useful to discuss the influences of the pressure group with local business people and compare these various views. Before carrying out visits, you would need to plan carefully the exact purposes of the visit (e.g. to clarify some part of the pressure group's policy).

Following the visits and the collection of information in general, you would then be in the position to analyse the information. The results of this analysis should allow you to then start examining Activity Two: the knowledge gained about the pressure group's influences should provide you with pointers to possible government influences. You may choose to compare the differences in influence, or to identify the different forms of influence by the pressure group and central/local government.

**Coursework assignment no. 4, 1989**

LEAG: GCSE BUSINESS STUDIES COURSEWORK ASSIGNMENT NO. 4
INTERNAL STRUCTURE AND MANAGEMENT OF A FIRM

**Background Work**
You are required to investigate the internal organization of a firm. You should investigate the firm's internal services.

Select a firm that is organized into departments, sections or functions such as Personnel, Finance or Accounts, Sales and Marketing.

Identify its range of internal services, e.g. office administration, maintenance.

**Activity One**
Investigate how this firm organizes its departments or functions and explain how they link with one another.

**Activity Two**
Investigate and explain how the firm organizes one or more of its internal services.

*Possible approaches*

As with the first coursework assignment, a visit – to discuss the operation of your chosen firm – would be very helpful in undertaking this assignment. Again, before a visit is undertaken, much research needs to be carried out.

Large PLCs will have Annual Reports which can be obtained and studied. These organizations – and many smaller ones – have Public Relations officials, who are often willing to provide information and assistance. In addition, the 'quality' newspapers, or electronic databases such as Prestel, may prove further sources of information.

Published information about smaller firms is less easy to come by. If you chose to do this, or a similar, assignment, your choice of firm should be dictated by the ease with which you can obtain (and publish, in your coursework) relevant information.

An arranged visit to the firm should prove a profitable source of information. With any visit, careful planning before it is undertaken is necessary: you have to identify the types of questions that need to be asked.

It is likely that an assignment such as this one will give the opportunity to summarize the information collected in the form of a chart (such as an organization chart, in this case). A good answer to such an assignment will demonstrate that the candidate fully understands the links between the various departments or functions, e.g. by providing illustrations of how they work in practice (Activity 1). Also, in answering Activity 2, a good answer would probably include an analysis of different ways that the internal services could be organized.

### Coursework assignment no. 6, 1989

#### LEAG: GCSE BUSINESS STUDIES COURSEWORK ASSIGNMENT NO. 6
#### LOCAL MARKETS

**Background Work**

You are required to investigate two markets in a local area. One of these markets must be the local labour market.

You can select the other market that you wish to study for activity two. For example:

a local street market;
the local market for public or private transport;
the local market for agricultural machinery or for industrial robots;
the local capital/savings market;
the local entertainment market.

**Activity One**

Analyse the demand for, and supply of, labour in a local area. In your report, use appropriate headings such as 'skilled', 'semi-skilled' etc.

**Activity Two**

Investigate one other market in a local area and describe the nature of demand and supply within this market.

*Possible approaches*

Activity 1 is quite specific in what it requires candidates to do. Research into a local area's labour market could involve visits to the local Jobcentre or to private employment agencies, to check labour supply and demand. Local papers could also be examined, to see the type of job adverts that are being placed. Any local large employers could be contacted, for example by writing a letter to the Personnel Manager outlining the problem.

A major difficulty faced by candidates is how to organize the information they collect for this piece of coursework. The information collected could be analysed to discover the types of jobs – white collar, 'blue collar', etc – being advertised, any pockets of high unemployment, the type of labour demanded by newer firms or by firms in the different sectors of the local economy and so on.

Activity 2 gives candidates a choice, which should be based on the nature of the 'local area' studied. Examples are given in the coursework and these indicate that any form of market – such as an actual, physical, one – could be selected. It is likely that there will be little published information on local markets such as those for entertainments and so a questionnaire may have to be devised. This could involve a candidate researching into one specific area, for example into the market for a new, 10-screen, 'American-style' cinema.

## 24.6 Further Coursework Projects

Many of the principles for selecting and carrying out coursework have been covered in the Unit. Three coursework assignments have been given above: there are many other specific and general areas of business that could be used as a basis for successful coursework. Possible areas include the following:

1 How an institution such as a bank can assist local business, and how it is influenced by the local economy.

2 The way in which a local firm serves others in either (or both) the public and private sectors.

3 How two business organizations are 'gearing up' for 1992.

4 The way in which a local firm has approached marketing a new product and the problems this has caused.

5 A survey into the buying habits of consumers and how a local store plans its shop layout accordingly.

6 How the local branch of a firm overcomes problems of internal communication, external communication with other branches and/or external communications with other firms.

7 The ways that different firms approach the same problem, e.g. that of training.

8 How a local authority is adapting to changes in the local economy, national policies which influence it and/or the needs of its local population.

## 24.7 Assessing Coursework

The way in which coursework is assessed differs according to the Examining Group, although all Groups look for the same type of skills and performances. Two examples are now given:

you will have to check the scheme of assessment for your coursework by talking to your teacher or by reading your syllabus.

The Midland Examining Group (MEG) has published the following marking programme for teachers assessing coursework for the 1990 syllabus.

*Maximum mark*

1 An understanding of the aim is displayed together with an understanding of the facts, principles, terms, techniques or ideas central to that part of the syllabus to which it relates and appropriate to the particular assignment. **10**

2 Information chosen is appropriate for use in the assignment. **5**

3 Information is presented in an accurate, logical and effective manner. **4**

4 Data has been analysed involving the interpretation of information in narrative, numerical or graphical form using skills and techniques developed within the course. **5**

5 Main findings have been presented, which involve reasoned explanations, developed arguments, valid inferences, solutions and conclusions as appropriate. **6**

**Total marks 30**

The London East Anglian Group (LEAG) provides these guidelines for teachers marking coursework assignments, again for the 1990 syllabus.

*Marks*

**17–20** Excellent work. The work demonstrates outstanding evidence of individual investigation, selection and interpretation of the subject matter, and is logically arranged and carefully presented.

**11–16** Good work. The work demonstrates good evidence of individual investigation, selection and interpretation of the subject matter, and is logically arranged and carefully presented.

**5–10** The mid point (7/8) of the mark range reflects the Grade F range of ability. The work demonstrates some evidence of investigation, selection and interpretation of the subject matter.

**1–4** Work where there is some evidence of positive achievement.

Both sets of guidelines give a range of marks. The number of marks given to a particular piece of coursework depend on the quality of that coursework. For example, a MEG assignment where the candidate has selected appropriate information will score five marks out of five for this achievement: if it has been presented in a reasonably (but not quite) accurate and logical way, it will probably score two or three out of the four marks available for this part of the work.

# 25 LAST-MINUTE HELP

People facing a major examination often spend some time thinking and worrying about that exam. You therefore need to think **positively** about how best to tackle the questions that you will face.

*Before the examination*

Produce a rough 'minutes per mark' guide. Some of the GCSE Business Studies exams contain questions which carry different mark totals: other thing being equal, you should spend less time answering a 12-mark question than a 24-mark question.

You can use this guide to help your exam performance. For example, the SEG 1988 Paper 1 contained questions totalling 200 marks, to be answered in two hours (120 minutes). Question 1 was worth 40 marks – a fifth of the total of 200 – and so should take approximately a fifth of the exam time to answer: one fifth of 120 minutes is 24 minutes. If, therefore, you were still working on question one after, say, 45 minutes, this would suggest that you needed to finish this question quickly to stand a chance of gaining the marks on the rest of the paper.

If you can discover which room is to be used for the exam, you can visit the room beforehand (if it is not one of your regular rooms), to get a 'feel' for it. It will not then be a wholly new experience on the day; and you can work out where is the best place to sit, assuming you have this choice. Do sit where you can see the invigilator and be seen: there may be a need to attract the invigilator's attention. Also, try to avoid being trapped in the sun: GCSE summer exams are not the best time to sunbathe!

The final task before the exam – other than revising! – is to prepare a checklist of what you need to bring with you to the exam. Obvious items are pens (more than one, and use black or blue ink: not green, red or other colours), ruler, calculator, watch and so on.

*On the day*

Consult the checklist so that you do not forget anything. Also, arrive early, to settle down. It is natural to be a little nervous, so you need to allow time to get over this. Do remember that you cannot expect to get all questions completely correct – you don't have to produce a perfect set of answers, even to obtain a grade A.

*In the exam*

**Read** the examination paper carefully. Where there is a choice, answer those questions you feel most confident with first of all and then return to the ones that appear to be more difficult.

Be careful that you **don't spend too long** a time answering any one question. You are under time pressure, and it could pay to 'cut your losses' with one question: it may be better to start the next question (and possibly gain a lot of marks quite quickly) than to spend a lot of time trying to finish the current question and only gain the final two or three marks.

Do **show all workings**, including any rough plans of essay-type questions. There is nothing to be lost by doing this and quite possibly much to be gained. Marks can be awarded by the examiner for part-correct questions, where the examiner can see the correct workings. If the final answer only to a numerical question is given by you (i.e. no workings are shown), and that answer is wrong, the examiner may not be able to award it any marks.

Do **write legibly**, because the examiner has to be able to read your answer before marking it. Time pressure may cause you to rush, but you have to balance the need for speed with the need for legibility.